JAPANESE
AIRCRAFT CARRIERS

JAPANESE AIRCRAFT CARRIERS 1920–1945

Ermanno Martino

Naval Institute Press
Annapolis, Maryland

Page 2, above: The camouflage of *Unryu* was modified at the end of 1944 with the application of a complex multicolour scheme on the flight deck in order to make it difficult to identify the elevators, one of the weak points of an aircraft carrier often attacked by enemy bombers. (M Brescia, from E Bagnasco & M Brescia, *La mimetizzazione delle navi italiane 1940–1945)*

Page 2, below: The half-sunken wreck of the aircraft carrier *Amagi* in the Bay of Kure in 1946. The two-tone green no 1 and no 2 paint scheme is still evident, although deteriorated and faded due to long exposure to the elements a year after the end of the Second World War. (US Navy Investigation Board, NHHC)

See page 109 for appendix on painting schemes.

Frontispiece: *Akagi* at anchor, 1933 (Kure Naval Museum)

First published in Great Britain in 2025 by
Seaforth Publishing
An imprint of
Pen & Sword Books Ltd
Yorkshire

Published and distributed in the
United States of America and Canada by the
Naval Institute Press,
291 Wood Road, Annapolis,
Maryland 21402-5034

www.usni.org/press/books

Library of Congress Control Number: 202594298

ISBN 978 1 68247 782 3

Designed and typeset by Ian Hughes, Mousemat Design Limited

CONTENTS

PUBLISHER'S NOTE

This work on Japanese aircraft carriers first appeared in Italian, published by Storia Militare in 2021. It was issued in their monograph series and written by Ermanno Martino, certainly one of the greatest Italian experts on Japanese warships. This English-language edition has been redesigned but incorporates all the material that appeared in the original Italian edition. The English translation was made by two well-known Italian naval historians, Ruggero Stanglini and Michele Cosentino. They have written two books for Seaforth Publishing in the last few years and their grasp of both naval history and the English language has been of great benefit.

PHOTO CREDITS

All the images in this book, with the exception of a very few whose source was impossible to trace, are accompanied by the indication of the archive, collection or documentary fund from which they are taken.

The Kure Naval Museum is the custodian of a large number of photographs, many of them coming from the collection of well-known Japanese naval historian Shizuo Fukui. Quite a few images (in particular those referring to operational aspects and aircraft carriers that survived the conflict) are of American origin. Whenever possible, the archival position in the collections of the Naval History and Heritage Command (NHHC) of the US Navy (indicated by the acronym NH followed by the relevant number) has been reported.

Special thanks go to the passionate Japanese graphic designer, J Irotoko, author of the colour renderings of originally black and white photographs, created with professionalism and adherence to the ships' original colours.

ABBREVIATIONS

abt	about
AVD	seaplane tender (destroyer)
B	beam
CA	heavy cruiser
CL	light cruiser
CNC	copper alloy non cemented
CV	aircraft carrier
CVL	aircraft carrier (Light)
DD	destroyer
DS	Ducol steel
HMS	His/Her Majesty's Ship
HP	high pressure
hp	horse power
HT	high tensile
IJN	Imperial Japanese Navy
L	length (oa overall, wl waterline, btwn pp between perpendiculars)
LP	low pressure
max	maximum
MNC	molybdenum alloy non cemented
MP	medium pressure
Mod	model
n/a	not available
nm	nautical mile(s)
NHHC	Naval History and Heritage Command
NVNC	new Vickers non cemented
rpm	rounds per minute
shp	shaft horse power
SS	submarine
tbc	to be confirmed
USN	United States Navy
USS	United States Ship
VH	Vickers hardened
wl	waterline
WW	World War

NOTES ON TABLES

DATES – Dates in brackets refer to those foreseen when the Japanese decided to build the warship(s).

DISPLACEMENT – Until the end of 1923, displacement of Japanese warships was measured in British tons (1 long ton = 1,016kg). After that date, it was always measured in metric tons (1 ton = 1,000kg).

Standard displacement: expressed in British tons, this represents the weight of the ship including crew, equipment, ammunition and fresh water, but without fuel and reserve water for boilers. Although adopted by the Imperial Japanese Navy only for official use and/or at international organisations, it is reported for the carriers up to and including *Hiryu*, in order to allow the evaluation of the progressive exhaustion of the aircraft carrier tonnage (81,000 standard tons) allocated to Japan by the Washington Treaty and subsequent agreements.

Normal displacement: expressed in British tons, this represents the weight of the warship ready to get underway, with one-quarter of fuel, three-quarters of ammunition and one-half of fresh water provisions.

Displacement at trials: expressed in metric tons, this represents the weight of the warship ready to get underway, with two-thirds of its fuel, food and reserve water for boilers. The Japanese considered this as 'battle displacement', assuming that, before reaching the area of operations, the warship would consume about one-third of its fuel and food provisions. Another third would be consumed during the battle, and the remaining third was to allow the return to base.

Full load displacement: expressed in British or metric tons, this represents the highest displacement, with the maximum amount of fuel and equipment.

DIMENSIONS

Length, overall (oa): measured from the extreme bow to the extreme stern, this is one of the few dimensions not dependent on displacement. It coincides with the maximum longitudinal warship size.

Waterline length (wl): this is the maximum length of the hull at the waterline. It varies with displacement, due to the shape of the bow and stern.

Length between perpendiculars (btwn pp): this is generally defined as the hull length measured between the intersection, at the waterline, of the bow and the rudder shaft. It depends on displacement and is not equally defined by various navies.

Beam: this represents the maximum transverse warship size, calculated approximately amidships and corresponding to the midship section. When possible, it is indicated whether the data indicates the maximum or the waterline (wl) beam. It does not depend on displacement.

Draft/draught: this represents the submerged hull depth, not including appendages (rudders and propellers). It depends on displacement.

FLIGHT DECK – Both length and maximum beam amidships are indicated. When possible, beam of both forward (fore) and aft sections are also shown.

MACHINERY – Its composition, as well as the maximum power delivered, refers to the warship design, or that derived from any modernisation.

SPEED – Expressed in knots (1 knot = 1 nautical mile per hour), this is generally the design speed, corresponding to the maximum power developed by machinery.

FUEL – Indicates the maximum provision of fuel on board.

ENDURANCE – Expressed in nautical miles (1 nm = 1,852m), this indicates the maximum distance the warship can steam at a given speed.

PROTECTION – Expressed in millimetres, this indicates the maximum armour thickness, including supporting plates.

ARMAMENT – Includes artillery and aircraft. Artillery indicates type and number of weapons as planned by the design or resulting from subsequent modernisations or conversions. As for aircraft, the maximum number planned to be hosted on board is shown and, in brackets, those in reserve.

COMPLEMENT – Indicates the number of officers and men (or total personnel) foreseen at the design stage.

COMPOSITION OF THE EMBARKED AIR WING – The composition of the carrier air wing in particular circumstances (design, main battles and deployments) is indicated at the end of the description of each type/class of aircraft carriers. However, given the disparity of sources, the composition of the embarked air wings do not always faithfully reflect the actual one.

FOREWORD

Between the 1920s and the Second World War, Japan undertook the construction of twenty-nine aircraft carriers, twenty-five of which were completed. Thirteen of them originated from the conversion of different types of vessels, such as passenger ships (seven), seaplane carriers (two), submarine support ships (two) and fast oilers (two). The fact that 52 per cent of the completed aircraft carriers were the result of conversions clearly demonstrates that the Japanese military-industrial complex was not capable of competing with those of the United States and Great Britain, the two major naval powers of that period.

The remaining thirteen aircraft carriers can be divided into four groups: light carriers (*Hosho* and *Ryujo*), medium-sized carriers (*Soryu*, *Hiryu*, *Unryu*, *Amagi* and *Katsuragi*) and fleet carriers, either built from scratch (*Shokaku*, *Zuikaku* and *Taiho*) or derived from battlecruisers or battleships (*Akagi*, *Kaga* and *Shinano*).

Considering just the fleet aircraft carriers built from scratch, their small number is not only a consequence of industrial and financial shortcomings, but also of the fact that in the second half of the 1930s, the primary effort of the Imperial Navy was directed towards the design and construction of the first two *Yamato*-class battleships. To give an idea of how much these battleships drained resources, it is sufficient to point out that just to 'hide' the construction site of *Musashi*, 2,710km of cables and hemp ropes were used, depriving fishermen of the materials necessary to weave their nets.

What judgement can be formulated regarding the Japanese aircraft carriers? The primary requirement was to operate the greatest possible number of aircraft, hence the almost generalised adoption of two closed superimposed hangars and the need to embark large supplies of aviation gas. However, this resulted in a reduced capability to absorb damage, in other word: a lower survivability. In short, it produced ships of high offensive value, with very high levels of efficiency (at least in the first period of the Second World War) and proficiency of technical personnel and pilots, but with limited self-defence capabilities.

As with my previous work about Japanese battleships, I enjoyed the help of both my dear friend Augusto de Toro and of Fulvio Petronio from Trieste, from whose library I was able to draw much indispensable material. I extend my gratitude to you both.

Ermanno Martino

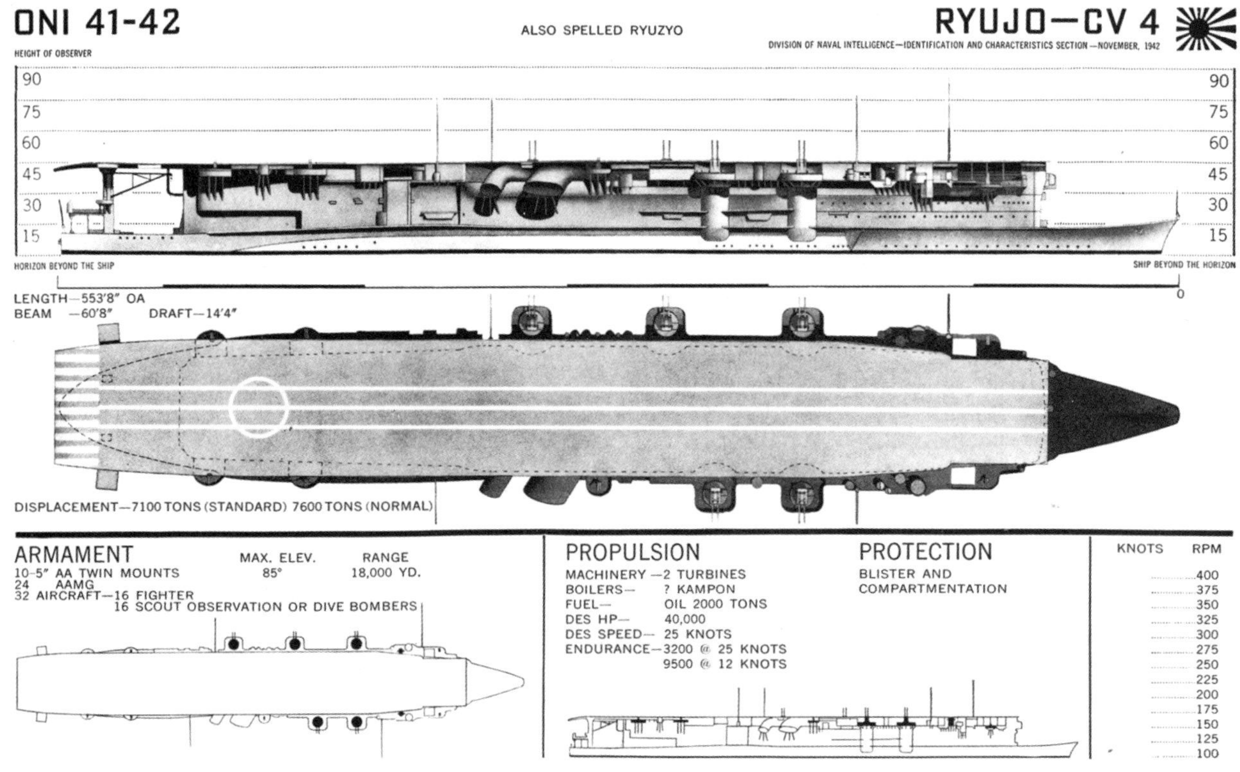

Drawings and main features of the aircraft carrier *Ryujo*, taken from an official document of the US Navy Office of Naval Intelligence dated November 1942. (*Japanese Naval Vessels of World War Two as seen by the US Naval Intelligence*)

POLICY AND PROGRAMMES

The 1922 Washington Treaty is generally associated with its provisions relating to capital ships (battleships and battlecruisers), but nevertheless aircraft carriers were also the subject of discussions and negotiations. Although a recent development, the major maritime powers (the United States, Great Britain and Japan) had begun to appreciate the potential of the aircraft carrier as a 'force multiplier', both in favour of their own battle forces and against those of their opponents. As a consequence, this relatively new and distinct category of warship was the subject of a long and in-depth debate, where each participating nation tried to ensure its own interests prevailed.

Even before the Washington Naval Conference commenced, the Royal Navy had a requirement for five 25,000-ton aircraft carriers. Therefore, Great Britain immediately proposed a limit of 125,000 tons for each of the two English-speaking powers. However, this proposal was quickly rejected by the United States, which not only aimed at becoming the world's leading naval power, but was also keen to make the most of the hulls of their *Lexington*–class battlecruisers being built at the time.[1]

A counterproposal of an 80,000-ton limit for the United States and Great Britain would have meant that, by applying the same percentages established for battleships, Japan would have been allowed to build 48,000 tons, while for Italy and France it would be just 28,000 tons.

This approach was immediately met with the strongest opposition from the other parties involved. Great Britain countered that, given the maximum standard displacement of 35,000 tons agreed for battleships, a 40,000-ton aircraft carrier would prove an anomaly. Conversely, a proposed displacement of 25,000 tons, also supported by France, would have allowed the Royal Navy and the Marine Nationale to convert some of the battleships in service or being constructed to aircraft carriers.[2] As for the Americans and Japanese, they were well aware that limiting the displacement of aircraft carriers to 25,000 tons could prevent the conversion of the battlecruisers they were already building.[3]

After exhaustive negotiations, a final decision was reached in the following terms: 135,000 standard tons of aircraft carriers were assigned to both Great Britain and the United States, 81,000 tons to Japan and 60,000 tons to France and Italy, thus respecting the 5–3–1.75 ratio already in place for battleships. Within the limits of the authorised displacement, each nation could build two 33,000-ton aircraft carriers, using for this purpose an equivalent number of battleships in service or being constructed and slated for scrapping. Aircraft carriers were limited to a 27,000-ton standard displacement and could carry up to ten 8in heavy guns. All aircraft carriers in service or under construction on 12 November 1921 were to be considered as experimental ships and therefore replaceable, within the limits of the allowed displacement, whatever their age.

In Japan, it is noteworthy that, after the experience of *Wakamiya*,[4] they had already identified the aircraft carrier as a suitable tool for carrying out long-range operations in the vastness of the Pacific. Therefore, the construction of *Hosho* had already been included in the '8-6 Programme for Fleet Completion' approved in 1918. *Hosho* was the first aircraft carrier in the world built as such, and not as the result of conversion from a different vessel. The '8-8 Programme for Fleet Completion', dated 1920, included the construction of two new 12,500-ton aircraft carriers (the first of which was to be named *Shokaku*), later cancelled following the decision to convert the battlecruisers *Amagi* and *Akagi*. Before the opening of the negotiations in Washington, Japan was also considering the construction of three 34,500-ton aircraft carriers, even if such a project would definitely have been more than the country could achieve, for both financial and industrial reasons.

In light of the Washington Conference's results, as well as of the changed political situation in the Pacific, on 28 February 1923 the Imperial Defence Council promulgated the Second Revision of the Imperial Defence Policy. Considering the United States, Russia, China and Great Britain as potential enemies (the latter due to its failure to renew the 1902 Anglo-Japanese Alliance Treaty), the revised policy called for a requirement for a fleet of no less than 1,210,840 tons.[5] However, this policy immediately encountered strong opposition from the liberal political circles

The seaplane tender ship *Wakamiya*, the first Japanese air-capable ship. She was classified as an aircraft carrier in 1920 and decommissioned in 1931. (W Stöhr collection)

Hosho, the first true aircraft carrier of the Imperial Japanese Navy, in Yokosuka shortly after entering service on 24 September 1924. (Kure Naval Museum, digitally coloured photo, courtesy J Irotoko)

which opposed the extremist parties and who had been very happy with the Washington Conference's results. The treaty actually allowed the redirection to other purposes of the huge financial resources that would have been absorbed by the planned strengthening of the fleet.

However, the construction of a 27,000-ton aircraft carrier and three aircraft support ships was foreseen within the '1924 Subsidiary Replacement Programme' but, due to the high expenditure required, economic considerations prevailed once again, preventing the programme from being implemented.

The topic of aircraft carriers was discussed again with the '1927 New Replacement Construction Programme', which envisaged the construction of *Ryujo*, the first example of a category of warship that had achieved consensus by the end of the 1920s, not only within the Japanese Navy but also to some degree in the US Navy.[6] Small aircraft carriers, it was argued, represented the best antidote to the vulnerability of a type of ship that could be put out of action by a single lucky bomb or torpedo hit. Additionally, the Imperial Navy – which now considered the US Navy as the likely future enemy – perceived the 'small' aircraft carrier (and therefore, given the treaty constraints, built in greater numbers) as the most suitable choice to offset an almost certain numerical inferiority compared to the US fleet.

In January 1930, with the aim of resolving what the Washington Treaty had left in limbo relating to other types of warships (cruisers, submarines and destroyers), a conference was convened in London with the participation of the same nations that had agreed in 1922 the limits concerning battleships and aircraft carriers. Regarding the latter, it was established in London that their displacement could be even less than 10,000 tons, while the maximum calibre of their artillery was limited to 155mm (6.1in). The results of the 1930 London Conference, which ended on 22 April and came into force on 27 October, were regarded in Japan with profound dissatisfaction, since their requests for parity about 'minor combatants' had been rejected. As a result, the idea began to take shape of designing some future merchant ships – notably passenger ships – so that they could be converted into aircraft carriers if necessary.

The Conference on Disarmament, which started in Geneva on 2 February 1932 under the aegis of the League of Nations and with the participation of around sixty countries, was a further failure as regards naval armaments. Among other things, Japan proposed the abolition of both aircraft carriers and flight decks on all other warships, but these requests were rejected. This was one of the reasons for Tokyo's withdrawal from the League of Nations (24 January 1933), following the 'Lytton Report' which censured Japan for its actions in Manchuria.

With the completion of *Ryujo*, the Japanese Navy had used 68,370 of the 81,000 tons allowed by the Washington Treaty regarding aircraft carriers. There were therefore still 12,630 tons available, to which 7,470 tons of *Wakamiya* could be added. Pursuant to Article VII of the Washington Treaty and Article 9 of the London Conference,[7] *Wakamiya* was considered, like *Hosho*, an experimental ship and as such replaceable. The displacement available for new construction would therefore rise to 20,100 standard tons.

In this scenario, the construction of a 9,800-ton aircraft carrier was envisaged in the '1930 First Naval Replacement Programme'.

However, this aircraft carrier was cancelled in the final draft of this programme. Pursuant to and for the purposes of paragraph 5 of Article 16 of the Convention signed by the three major maritime powers alongside the London agreements, 25 per cent of the commissioned cruisers could be equipped with a flight platform or deck. Thus, a number of studies and designs relating to this type of warship had been initiated in both Japan and the United States.

The construction of two 'cruiser-aircraft carriers' of 10,050 standard tons was envisaged in the '1934 Second Naval Replacement Programme'. However, this project was interrupted immediately after the capsizing of the torpedo boat *Tomozuru* and the '4th Fleet Incident', the latter leading to a complete review of the designs for all types of Japanese surface ships, excluding battleships and aircraft carriers.

Increasingly convinced that the 'unreasonable' clauses of the Washington and London Conferences were penalising their security, Japan officially declared it would consider all previous naval armament treaties null and void starting from 1 January 1937, unless new agreements were reached before that deadline.[8] In the meantime, according to Article 23 of the London Treaty (9), on 24 October 1935 the British government had issued a formal invitation to the five signatory powers of the Washington Treaty, in order to find a common formula capable of balancing each other's requirements. The new conference started in London on

The aircraft carrier *Akagi*, leaving Osaka harbour in the late 1920s. (NHHC)

The American aircraft carrier *Lexington* (CV-2), entering a dry dock at the Boston Navy Yard in January 1928. (Boston Public Library)

5 December, but was immediately postponed to 6 January 1936.

The Japanese delegation, led by Admiral Osami Nagano, immediately proposed the abrogation of the 5–5–3 capital ships ratio introduced with the Washington Treaty, which had created a 'humiliating hierarchy among nations' and introduced, for the other categories of warships, the qualitative limits currently in force. After its requests were rejected, the Japanese delegation abandoned the conference on 15 January 1936.

Just a month later, on 26 February, at a critical moment for Japanese domestic politics, a group of young officers mutinied, accusing the higher echelons of 'lukewarmness' towards the 'supreme interests' of the nation. Some Army units also mutinied, although the rebellion quickly subsided, but not before the removal of some important political authorities. The leaders of the revolt were court-martialled and executed, while the government in office was replaced.

After these events, the Imperial Defence Council rejected the treaty's constraints and drafted a new set of strategic directives during various meetings held between 21 April and 3 June 1936.

In addition to defining the United States, Soviet Union, China and Great Britain as potential enemies, the new policy reiterated the intention to 'strike south' in the direction of the Dutch East Indies, rich in oil and raw materials, as the Imperial Navy had already planned.

Taking into account the emerging political-strategic situation and the increasingly deteriorating relations with the Western powers, especially the United States, on 3 July 1936 the new Minister of the Navy, Admiral Osami Nagano,[10] submitted to the Japanese Cabinet a new construction programme, which had been under consideration since 1934. The programme, known as the '1937 Third Replacement Construction Programme' (*Maru-San*), was definitively approved on 31 March 1937. It included the construction of seventy warships (of which sixty-six were actually completed), including the first two *Yamato*-class super-dreadnoughts and the two large *Shokaku*-class aircraft carriers, as well as additional vessels.[11] The approval of the new warships only involved the related financial resources, while their technical characteristics were kept strictly secret.

While the 1937 construction programme was being discussed and approved, relations between Tokyo and Washington were steadily worsening, particularly after the sinking of the American gunboat *Panay* on 12 December 1937 on the Yangtze River by aircraft from the aircraft carrier *Kaga*, as well as the 'Rape of Nanjing' (following the occupation of this town, the Japanese troops carried out atrocities against the Chinese population). After Japan abandoned the London Conference and refused to reveal the characteristics of the new battleships, relations between Washington and Tokyo were further eroded, also affecting the respective fleets' modernisation plans.

Following the approval of the 1937 *Maru-San* programme, the Japanese Navy started to draft the '1939 Fourth Constructive Replacement Programme', using the detailed information acquired regarding the American decision to significantly increase the number of both fleet aircraft carriers[12] and other types of warship. The new construction plan proved difficult to manage due to the concurrent pressing requests from the Army, now bogged down within Chinese territory. As a result, the Navy's initial request for three additional *Shokaku*-class fleet aircraft carriers was reduced to just one, *Taiho*, although of an improved type. Other types of warships suffered similar cuts.[13] The new programme, officially known as the 'Showa Era 14th Year Completion Naval Armament Programme (1939)' – known as *Maru-Yon* within the Imperial Navy – was submitted to the Imperial Diet (Japan's national legislature) on 26 December 1938 and approved on 5 March 1939.

The year 1940 was notable for Japan, marked by recurrent government crises and the progressive deterioration of relations with the United States.[14] After the signing of the Molotov–Ribbentrop Pact, a prelude to the outbreak of the Second World War, the incumbent prime minister Kiichiro Hiranuma, known for his anti-communist beliefs, was replaced by General Noboyuki Abe (August 1939). However, on 16 January 1940, the latter was replaced by Admiral Mitsumasa Yonai, who was apparently pursuing a policy of moderation towards the United States. However, his real aim was to increase the reserves of strategic materials which Japan was lacking. Furthermore, this policy could have softened Washington's position, thus indirectly favouring the now-decided 'push' towards the south.

The great victories achieved by Germany in the first half of 1940, culminating in the fall of France, convinced the Japanese ruling class of the possibility of establishing a 'New Order' in Asia, despite the risk of war with the United States.

The Yonai cabinet was replaced on 22 July 1940 by a 'war cabinet' chaired by Prince Fumimaro Konoye, with General Hideki Tojo as Minister of War and Admiral Zengo Yoshida as Minister of the Navy. One of the first steps of the new government, in addition to the dissolution of all domestic political parties, was to convince the pro-German Vichy government, established in France after the nation's defeat, to allow Japan to establish bases and airfields in southern Indochina. Admiral Yoshida, opposed to collaboration with Germany and Italy, resigned and was replaced by Admiral Koshiro Oikawa, paving the way for the accession of Japan to the Tripartite Pact signed in Berlin on 27 September 1940.

By mid-1941, the Pacific war was approaching, leading to further political changes. The Konoye government, with the aim of ousting Foreign Minister Yosuke Matsuoka who opposed the war against the United States and advocated a 'push north' towards China, resigned on 16 July. A cabinet, still chaired by Konoye, was immediately in charge, with Admiral Soemu Toyoda as Foreign Minister.

After Japanese troops entered Saigon on 24 July 1941, in accordance with the 'Treaty for the Defence of Indochina' signed with the French Vichy government, the United States, Great Britain and the Netherlands reacted by freezing all Japanese financial assets in their respective territories and interrupting any commercial relationship, including oil supplies.

This situation would almost certainly lead to war. Since the spring of 1941, the Naval Headquarters (Gunreibu) and the Ministry of the Navy (Kaigunsho) had been considering how to counteract the massive American naval programmes, even though an effective response was beyond the reach of Japanese financial and industrial resources. However, since it was necessary to react in some way, the '1942 Fifth Replacement Construction Programme' (*Maru-Go*) was developed, which envisaged the construction of 159 ships for a total of 650,000 standard tons.

The programme included three aircraft carriers, namely two of the *Taiho* class (No 801 and No 802) of 33,000 tons each and one of a new type (No 800), displacing 17,500 tons. The Japanese were well aware that the 1942 Programme was difficult, if not impossible, to carry out in their current situation. In fact, considering the materials and manpower requirements, it was estimated that at least nine years (*ie* until 1950) were necessary for its completion.

At the same time, the 'Sixth Replacement Construction Programme' (*Maru-Roku*) was drafted, which outlined the construction of 197 vessels for a total of 800,000 standard tons, including three large fleet aircraft carriers. With reference to the last two shipbuilding programmes, it is noteworthy that a total of

Military and civilian personnel of the Kure Arsenal posing in front of the bow of *Shokaku* just before her launch on 1 June 1939. (Kure Naval Museum)

The aircraft carrier *Hiryu* undergoing machinery trials in the late summer of 1938. (Kure Naval Museum, digitally coloured photo, courtesy J Irotoko)

thirteen battleships were planned,[15] compared to just six aircraft carriers – a clear sign that the 'big gun club' still held a leading position inside the upper echelons of the Imperial Navy.

On 2 July 1941, during a conference between the Imperial Headquarters and the government, a 'Synthesis on the Policy of the Japanese Empire in Relation to the Change of Circumstances' was approved. The document, reiterating the decision to 'strike south', took into account the possibility of a war against the United States and Great Britain. Consequently, on 28 July, an 'Urgent War Construction Programme' (*Maru-Kyu*) was adopted, which provided for 293 new-builds, including an improved *Hiryu*-class aircraft carrier which would later become the *Unryu*.

After the Battle of Midway, where Japan lost four aircraft carriers (in addition to *Shoho*, sunk the previous month), between 20 and 21 June 1942 several high-level meetings took place on board *Yamato*, flagship of the Combined Fleet (Rengo Kantai), in order to somehow remedy this critical situation. After long discussions, a complete revision of the *Maru-Yon* and *Maru-Go* Programmes was decided, merging them into a single plan identified as the 'Fifth Emergency Replacement Programme' (*Kai-Maru-Go*), envisaging the construction of 361 ships, including eighteen aircraft carriers.[16] According to this programme, nine ships were also to be converted into aircraft carriers: the third *Yamato*-class battleship, a submarine support ship, two seaplane carriers and five passenger ships.[17]

For the aircraft carriers converted from auxiliary and merchant ships, essentially intended for escort and/or air transport missions, it proved possible to keep to the delivery schedule almost entirely. However, this was not the case for aircraft carriers to be built from scratch or, as in the case of *Shinano*, requiring extensive and complex works. As described later, these ships, once completed, did not embark even a single aircraft, an unmistakable sign that the warship–aircraft combination peculiar to the Imperial Japanese Navy, which had proved its worth in the first months of the Pacific war, by then was only a fading memory.

HOSHO

HOSHO

	Shipyard	Laid down	Launched	Completed
	Asano, Tsurumi*	16 December 1920	13 November 1921	27 December 1922*
Displacement	7,470t standard, 9,494t normal			
Dimensions	Length 168.25m oa; 165.05m wl; 155.45m pp. Beam 17.98m wl. Draft, 6.17m			
Flight deck	168.25 x 22.62m (7.5m forward, 10.5m aft)			
Machinery	8 Kanpon boilers and 2 Parsons geared turbines: 30,000shp, 2 shafts			
Speed	25 knots			
Fuel	Oil, 2,700 tons; coal, 940 tons			
Endurance	8,680 miles at 12 knots			
Armament	4 Third Year type 140mm/50 single mounts; 2 Third Year type 76.2mm/40 single mounts; 2 Vickers 40mm/62 single mounts; 15 (+6) aircraft			
Complement	59 officers and 459 men			

* Fitted out and completed at the Yokosuka Arsenal

The '1918 8-6 Fleet Completion Programme' also provided for six 'special service' ships, including five *Shiretoko*-class tankers,[18] which were thus to be added to the two tankers included in the previous programme. However, the sixth tanker was destined to become not only the Imperial Japanese Navy's first aircraft carrier, but also the world's first ship of this type built as such to enter service.[19]

At the time, the close relations existing between Tokyo and London had allowed several Japanese officers to study in Great Britain. Therefore, the design for a Japanese aircraft carrier was the subject of various proposals derived from British developments, especially regarding the embarked air wing. Influenced by the work done on *Campania* and *Furious* (the latter before being fully converted), the Japanese Navy initially envisaged a seaplane carrier equipped with a forward platform inclined by 2°, a structure including bridge and funnel placed amidships, and a large hangar. However, after receiving further information from the Japanese naval attaché in London relating to the characteristics of *Eagle*[20] and *Hermes*, the Japanese Navy decided to build a vessel equipped with a continuous flight deck and a small island, this including the bridge and supporting a short mast.

The construction of this new vessel, initially named *Hiryu* but later definitively named *Hosho*, was to be assigned to the Yokosuka Arsenal. It was, however, decided to divert the order to the Asano yard in Tsurumi (near Tokyo), which had been selected as a 'reserve' shipyard for the construction of warships but at the time was suffering a serious financial crisis.

After her launch, *Hosho* was towed to the Yokosuka Arsenal for completion and fitting out. At the time, Yokosuka was the 'cradle' of Japan's nascent naval aviation. The hull of *Hosho* was shaped like contemporary Japanese light cruisers, but was provided with a double bottom in order to maintain sufficient structural strength. Additionally, and given her small displacement, *Hosho* was fitted with a pair of Sperry-type stabiliser fins that would reduce rolling and ensure transverse stability during flight operations.

The flight deck was as long as the ship's overall length: its 28m-long forward section was sloped down at an angle of -5° to help aircraft during take-off, and the flight deck's aft section was partially rounded at the edge to facilitate landing. Two elevators (10.35 x 7.86m the forward one, and 13.7 x 6.34m the aft one) were used to move aircraft up and down. There were two hangars, arranged at different levels and linked by a connecting passage. The forward hangar, located on the forecastle deck, was crossed by the boilers' exhausts and was used for housing the fighter aircraft.

The two-deck aft hangar was split into two sections (of 16.5 x 14m and 29.4 x 12m, respectively), the latter likely devoted to stowing Type 10 triplane torpedo bombers.[21] Arresting gear equipment included both a British-manufactured type with longitudinal steel cables and a French Fieux-type with transverse steel cables.

On the starboard side of the flight deck, just abaft the forward elevator, there was a small island fitted with a tripod mast. A collapsible crane, located forward of the island, was used to embark aircraft when *Hosho* was alongside. Three hinged funnels were placed abaft the island. During flight operations, they were pivoted horizontally outboard so that the flight deck was not affected by smoke. However, since these funnels protruded from inside the flight deck, they reduced the area available for flight operations.

1 • The aircraft carrier *Hosho* when commissioned (1922).
2 and 3 • *Hosho* in 1941. (From M Ledet, *Samourai sur porte-avions*)

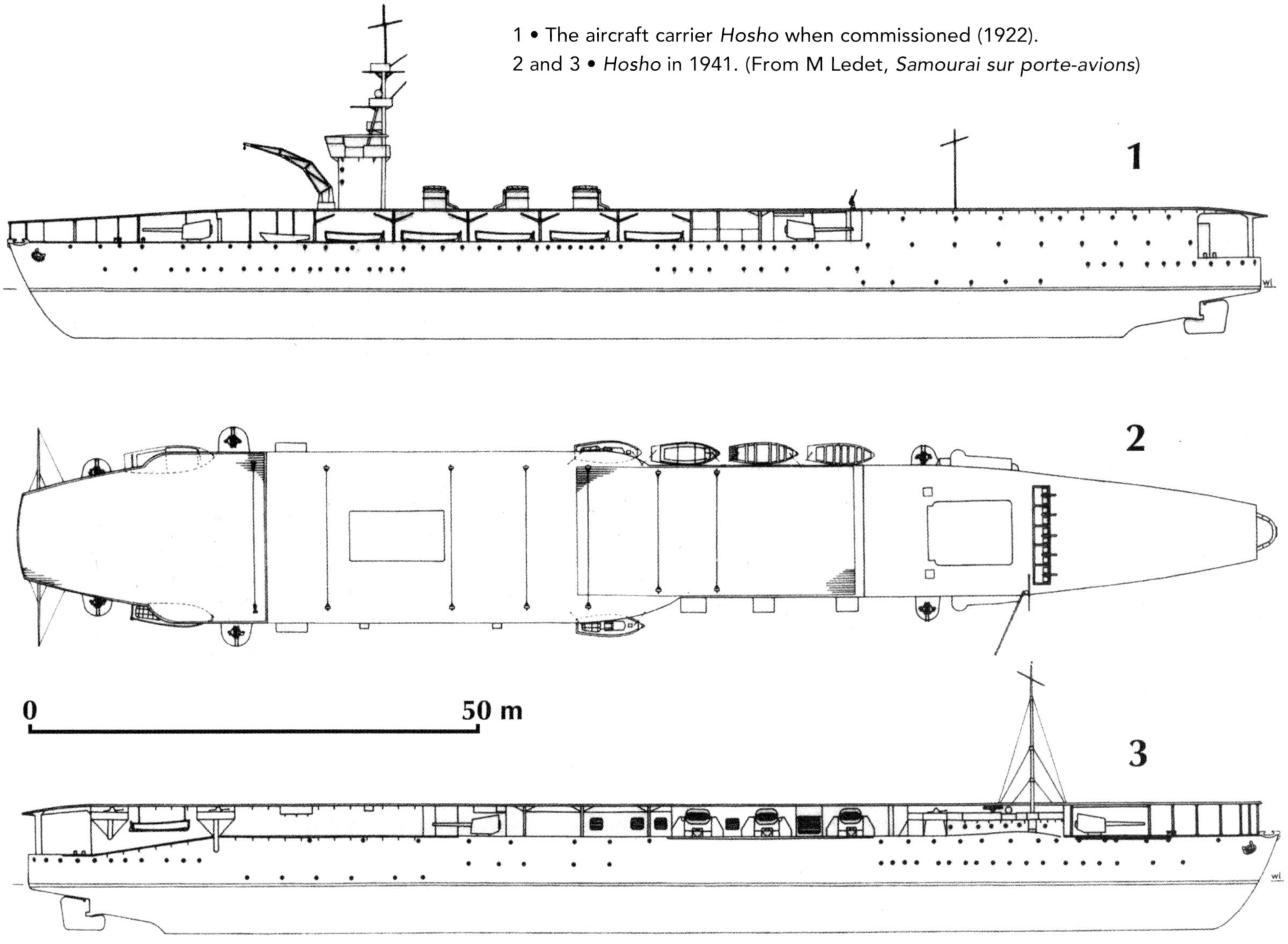

1

2

0 50 m

3

The aircraft carrier *Hosho* one week after launch, moored at the Asabo shipyard in Tsurumi on 20 December 1921. Fitting out was completed at the Yokosuka Arsenal. (Kure Naval Museum)

The aircraft carrier *Hosho* in early December 1922, shortly before commissioning, which took place on the 27th of that month. (Kure Naval Museum)

Machinery included two Parsons geared turbines of 15,000shp each, purchased from Britain. Steam was provided by eight Kanpon boilers, four oil-fired and four oil- and coal-fired, the latter being replaced in 1928 by oil-fired equipment. Boilers provided steam at 18.3kg/cm^2 and 138°C for 30,000shp, achieving a speed of about 25 knots.

Armament included four Third Year-type 140mm/50 single guns (two fore and two aft) and two Third Year-type 76.2mm/40 retractable single guns, the latter being placed, one on each side, forward of the aft elevator. Anti-air defence was also provided by two Vickers 40mm/62 single mounts.

During *Hosho*'s first take-off and landing trials, it was found that the island and the narrow width of the flight deck were dangerous, even for small aircraft such as those of the time. Furthermore, although facilitating flight operations, the inclination of the flight deck had drawbacks in terms of longitudinal stability. Thus, from June to August 1924, *Hosho* was modified at the Yokosuka Arsenal. The aircraft crane and the island were removed, the latter being replaced by a small deckhouse placed below the flight deck and fitted with small wings for flight operations control. As requested by aircrews and to improve visibility during flight operations, the aft section of the flight deck was levelled horizontally. The 76.2mm guns were moved to where the island had previously been located, the reason being the length

Hosho's side view in 1924, after the removal of the island. (Kure Naval Museum)

Kure, October 1945: after the end of the Second World War, *Hosho* was used for a few months for the repatriation of Japanese soldiers still present in various war zones. Note the greater extension towards the stern of the flight deck, compared to when *Hosho* entered service. (Kure Naval Museum)

of time (30–60 minutes) required to bring them into action in their original position due to the presence of the horizontal arresting cables. The small tripod mast was replaced by a shorter mast, fitted on the starboard side.

After additional take-off and landing trials, the Yokosuka Arsenal carried out some further minor improvements from March–July 1925, including the installation of a crash barrier abaft the forward elevator.

From 1927–34, additional works were carried out to allow flight operations with new types of aircraft progressively introduced into Japanese naval service. During the '4th Fleet Incident (26 September 1935), *Hosho*'s small navigation bridge collapsed. Therefore, from November 1935 to March 1936, *Hosho* was again modified. The flight deck was shortened by 3m; six Type 93 13.2mm/76 twin gun mounts were installed in place of the 76.2mm/40 mounts; an internal passage was created connecting the two hangars; and the funnels were fixed in the horizontal position with the ends angled slightly downwards and the folding mechanisms were eliminated, thus saving 60 tons. In 1939, the elevators were enlarged to 12.8 x 8.5m (forward) and to 13.7 x 7m (aft), thus permitting operations with Type 90 and Type 95 fighters and Type 92 torpedo bombers.

Shortly before the outbreak of the Pacific war, it was judged that *Hosho* could not operate the new Type 0, Type 99 and Type 97 aircraft.[22] Therefore, the Japanese Navy decided to use her as a training carrier from November 1942 onwards. In this new role, it was assessed that Tenzan- and Judy-type aircraft could be operated with some additional modifications. Therefore, the flight deck was increased to 180m in length and 22.7m amidships. Six Kure-type Mod 10 and Mod 11 arrester wires and a Kusho-type Mod 3 barrier were also fitted. About 20 Type 96 25mm/60 single and twin mounts replaced the old 140mm guns.

At the end of the war, dismantling *Hosho*'s flight deck allowed her to be used as a transport to repatriate Japanese soldiers stationed overseas. This ended her role as an aircraft carrier.

Hosho's capstans, located at the forward end of the main deck. Above, the lower structure of the forward end of the flight deck is visible. (Kure Naval Museum)

COMPOSITION OF THE EMBARKED AIR WING

- **When commissioned**
  10 1MF3, 3 B1M3
- **China Sea (January/March 1932)**
  10 A1N2, 9 B1M3
- **China Sea (August 1937)**
  9 A4N1, 6 B3Y1
- **May/June 1942**
  6 B4Y1

AKAGI – KAGA

AKAGI

	Shipyard	Laid down	Launched	Completed
	Kure Arsenal	6 December 1920	19 November 1923	22 April 1925 (*)
Displacement	26,900t standard; 34,364t at trials; 37,300t full load			
Dimensions	Length: 261.20m oa; 248.95m wl; 234.7m btwn pp. Beam: 31m max; 28.96m wl. Draft: 8.08m			
Flight deck	190m x 30.48m			
Machinery	19 Kanpon boilers and 4 GiHon geared turbines: 131,000shp, 4 shafts			
Speed	32.5 knots			
Fuel	Oil, 3,900 tons; coal, 2,100 tons			
Endurance	8,000 miles at 14 knots			
Protection	Belt, 142mm; deck, 38mm			
Armament	10 Type 3 200/50 mounts (2 twin, 6 single); 6 Type 10 120/45 twin mounts; 60 aircraft			
Complement	Not known			

(*) Fitted and completed at the Yokosuka Arsenal on 25 February 1927.

After modernisation

	Shipyard	Commencement	Completion
	Sasebo Arsenal	24 November 1935	31 August 1938
Displacement	41,300t at trials, 43,725t full load		
Dimensions	Length: 260.67m oa; 250.36m wl; 234.7m btwn pp. Beam: 31.32m wl. Draft: 8.71m		
Flight deck	249.17m x 30.48m (19m fore, 23.77m aft)		
Machinery	19 Kanpon boilers and 4 GiHon geared turbines: 133,000shp, 4 shafts		
Speed	31.2 knots		
Fuel	Oil, 5,770 tons		
Endurance	8,200 miles at 16 knots		
Armament	6 Type 3 200/50 single mounts; 6 Type 10 120/45 twin mounts; 14 Type 96 25/60 twin mounts; 69 (+25) aircraft		
Complement	2,000 officers and men		

The Washington Treaty granted the conversion into aircraft carriers of two warships which at the time were still on the slipways. The Japanese chose the battlecruisers *Amagi* and *Akagi*, being built respectively at the Kure and Yokosuka Arsenals. The hulls of the battleships *Kaga* and *Tosa* would also have been available – both of them being in a more advanced phase of construction – but the greater length and speed of the battlecruisers were the main reasons for their selection.

However, following an earthquake (8.3 on the Richter scale) which struck the Tokyo area on 1 September 1923, the *Amagi*'s hull suffered such extensive damage that it was scrapped, being replaced for the purpose of conversion with that of the battleship *Kaga*, which, under the terms of the Washington Treaty, should have been scrapped.

In contrast to the US Navy, which on the contemporary *Lexington*s had immediately adopted the continuous flight deck for almost the entire hull length, the Japanese, perhaps influenced by what was undertaken by the Royal Navy with the second reconstruction of *Furious*,[24] chose a three-level flight deck. Owing to the characteristics of the original hull (a battleship), this included: an upper or main flight deck, 190.2m long and 30.48m wide (*Kaga*, 171.3m and 30.48m); a middle flight deck, located immediately forward of the main deck, only 15m long and thus difficult to operate; and a lower flight deck, 55.02m long and

The final configuration of the aircraft carrier *Akagi* in 1940. Top and side views, machinery layout, B-B and A-A cross sections (armour thickness in mm). (Drawings by A Nani)

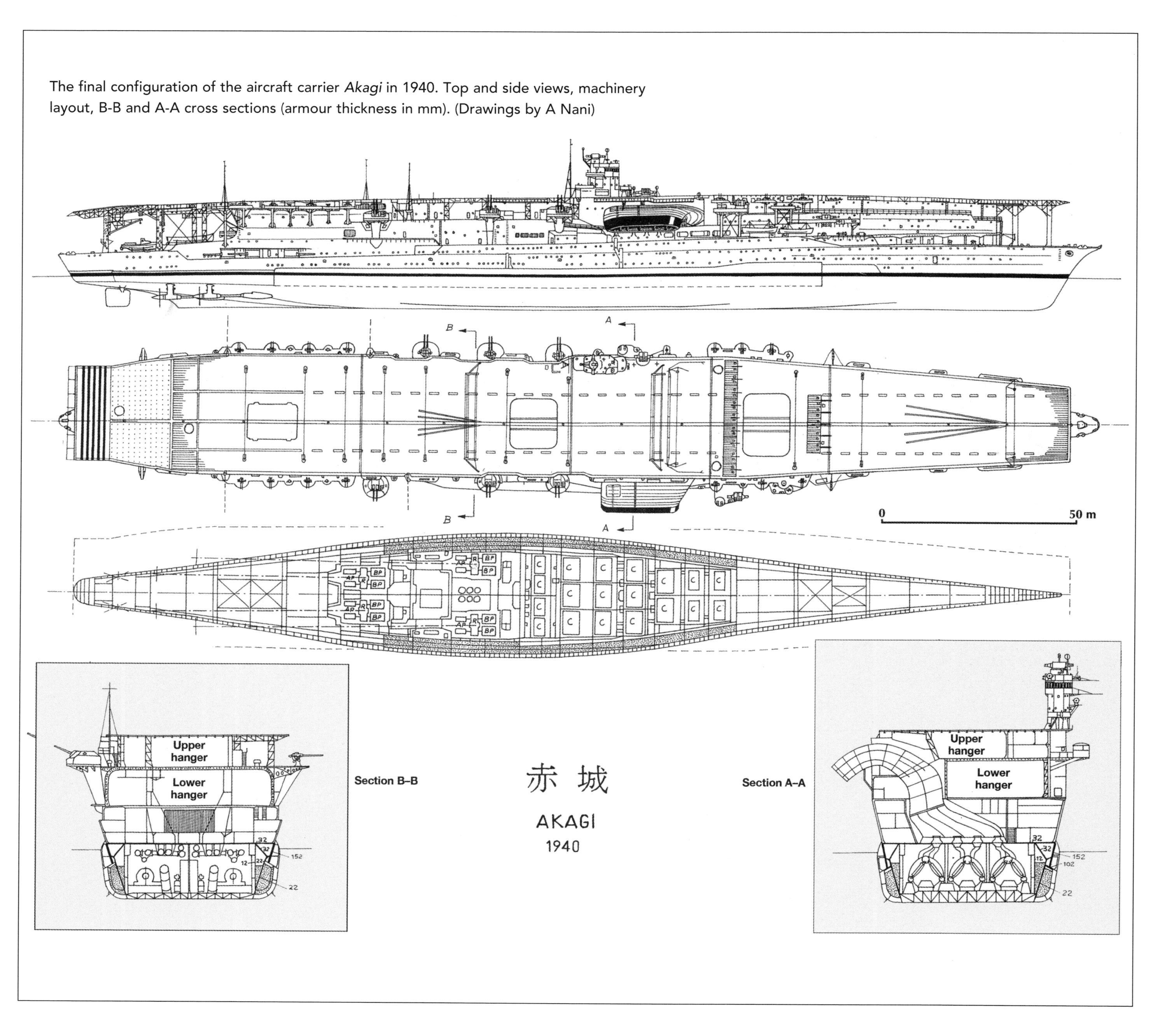

The aircraft carrier *Akagi* in the final stages of construction at Kure Arsenal on 6 April 1925, in preparation for her official launch on 22 April. (Hiroshima Prefectural Museum of Science and History)

22.86m wide (*Kaga*, 48.8m and 24.38m), used for take-off of torpedo planes. Theoretically, this three-level configuration should have allowed simultaneous take-off and landing operations, thus representing a kind of angled deck well before such things had been developed. However, the rapid development of increasingly heavy and better-performing aircraft would quickly make this complicated configuration obsolete.

In order to house the sixty planned aircraft, both *Akagi* and *Kaga* were equipped with a hangar whose stern and bow sections consisted of three and two levels, respectively.

As for the two axial elevators, there were some size differences because they were to operate respectively heavier and lighter aircraft. Elevator sizes were as follows: forward lift, 11.8 x 13m (*Kaga*, 10.67 x 15.85m); aft lift, 12.8 x 8.49m (*Kaga*, 12.8 x 9.15m).

Akagi at full speed during machinery trials in the Iyonada Sea (northern coast of Kyushu) on 17 June 1927. Note the initial configuration of the carrier, with three superimposed flight decks. (Kure Naval Museum)

The aircraft carrier *Akagi* at anchor in the waters off Kure Arsenal in June 1929. (Kure Naval Museum)

The final configuration of *Akagi* in 1941, with a single flight deck extending almost to the edge of the bow. (S Fukui collection)

Twin 127/40 mounts on the port side of *Akagi*, abaft the island, in December 1941. (Kure Naval Museum – digitally coloured image, courtesy J Irotoko)

Since both carriers had no island, all command and control spaces were located below the starboard side of the upper deck and positioned behind the corresponding 200mm twin turret.

Protection of *Akagi* and *Kaga* was based, with reduced thicknesses, on that envisaged by their original designs. On both carriers, the VC steel armoured belt was 152mm,[25] while the 38mm horizontal protection was maintained as in the original design so that it would not interfere with the planned insertion of bulges.

Should a gunnery engagement with cruisers equipped with 8in main armament occur, both carriers were armed with ten 7.9in/50 Type 3 guns: two twin mounts were located on the sides of the middle flight deck and six single mounts were placed in the aft casemates, three on each side. The anti-aircraft battery included six 120/45 Type 10 twin mounts distributed amidships, three on each side.

Machinery configuration remained as in the original designs. *Akagi* was fitted with four GiHon geared steam turbines fed by nineteen Kanpon Type B boilers (eleven oil-fired and eight with mixed firing), while *Kaga* featured four Kawasaki-Brown Curtis geared steam turbines fed by twelve Kanpon Type B boilers (eight oil-fired and four mixed firing).

Due to the differences between the original designs, *Akagi* and *Kaga* had different power and speed characteristics. With 131,200shp, *Akagi* achieved 32.5 knots, while *Kaga*, developing 91,000shp, managed only 27.5 knots.

KAGA

	Shipyard	Launched	Completed
	Kawasaki, Kobe	19 July 1920	17 November 1921
Displacement	26,000t standard; 33,693t at trials; 36,000t full load		
Dimensions	Length: 238.5m oa; 230m wl; 217.93m btwn pp. Beam: 31.67m max; 29.75m wl. Draft: 7.92m		
Flight deck	171.3 x 30.48m		
Machinery	12 Kanpon boilers and 4 Kawasaki-Brown Curtis geared turbines: 91,000shp, 4 shafts		
Speed	27.5 knots		
Fuel	Oil, 3,600 tons; coal, 1,700 tons		
Endurance	8,000 miles at 14 knots		
Protection	Belt, 152mm; deck, 38mm		
Armament	10 Type 3 200/50 mounts (two twin, six single); 6 Type 10 120/45 twin mounts, 60 aircraft		
Complement	Not known		

(*) Fitted and completed at the Yokosuka Arsenal on 25 February 1927.

After modernisation

	Shipyard	Commencement of works	Completion
	Sasebo Arsenal	25 June 1934	25 June 1935
Displacement	26,000t standard; 33,693t at trials; 36,000t full load		
Dimensions	Length: 248.6m oa; 240.30m wl; 217.95m btwn pp. Beam: 32.48m wl. Draft: 9.48m		
Flight deck	248.6 x 30.48m (14.32m fore, 30.48m aft)		
Machinery	8 Kanpon boilers and 4 Kanpon geared turbines: 127,400shp, 4 shafts		
Speed	28.34 knots		
Fuel	Oil, 7,500 tons		
Endurance	10,000 miles at 15 knots		
Armament	10 Type 3 200/50 single mounts; 8 Type 89 127/40 twin mounts; 11 Type 96 25/60 twin mounts; 72 (+18) aircraft		
Complement	2,016 officers and men		

The solution adopted for smoke emissions was also different. *Akagi* had a double smokestack jutting out and positioned on the starboard side, while *Kaga* adopted a configuration echoing that of HMS *Furious*, consisting of two large 90m-long pipes running on each side of the hull, towards the stern, at the height of the middle flight deck. This configuration would not be considered satisfactory, as hot gases in the stern area created turbulence on the main flight deck, particularly in the critical landing area.

Although her conversion was completed after that of *Akagi*, *Kaga* was the first carrier to undergo modernisation. In addition to the complexity of air operations due to the triple flight deck, other reasons that led to this decision were the insufficient speed and the configuration of the exhaust ducts. Approved in 1933, but for financial reasons postponed to the following year, the works were awarded to the Sasebo Arsenal and lasted from June 1934 to June 1935.

The hull was lengthened by approximately 10m to provide additional internal spaces and to compensate for the negative effects on speed as a result of the increase in waterline the beam from 29.57 to 32.48m, following the installation of an additional bulge to improve underwater protection and reduce rolling.

A continuous flight deck was installed for almost the entire hull length, supported at the bow and stern ends by large pillars which relieved the weight on the hull structure; a third 10.67 x 15.85m elevator was also installed.

The elimination of the middle flight deck created a notable increase in internal spaces, thus allowing the stowage of ninety aircraft,[26] eighteen of them partially dismantled and intended as a reserve to replace losses. The upper and lower hangars, 180m and 160m long respectively, both 24m wide and 5m high, had a total surface area of 8,160m^2 and a volume of 40,800m^3.

In addition, the armament was modified. The two 7.9in twin mounts were replaced by an equal number of casemated guns (two on each side), placed forward of the existing ones. The anti-aircraft battery was also strengthened, replacing the original 120/45 twin mounts with more modern Type 89 127/40 mounts. Eleven Type 96 25/60 twin mounts were also installed.

As for protection, belt thickness remained unchanged, with a slight increase in deck thickness.

The final configuration of the aircraft carrier *Kaga* in 1940; side and top views, machinery layout and A-A cross section (armour thickness in mm). (Drawings by A Nani)

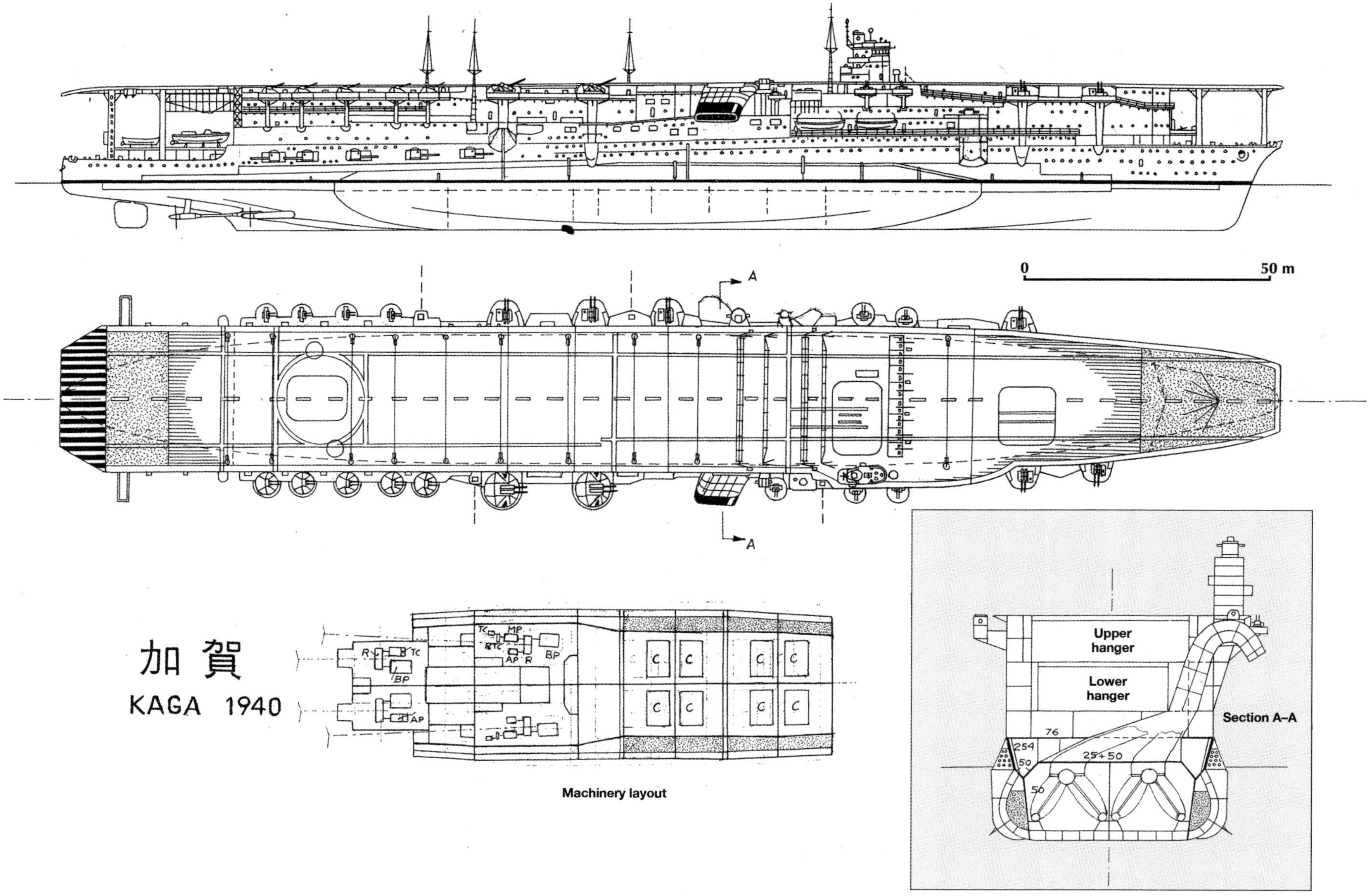

0 50 m

A

A

加賀

KAGA 1940

Machinery layout

Upper hanger

Lower hanger

Section A–A

76

254

50

25+50

50

To increase speed, the previous machinery was completely replaced with four Kanpon geared steam turbines fed by eight Kanpon boilers. Power rose to 127,400shp and speed to 28.34 knots. The cumbersome horizontal smokestacks were replaced with a single smokestack placed on the right side, with exhaust emitted downwards. A small island including a navigation bridge, fire control and observation posts was installed on the forward starboard side of the flight deck.

Around 1940, pneumatic catapults (two on *Akagi* and three on *Kaga*) were installed for experimental purposes in the forward area of the flight decks, probably with some strengthening of the structures below.

The issue of not having developed an efficient catapult would emerge when new types of aircraft entered service.[27] In order to accelerate take-off operations, starting from the summer of 1942, the Japanese Navy began to test a new device for assisted take-off, consisting of a platform which passed through the aircraft's centre of gravity and ended under its tail. This platform was equipped with two accelerators (one on each side) which, fed by a blend of chemicals (nitrocellulose, nitroglycerine, etc), developed thrust of 700kg for three seconds, thus allowing a 30 per cent reduction of launch time. Despite not being widely used, this system was adopted a few times for launching Zeros, Judys and Jills.[28]

Works carried out on *Akagi* were more limited than those on *Kaga*, the size of her flight deck being sufficient and speed not being an urgent matter. Contrary to what happened with *Kaga*, whose modernisation took just one year, that of *Akagi* required almost three years. In all likelihood, the causes of this delay can be ascribed to financial issues and the workload of the Sasebo Arsenal.[29]

As with *Kaga*, a single flight deck replaced the three-deck configuration. Until *Taiho* was built, *Akagi*'s flight deck became the largest of all Japanese aircraft carriers. A third 11.80 x 16m elevator was installed forward, moving amidships the one that previously was in the same position, as was the case for *Kaga*.

Due to the availability of more internal space, the size of hangars was also increased, to a surface area of 8,280m^2 and a volume of 41,400m^3. Furthermore, the capacity of magazines and petrol tanks located below the protective deck was increased, the thickness of the latter being raised to 68mm (57mm of NVNC steel + 11mm of HT steel).

To contain costs, *Akagi*'s armament was not modified. The two 200/50 twin mounts were not replaced and the new Type 89 127/40 mounts were not installed, leaving on board the less-efficient Type 120/45. The only change was the installation of fourteen Type 96 25/60 twin mounts.

Although refurbished, machinery remained unchanged. However, the original mixed combustion boilers were replaced by oil-fired ones. Despite the increase in displacement, speed decreased only slightly. The previous small smokestack, angled upwards and placed behind the main one, was incorporated into a single enormous horizontal smokestack placed on the starboard side and equipped with an anti-smoke screen.

The aircraft carrier *Kaga* in two phases of her construction: the top photo shows the side structures of the aft elevator, the bottom one the twin 200/50 turret on the forward port side.

Kaga after completion at the Yokosuka Arsenal in March 1928, shortly before entering service with the Imperial Navy. (S Fukui collection)

Unlike on *Kaga*, the *Akagi*'s island was positioned approximately amidships, on the port side. Modernisation also affected the flight deck equipment, which included ten Kure-type Mod 4 arresting gears (eight on *Kaga*), two Kusho-type Mod 3 fixed and three mobile safety barriers (two fixed and two mobile on *Kaga*), and two windbreakers (one on *Kaga*).

Akagi at anchor in 1933. The twin 200/450 forward turrets and the three superimposed flight decks are clearly shown. (Kure Naval Museum – digitally coloured image, courtesy J Irotoko)

COMPOSITION OF THE EMBARKED AIR WING

- ***Akagi* and *Kaga*, when commissioned**
16 1MF3, 28 B1M1, 16 2MR1

- ***Kaga* in the East China Sea (January/March 1932)**
16 A1N2, 32 B1M3

- ***Akagi* and *Kaga*, after modernisation**
12 (+ 4) A5M4 (*Kaga* 12 (+ 3)), 38 (+ 16) B4Y1 (*Kaga* 36 (+ 9)), 19 (+ 5) D1A2 (*Kaga* 24 (+ 6) D1A1)

- ***Kaga* in the East China Sea (August 1937)**
16 A2N1-3, 16 D1A1, 22 B2M2, unknown number of B3Y1

- ***Akagi* and *Kaga* at Pearl Harbor (December 1941)**
27 A6M2, 18 D3A1 (*Kaga* 26), 27 B5N2 (*Kaga* 26)

- ***Akagi* during the raid into the Indian Ocean (April 1942)**
27 A6M2, 18 D3A1, 27 B5N2

- ***Akagi* and *Kaga* at Midway (June 1942)**
21 A6M2, 21 D3A1 (*Kaga* 27), 21 B5N2 (*Kaga* 18)

Right: Aerial view of the aircraft carrier *Akagi* in her initial configuration in 1930, with three superimposed flight decks. (Kure Naval Museum)

A side view of the aircraft carrier *Akagi* in 1936, in her final single-deck configuration following the 1934–5 modernisation. (Kure Naval Museum)

RYUJO

RYUJO

	Shipyard	Laid down	Launched	Completed
	Yokohama Dock Co	26 November 1929	2 April 1931	9 May 1933*
Displacement	8,000t standard; 11,768t at trials; 12,829t full load			
Dimensions	Length: 180m oa; 175m wl; 167.2m btwn pp. Beam, 18.5m wl. Draft, 5.5m			
Flight deck	158.7 x 23m (17m forward, 23m aft)			
Machinery	6 Kanpon boilers and 2 Kanpon geared turbines: 65,000shp, 4 shafts			
Speed	29 knots			
Fuel	Oil, 2,290 tons			
Endurance	10,000 miles at 14 knots			
Protection	Belt, 46mm			
Armament	6 Type 89 127/40 twin mounts; 6 Type 93 13.2/76 quadruple mounts; 36 (+12) aircraft			
Complement	101 officers and 823 men			

* Fitted and completed at the Yokosuka Arsenal

With the completion of *Hosho*, *Akagi* and *Kaga*, the 81,000 standard tons allowance assigned to Japan for aircraft carriers gradually decreased. Thus, the Imperial Navy assessed that the best path to follow was building a type of aircraft carrier with limited displacement, but one that was fast and capable of embarking a large number of aircraft.

Consequently, in the 1930s an aircraft carrier with these features was evaluated positively not only by the Imperial Japanese Navy but also by the US Navy, and the construction of a small carrier, named *Ryujo*, was included in the '1927 New Replacement Construction Programme'.

Designed by Kikuo Fujimoto, *Ryujo* should have been built at the Yokosuka Arsenal. However, to meet the needs of the private shipbuilding industry, at the time in severe crisis, the Imperial Japanese Navy assigned her construction to the Yokohama Dock Co shipyards, which was to build the hull up to the main deck. Later, the Yokosuka Arsenal would complete the upper part, including the hangar and flight deck.

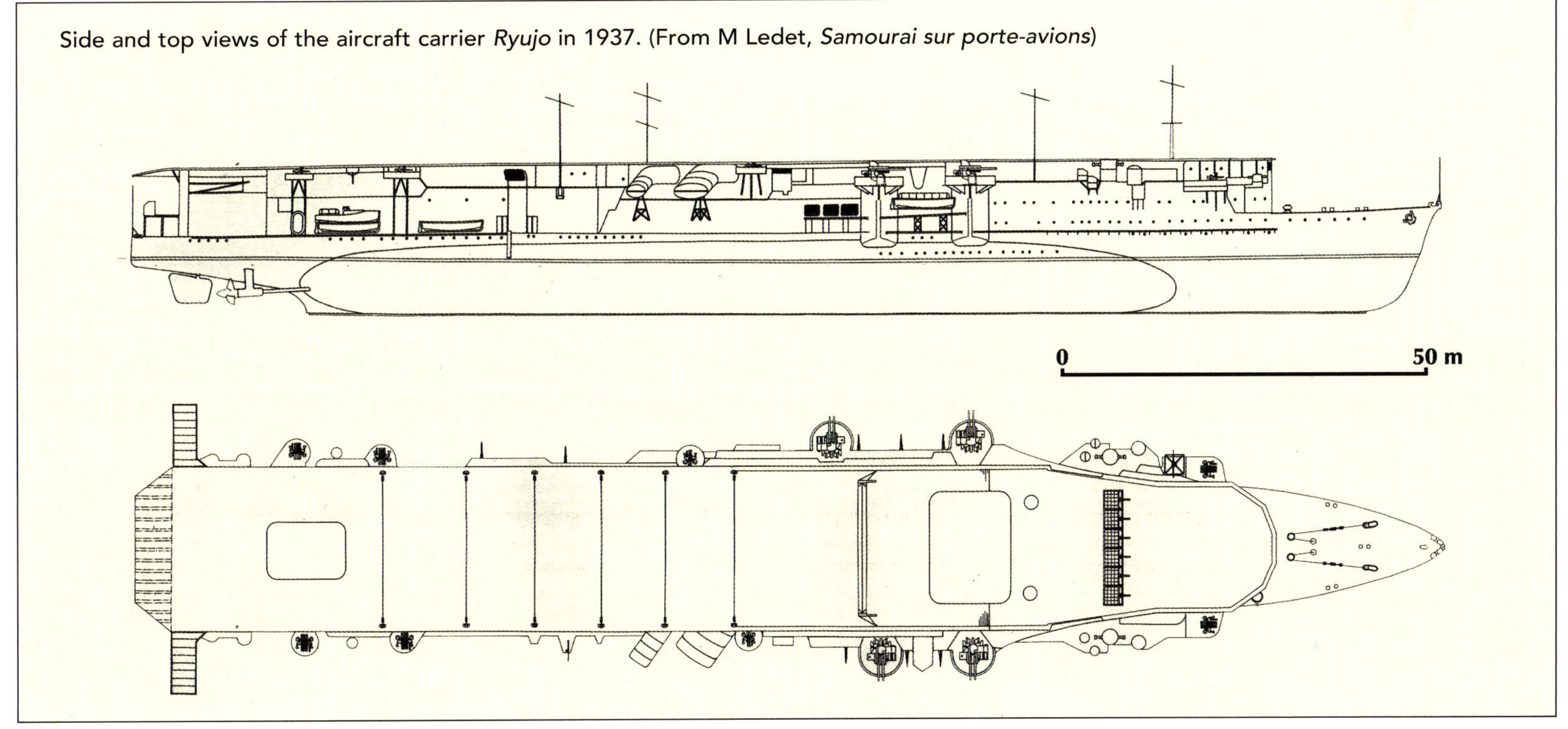

Side and top views of the aircraft carrier *Ryujo* in 1937. (From M Ledet, *Samourai sur porte-avions*)

The aircraft carrier *Ryujo* being completed at the Yokosuka Arsenal, on 20 October 1931. Note that in the background, as part of the Japanese secrecy of the time, the surrounding hills and the Arsenal installations have been hidden by white-out applied to the photograph. (Hiroshima Prefectural Museum of Science and History)

According to the initial design, *Ryujo* was to be equipped with a single hangar built above the main deck and able to house twenty-four aircraft (plus six spares). However, those plans did not come to fruition. A few months after her construction had started, according to the outcome of the first London Conference, the Japanese Naval Staff ordered a radical change of the planned design. Following the Japanese doctrine of building warships that were individually stronger than those of a potential adversary, it was decided that *Ryujo* should be equipped with a double hangar so as to house a greater number of aircraft than previously planned.

This drastic design change would have a negative impact on the general features of the new aircraft carrier, especially regarding structural strength and stability, but the Naval Staff nevertheless ordered the construction of a second hangar. Given a consequent hull depth increase from 16.25m to 20.60m, it was necessary to install bulges in order to maintain the design's metacentric height (ie, its stability) and compensate for the increase in weight.

These changes also impacted the contract signed with the Yokohama Dock Co shipyards, which would have preferred to continue building the ship according to the new design, but encountered strong opposition from the Navy. Thus, after launch, *Ryujo* was towed to the Yokosuka Arsenal for the final works, including the construction of the double hangar and the application of bulges. However, these works could only be resumed in January 1932, due to both lack of funds and the Arsenal's workload.[30]

Fore and aft views of *Ryujo*, *circa* mid-1930s. The forward view shows the bridge located immediately below the forward end of the flight deck. (Kure Naval Museum)

Delivered on 9 May 1933, *Ryujo* featured a hull similar to that of the *Aoba*-class heavy cruisers, which, above and below the waterline, were divided into 86 and 123 watertight compartments, respectively. Due to her limited displacement, only light armour with 46mm of NVNC steel was provided, essentially suitable for dealing with shrapnel or ammunition up to 5in.

The machinery, corresponding to half of that installed on the *Takao*-class cruisers, included two geared turbines fed by steam produced by six Kanpon boilers of the same type as those of the *Fubuki*-class destroyers. The designed power of 65,000shp should have allowed a speed of 29 knots, which was exceeded during trials (29.5 knots with 65,273shp). There were two 4.4m propellers. Combustion gases were emitted through two elliptical-shaped lateral smokestacks located amidships on the starboard side, at the height of the upper hangar deck.

Two innovations were introduced as regards artillery. Long-range anti-aircraft defence was provided by the new Type 89 127/40 gun (six twin mounts), being adopted for the first time on Japanese aircraft carriers, although the Type 93 13.2/76 quadruple mounts were no longer proposed.

The steel flight deck was covered with wooden planks placed transversely and was 158.70m long. At the bow, it ended slightly forward of the command post, this being located under the flight deck. Aft, the flight deck extended just beyond the stern. There were two elevators of different size: the forward one measured 11.1 x 15.70m, that at the aft 10.8 x 8m.

In order to house the greatest possible number of aircraft, the two hangars exploited almost the entire hull width. However, this created significant drawbacks, both for positioning ventilation ducts and bow–stern crew movements. The upper hangar, 125m long and 17.8m wide, was divided into three sections by the forward elevator and a firewall. The lower hangar, 110m long and 17.8m wide, had a forward section only partly capable of stowing aircraft.

Even after the addition of the second hangar, hull form and dimensions remained as originally planned. Thus, during the first sea trials, *Ryujo* highlighted a series of problems, ranging from poor stability to structural weakness. Additionally, she experienced a dangerous tendency to trim by the head when at high speed, thereby suffering water infiltrations in the bow spaces. The latter

Aerial view of the aircraft carrier *Ryujo* in the second half of the 1930s; note the paint scheme with red and white stripes at the aft end of the flight deck. (See also Appendix 4)

problem was due to three factors: the double hangar (which significantly raised the flight deck), the weight savings in some structural elements and a hull with a too-low freeboard.

Having taken note of these defects, combined with lessons learnt from the '*Tomozuru* Accident', *Ryujo* underwent a number of modifications carried out at the Kure Arsenal from 26 May to 20 August 1934. These included the replacement of the previous bulges with larger ones which, in case of war, could be filled with oil; loading approximately 500 tons of ballast; modifications of the forward section of the lower hangar, although at the cost of three fighters; partial replacement of the fireproof bulkhead of the upper hangar with lightweight fireproof barriers; replacement of the access door to the lower hangar with a watertight steel bulkhead, in order to prevent flooding; replacement of two 5in mounts with two Type 96 25/60 twin mounts; and an increase in the angle of inclination of smokestacks and modification of ventilation ducts. After these works, *Ryujo*'s displacement at trials rose to 12,575 tons.

After the 4th Fleet Incident, in which *Ryujo* was damaged, she underwent additional modifications at the Kure Arsenal, lasting from 11 October 1935 to May 1936.

Ryujo's forward section was strengthened and the command post was made round-shaped, thus shortening the flight deck from 158.7m to 156.5m. An additional watertight bulkhead was placed in front of the access door to the lower hangar and strengthening works were carried out in the upper hangar.

About two years later, works were also carried out to modernise the flight deck equipment, which, in its latest configuration, included six Type Kure Mod 4 arresting gears, a Type Kusho Mod 3 emergency barrier as well as a further windbreak barrier.[31]

Shortly before the war with the United States began, *Ryujo* was equipped with an anti-mine demagnetisation belt, while the short-range anti-aircraft battery was slightly enhanced; some unverifiable sources report that in May 1942, the six 13.2/76 quadruple mounts were replaced with the same number of 25/60 triple mounts.

COMPOSTION OF THE EMBARKED AIR WING

- **When commissioned (June/September 1933)**
9 (+ 3) B1M2, 3 (+ 2) A1N1

- **After the Second modernisation (May 1936)**
12 (+ 4) D1A1, 24 (+ 8) A4N1

- **East China Sea (July 1937)**
12 A4N1, 15 D1A1

- **East China Sea (March/April 1938)**
15 D1A2, 9 A5M4

- **Raid against British maritime shipping in the Gulf of Bengal (March 1942)**
12 A5M4, 13 B5N1, 4 B5N2

- **Aleutian Islands (June 1942)**
12 A6M2, 18 B5N2

- **Eastern Solomon Islands (August 1942)**
23 (+ 1) A6M2, 9 B5N2

Ryujo steaming at full speed on 6 September 1934. (Kure Naval Museum)

Right: The aircraft carrier *Ryujo* at anchor in 1936. (Kure Naval Museum – digitally coloured image, courtesy J Irotoko)

SORYU

SORYU

	Shipyard	Laid down	Launched	Completed
	Kure Arsenal	20 November 1934	23 December 1935	29 December 1937
Displacement	15,900t standard; 18,848t at trials; abt 20,000t full load			
Dimensions	Length: 227.5m oa; 222.46m wl; 206.52m btwn pp. Beam: 21.34m wl. Draft: 7.62m			
Flight deck	216.9 x 26m			
Machinery	8 Kanpon boilers and 4 Kanpon geared turbines: 152,000shp, 4 shafts			
Speed	34.5 knots			
Fuel	Oil, 3,400 tons			
Endurance	7,680 miles at 18 knots			
Protection	Belt, 140mm; deck, 40mm			
Armament	6 Type 89 127/49 twin mounts; 14 Type 96 25/60 twin mounts; 57 (+16) aircraft			
Complement	81 officers and 1,021 men			

After *Ryujo*'s completion, Japan had to decide how best to use the amount of tonnage still available for aircraft carriers under the Washington treaty. At the time, two schools of thought emerged, promoting respectively an aircraft carrier of limited displacement but capable of operating a large embarked air wing (such as Ryujo or the contemporary USS *Ranger*), and alternatively an aircraft carrier-cruiser hybrid, a concept being explored within the US Navy.

As the United States was considered the principal enemy, the Imperial Japanese Navy followed American developments closely. As a result, a hybrid design named G.6 was developed, with cruiser features that were disproportinate for a 12,000t standard displacement carrier. As a consequence it was necessary to reconsider such a proposal, falling back on a more 'reasonable' Design G.8 which, inter alia, featured a standard displacement of 10,050 tons. Respecting the treaty constraints, it would have been possible to build two carriers which, planned in the '1934 Second Construction Replacement Programme', should have been completed between 1936 and 1937.

For comparison, the preliminary features of the two designs are shown below:

	G 6	**G 8**
Standard displacement	12,000t	10,050t
Displacement at trials	17,500t	18,000t
Waterline length	240m	240m
Beam	21.7m	23.4m
Power	150,000shp	150,000shp
Speed	36 knots	35.5 knots
Armament	Three 7.9in twin mounts,	Five 6.1in mounts (1 triple, 1 twin),
	Six 5in twin mounts,	6 5in twin mounts,
	70 aircraft	Fourteen 25mm twin mounts, 74 aircraft

The first aircraft carrier was named *Soryu*. However, while materiel necessary for her construction was being readied, the capsizing of the torpedo boat *Tomozuru* forced a radical change of plan.

Since issues had become apparent from the start, in order to ensure a smooth coexistence of all requirements in an already contained displacement, the *Tomozuru* Accident[32] became the trigger for a complete design reassessment, moving from the concept of 'aircraft carrier-cruiser' to that of a true aircraft carrier. *Soryu* would actually become the first modern Japanese aircraft carrier. The Japanese Naval Staff dictated the following preliminary features: displacement at trials, 18,000 tons; fifty-one (+ seventeen) aircraft; top speed, 35 knots.

The aircraft carrier *Soryu* in 1940: side and top views, machinery layout and A-A cross section (armour thickness in mm). (Drawings by A Nani)

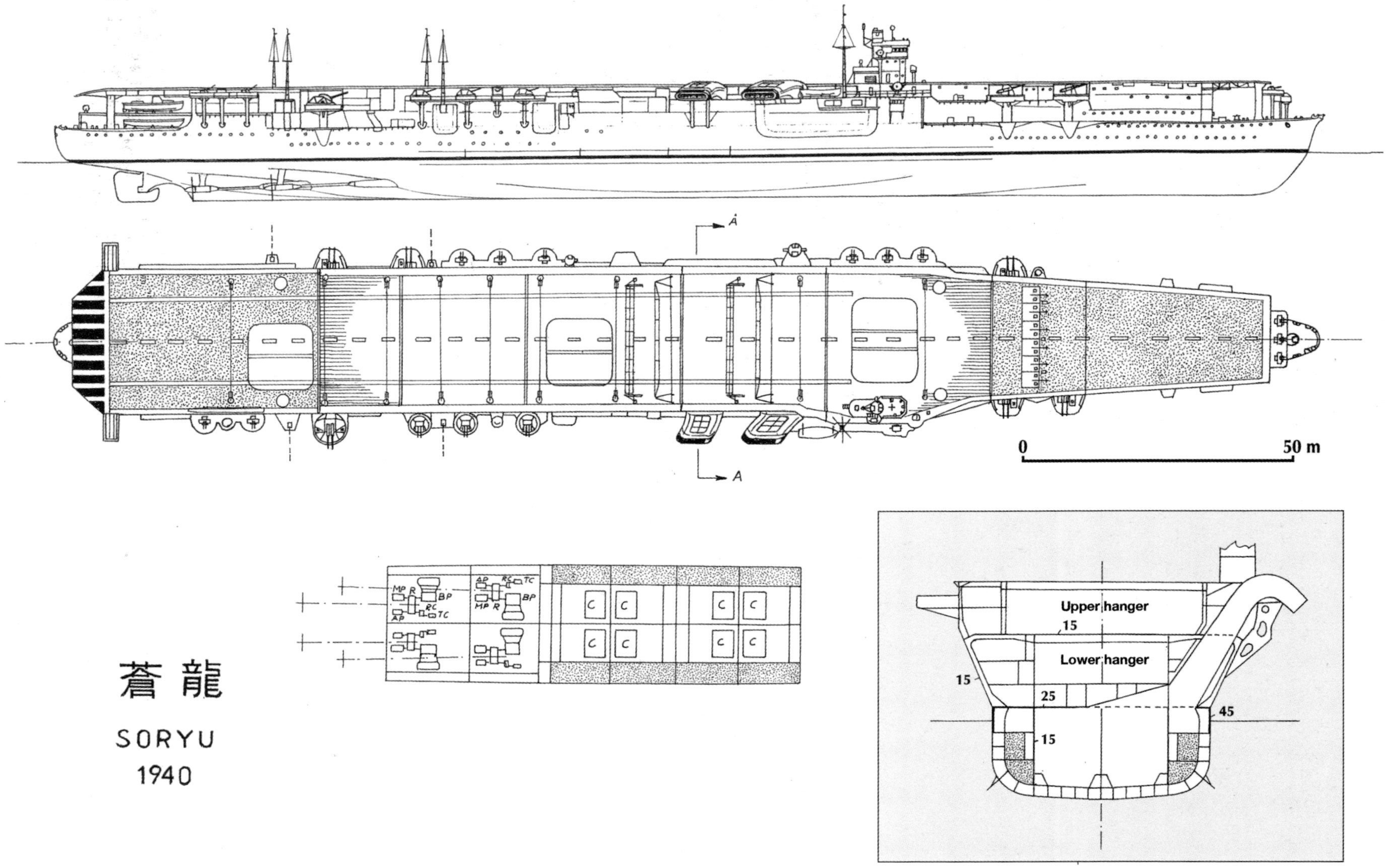

A
A
0
50 m
MP R BP
AP RC TC
AP RC TC
MP R BP
C
Upper hanger
15
Lower hanger
15
25
45
15

蒼龍
SORYU
1940

Soryu being fitted out at the Kure Arsenal in spring 1937. (Kure Naval Museum)

Laid down at Kure in December 1934, *Soryu* had a hull shape echoing those of a cruiser with a high length/beam ratio (ie, 10), and therefore suitable for high speeds. The forward-located island was placed on the starboard side, on a sponson connected down to the hull waterline. Two funnels emitting exhaust downwards were placed immediately abaft the island.

To contain weight and remain within the displacement limits established by the treaties, extensive use of welding was initially envisaged for the hull construction, as well as the use of light alloys. However, while construction was still in its initial phase, the 4th Fleet Incident[33] forced a further design review, especially in terms of robustness and stability.

The hull and hangar were thus strengthened with riveted plates. Furthermore, since the upper hangar deck was not part of the hull strength structure, the upper flight deck was fitted with expansion joints, in order to dampen stresses due to the succession of pitching and sheering.[34] To increase stability, *Soryu* was also equipped with bilge keels extending over one-third of the hull length. The flight deck did not contribute to the structural strength of the hull and had three elevators, all 11.5m wide and 16m, 12m and 10m long respectively.

The presence of three elevators was due to two linked factors: the almost generalised double hangar configuration in the most important Japanese aircraft carriers and the requirement to quickly move planes from the hangars to the flight deck and vice versa. However, this configuration took away useful space for housing aircraft in the hangar and weakened the flight deck structure, creating a dangerous concentration of forces in the central section.

The double hangar was split into three compartments by sliding fireproof bulkheads placed forward of each elevator. The two hangars had the same width (17m), but different lengths (170m the upper one, 140m the lower one). Their height was rather limited, especially that of the lower hangar, with consequent complications for moving, refuelling and rearming aircraft (the Japanese carried out these operations inside the hangars).

Both hangars were split into three compartments, each intended to accommodate a particular type of aircraft, this being standard procedure in the most important Japanese aircraft carriers. The first compartment, between the aft and the central elevator, was devoted to torpedo bombers; the second, from the central elevator to the forward one, was used for dive bombers; the third, located between the forward elevator and the bow bulkhead, was devoted to fighters.

The lower hangar was separated from machinery spaces by an underlying bridge which housed workshops, depots, engineer officers' and non-commissioned officers' quarters. Electrical equipment and passageways were arranged in front of the boiler rooms. Then followed, towards the bow section, bomb, torpedo and anti-aircraft ammunition magazines and petrol tanks. A similar arrangement was adopted in the stern section, abaft machinery spaces.

The flight deck equipment included nine Type Kure Mod 4 arresting gears (two forward of the crash barriers and seven behind them), capable of stopping a 4-ton aircraft in less than 40m. There were also three (two fixed and one mobile) Kusho Type 3 safety barriers, the first installation of such a device on a Japanese aircraft carrier. They were used together with a windbreaker. A hydraulically operated screen was placed in front of the forward elevator to protect flight deck personnel during aircraft launches.

According to *Soryu*'s design, aircraft should have embarked through a special ramp, located aft of the hangar deck. However, this ramp was eliminated after the 4th Fleet Incident because in rough weather it was a possible source of flooding. For the same function, a foldable crane was installed on the port side, next to the aft elevator.

Machinery included, as on the *Suzuya*-class cruisers, four Kanpon geared steam turbines fed by eight Kanpon boilers (operating at 22kg/cm^2 and 300°C). Designed power – 152,000shp – was calculated to achieve 34.5 knots. Considering that several of the new aircraft carriers tended to heel excessively, *Soryu* was equipped with two underhung rudders, instead of the usual semi-compensated rudders.

Hull protection was provided only by a narrow armoured belt of NVNC steel with a thickness ranging, depending on the areas, from 35–140mm. The lower hangar deck, which served as a protection deck, had 40mm NVNC steel plates. Underwater protection was provided by a 15mm central bulkhead, which would not have been particularly effective, especially on a warship of limited beam.

Artillery included six Type 89 127/40 machine guns and fourteen Type 96 25/60 machine guns, both in twin mounts. The 5in mount positioned immediately abaft the funnels was equipped with a smoke screen, as well as the three 25mm mounts abaft the second funnel.

COMPOSITION OF THE EMARKED AIR WING

- **Design**
12 (+ 4) A5M4, 27 (+ 9) D1A2, 9 (+ 3) B5N1, 9 C3N1 (S)

- **Pearl Harbor (December 1941)**
26 A6M2, 17 D3A1, 18 B5N2

- **Indian Ocean Raid (April 1942)**
21 A6M2, 21 D3A1, 21 B5N2

- **Midway (June 1942)**
21 A6M2, 21 D3A1, 18 B5N2, 2 D4Y1-C

Detail of the stern of the aircraft carrier *Soryu*, with the impressive wake generated by the ship's high speed. (Kure Naval Museum)

Soryu at anchor in Sukumo Bay (southern coast of Shikoku Island) in 1939. (Kure Naval Museum – digitally coloured image, courtesy J Irotoko).

HIRYU

HIRYU

	Shipyard	Laid down	Launched	Completed
	Yokosuka Arsenal	8 July 1936	16 November 1937	5 August 1938
Displacement	17,300t standard; 20,250t at trials; abt 21,800t full load			
Dimensions	Length: 227.35m oa; 222.93m wl; 210m btwn pp. Beam: 22.04m wl. Draft: 7.74m			
Flight deck	216.9 x 27m			
Machinery	8 Kanpon boilers and 4 Kanpon geared turbines: 153,000shp, 4 shafts			
Speed	34.3 knots			
Fuel	Oil, 3,750 tons			
Endurance	7,670 miles at 18 knots			
Protection	Belt, 140mm; deck, 56mm			
Armament	6 Type 89 127/49 twin mounts; 31 Type 96 25/60 mounts (7 triple and 5 twin); 57 (+16) aircraft			
Complement	79 officers and 1,251 men			

Hiryu was laid down in July 1936, six months after Japan released itself from any previous agreement on naval armaments. At least initially, *Hiryu* was supposed to be a replica of *Soryu*. However, following the lessons learnt from *Kaga*'s modernisation and the outcome of the 4th Fleet Incident, it was deemed essential to modify and improve some features, so that *Hiryu* could meet the up-to-date operational requirements of the Japanese Navy. *Hiryu*'s general layout was similar to that of *Soryu*, but while still aiming for a light and fast aircraft carrier, capable of operating a large number of aircraft, modifications made *Hiryu* a one-off carrier.

Her hull was largely strengthened by riveting plates of any structural elements which might be subject to longitudinal stresses. Made of DS, 80 per cent of the plating in the hull central section was also riveted on. Side protection was increased, ranging from 50mm to 140mm of NVNC steel. Thickness of the NVNC steel in the lower hangar deck was also increased to 56mm. As in *Soryu*, this level acted as a protection deck. Additionally, a number of HT steel transversal bulkheads were installed to protect various sensitive areas.

These changes led to a trials displacement increase (20,250 tons, compared to *Soryu*'s 18,4487 tons), but with a speed decrease of only 0.2 knots. On the other hand, fuel stowage was higher, which, despite the increased displacement, allowed an endurance almost equal to *Soryu*'s. A noteworthy difference from *Soryu* was the use of a single semi-compensated rudder.

The configuration of the short-range anti-aircraft armament slightly differed from that on *Soryu*, which was laid out for long-range engagements. As well as 25mm triple mounts being installed

Hiryu's machinery trials off Tateyama (east coast of Honshu Island) on 22 January 1938. (Kure Naval Museum – digitally coloured image, courtesy J Irotoko)

The aircraft carrier *Hiryu* in spring 1942: top and side views, inboard profile, machinery layout and cross section (armour thickness in mm). (Drawings by A Nani, coloured by M Brescia)

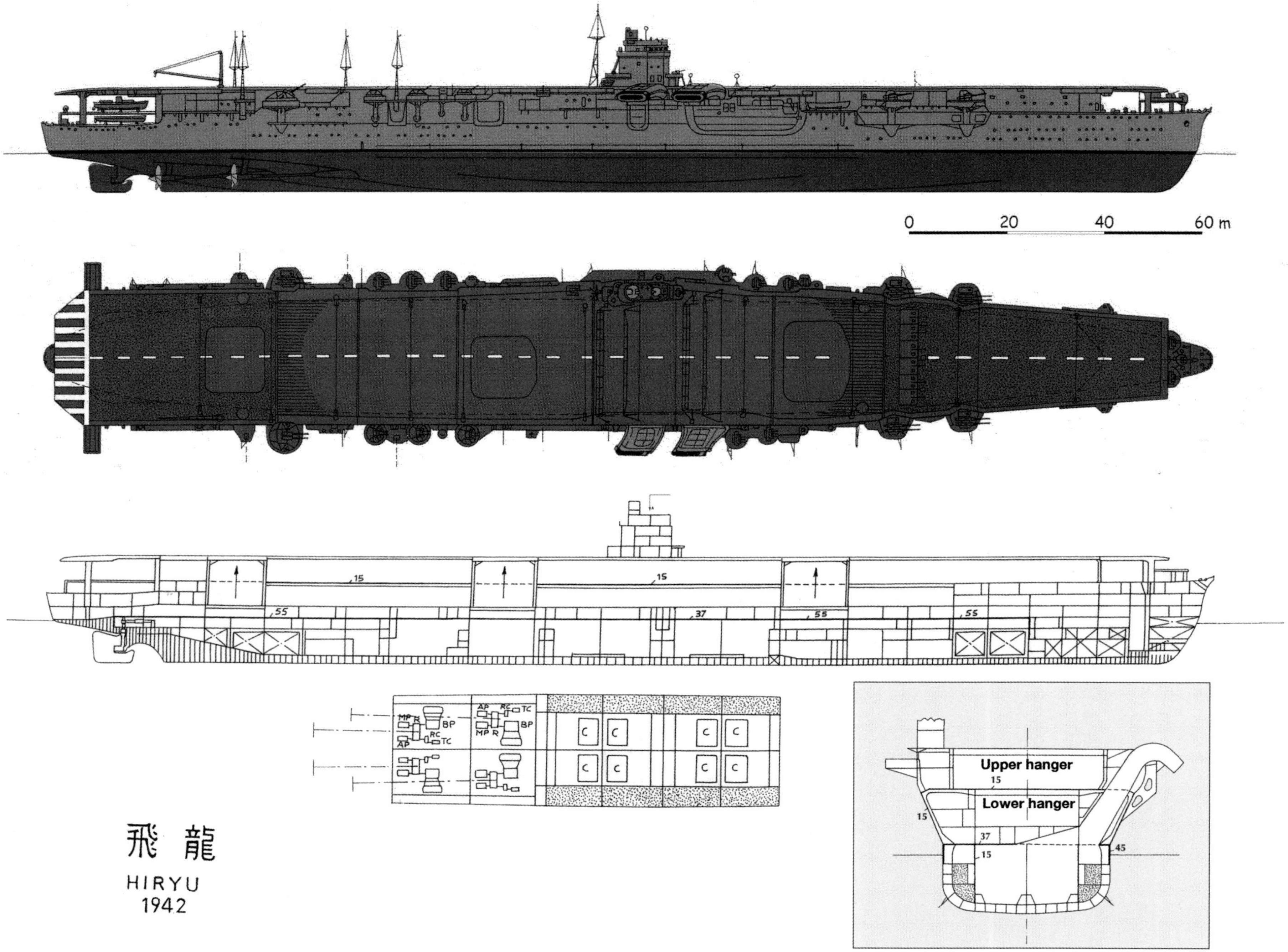

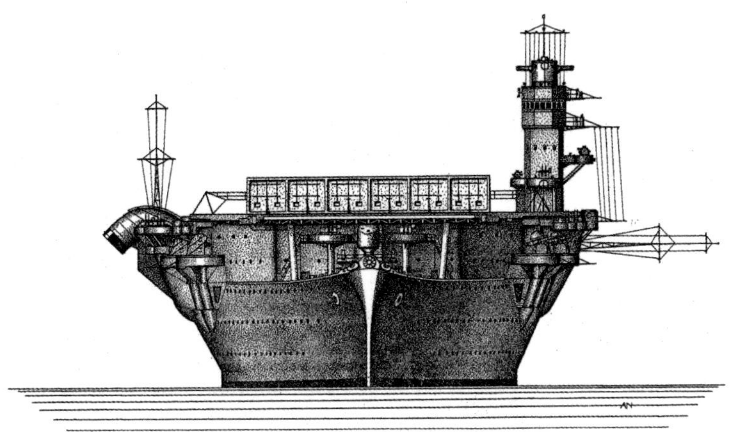

Forward view of the aircraft carrier *Hiryu* when commissioned, with the island located on the port side. (Drawing by A Nani)

for the first time in Japanese aircraft carriers, there were six 5in twin mounts – four placed forward of the funnels and two aft.

The flight deck equipment also had some differences; for example, elevators were larger, the forward one being 16 x 13m, the central one 12 x 13m and that aft 13 x 11.8m.

In addition, a third Type Kusho Mod 3 safety barrier was placed forward of the aft elevator. *Hiryu*'s island was larger than that of *Soryu*, was fitted with an additional level and, like in *Akagi*, was placed on the port side. To aid stability, the two lateral funnels were positioned on the starboard side. After *Akagi*'s trials, it became clear that this arrangement, although freeing the bridge from smoke, threatened to prove counterproductive. Indeed, in certain conditions of wind and speed, hot air enveloped the flight deck, generating variations in lift for landing aircraft. However, since *Hiryu*'s construction was by then too advanced, it was no longer possible to remedy this issue, except to establish that this configuration would not be repeated in future carriers.

As far as air operations were concerned, according to the indications of the Naval Aviation Department, the width of the flight deck was increased by 1 metre (*Soryu*'s 26m-wide flight deck was considered too small), with a similar increase in the hull beam.

COMPOSITION OF THE EMBARKED AIR WING

• **Design**
12 (+4) A5M4, 27 (+9) D1A2, 9 (+3) B5N1, 9 C3N1

• **Pearl Harbor (December 1941)**
23 A6M2, 17 D3A1, 18 B5N2

• **Indian Ocean Raid (April 1942)**
21 A6M2, 21 D3A1, 21 B5N2

Midway (June 1942)
21 A6M2, 21 D3A1, 21 B5N2

Hiryu at anchor, probably at Yokosuka, in 1939. (Kure Naval Museum)

The aircraft carrier *Hiryu* underway on 28 April 1939. (NHHC, NH-73063)

SHOKAKU CLASS

SHOKAKU Class

	Shipyard	Laid down	Launched	Completed
Shokaku	Kure Arsenal	12 December 1937	1 June 1939	8 August 1941
Zuikaku	Kawasaki, Kobe	28 May 1938	21 November 1939	25 November 1941
Displacement	29,800t at trials; 32,105t full load			
Dimensions	Length: 257.5m oa; 250m wl; 238m btwn pp. Beam: 29m wl. Draft: 8.87m			
Flight deck	242.2 x 29m (fore 18m; aft 26m)			
Machinery	8 Kanpon boilers and 4 Kanpon geared turbines: 160,000shp, 4 shafts			
Speed	34 knots			
Fuel	Oil, 5,000 tons			
Endurance	9,700 miles at 18 knots			
Protection	Belt, 165mm; deck, 132mm			
Armament	8 Type 89 127/40 twin mounts; 36 Type 96 (12 25/60 triple mounts); 72 (+12) aircraft			
Complement	131 officers and 1,529 men			

There were two key aspects to the approval of the '1937 Third Replacement Construction Programme' (*Maru-San*). The first implied that Japan, after having unilaterally freed itself from previous naval armaments agreements, had chosen to follow the path to war with the Western powers. The second concerned the coexistence of two opposite schools of thought within the Imperial Japanese Navy. Most senior officers were still stubbornly linked to the 'myth of Tsushima', and thus supported the construction of battleships. They were opposed by a group of younger officers who believed that the time for aircraft carriers and naval aviation had arrived.

The 1937 construction programme included two categories of major warships: the first two *Yamato*-class super-dreadnoughts and the two *Shokaku*-class fleet aircraft carriers. These ships would have very different impacts upon the coming war: the *Yamato*s had almost no influence on the course of the conflict, proving to be useless giants, whereas the *Shokaku*s would become the spearhead of the Imperial Japanese Navy.

Naval Staff specifications for the *Shokaku*s included the following: eighty-four embarked aircraft (plus twelve in reserve); sixteen 5in and thirty-six 25mm guns; speed, 34 knots; endurance, 9,700 miles at 18 knots; protection of magazines against 800kg bombs and 7.9in shells; and machinery spaces protected against 250kg bombs from dive-bombers and 5in shells.

Finally free from the limitations imposed by previous treaties,

Shokaku shortly after her launch at Kure Arsenal, on 1 June 1939. It was a foggy day, a rather frequent occurrence in the area at that time of year. (Kure Naval Museum)

The aircraft carrier *Zuikaku* in 1943: side and top views, machinery layout and cross section (armour thickness in mm). (Drawings by A Nani, coloured by M Brescia)

0 20 40 60 m

MP C BP TC R AP

瑞鶴

ZUIKAKU 1943

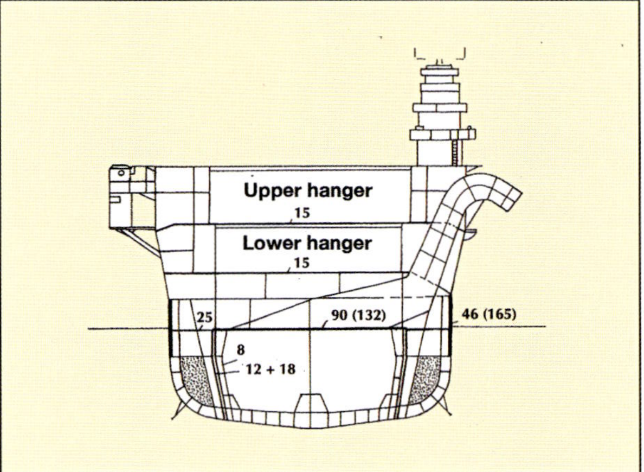

Shokaku a few weeks after commissioning, which took place on 8 August 1941. (Kure Naval Museum)

the Japanese designers not only managed to meet all these requirements, but exceeded them, as highlighted during the trials.

Apparently resembling a scaled-up version of *Soryu*, the *Shokaku*s were actually very different, especially through their improved protection provided by a more robust hull. Furthermore, although their dimensions and displacement did not allow maintaining the same block coefficient as in the *Soryu* and *Hiryu*, they achieved the expected 34 knots, thanks to a better hull design and the excellent performance of their engines.

The bow, very high and raked, had a small bulb, as well as flare and deadrise lines in order to improve speed and seaworthiness.

The *Shokaku*s' stability was compromised by their length, to overcome which, especially in the case of suffering damage, they were equipped with two rudders in tandem. The larger one was located at the stern, while the smaller, auxiliary one was positioned further forward. Seaworthiness was satisfactory, making the *Shokaku*s excellent seagoing boats, with dry decks even in rough seas.

According to design calculations, during trials the flight deck would have been 14.13m above the waterline, facilitating aircraft take-off and landing. However, this would lead to a very low freeboard, with a negative impact on stability. To prevent this, the Japanese designers were able to reduce the flight deck height to 13.7m at full load displacement.

At trials, the summary of weights was as follows:

Weight element	Weight, t	%
Hull	12,460	41.81
Protection	5,153	17.29
Machinery	12,750	9.23
Armament and ammunitions	648	2.18
Fixed and mobile weights	2,873	9.64
Air wing-related weights	2,196	7.37
Fuel	3,335	11.19
Reserve fresh water	385	1.29
Total	29,800	100

The small island, located on the starboard side and moved forward, housed four levels: admiral bridge, navigation bridge, air operations control room, and wheelhouse/command and control spaces. During the concept design phase, placing the island on the port side and amidships was also considered, with the traditional smokestacks emitting smoke downward, on the opposite side. However, after lessons learned from initial operations of *Akagi* and *Hiryu*, in which this latter configuration had been adopted, the Naval Aviation Department expressed its preference for *Soryu*'s configuration, later repeated on all future Japanese carriers. Fitted with eight expansion joints, the flight deck was covered with 12–15cm-thick, longitudinally arranged wooden planks. At its fore and aft ends, the flight deck was made of steel and covered with anti-slip paint.

There were three elevators, one measuring 13 x 16m placed forward and two (central and aft) both measuring 13 x 12m. Fitted with a speed controller, they worked at 0.8m/sec. Thus, an aircraft could be raised from the lower hangar to the flight deck in approximately fifteen seconds (or forty seconds, including the time needed to disengage the elevator basement from its position). There were two smaller auxiliary elevators for moving bombs and torpedoes up to the hangar during aircraft rearming operations.

Landing operations were supported by a number of Type Kure Mod 4 arresting gears. To stop a plane that had missed these, there were five Type Kusho Mod 3 safety barriers (three fixed and two mobile). Flight deck equipment also included a windbreaker.

The two superimposed hangars were of different sizes. The upper hangar was 200m long and 24m wide (18.5m in the boiler spaces). The lower hangar was 180m long and 17.5–20m wide. Their heights also varied, from 4.85m for the upper hangar to approximately 4.7m for the lower hangar. Since refuelling and rearmament operations took place inside the hangars, where air was exchanged every ten minutes, this could lead to extremely dangerous situations in the event of the ship being hit or malfunction of the ventilation system, as petrol vapours could saturate these spaces. Later, measures were taken to mitigate this risk, making refuelling and rearmament also possible on the flight deck.

Machinery was similar to that of *Soryu* and *Hiryu*, but was upgraded in order to reach the required speed. The eight Kanpon

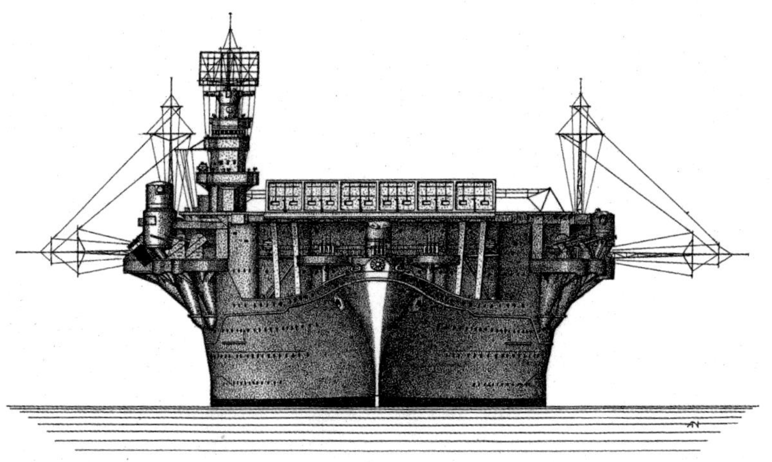

Forward view of the aircraft carrier *Shokaku* in late 1943. (Drawing by A Nani)

boilers (operating at 30kg/cm^2 and 350°C) were arranged amidships, gathered in two groups of four, separated by a double bulkhead. To improve safety, each group was divided into four separate spaces (one for each boiler). The four Kanpon geared turbines groups were placed in separate spaces, abaft those of the boilers. The two forward groups drove the external shafts, the others the internal ones. The total power output of 160,000shp allowed a maximum speed of 34 knots.

Compared to previous Japanese aircraft carriers, the *Shokaku*s were efficiently and precisely armoured. Horizontal protection extended from the bow to the stern petrol tanks, and also included machinery spaces and magazines. NVNC and CNC armour steel plates, connected with 25mm DS plates, were distributed over two decks: the gallery deck, from machinery spaces to the bow elevator; and the main deck, above the bow and stern storerooms. The thickness of the NVNC plates varied from 105mm (petrol tanks) to 132mm (magazines). There were also 65mm CNC steel plates above the machinery rooms.

Vertical protection included a 46mm CNC steel belt, 4.1m wide (2m below the waterline); its lower part was reinforced with 50mm DS plates.

Magazines and storerooms not covered by the armoured belt were shielded by 165mm of NVNC steel inclined at 25° and then tapered to 75–55mm.

The underwater protection scheme resembled that of the American *Colorado*-class battleships and represented a real innovation, as the adoption of bulges would have prevented achieving the required 34 knots.

The *Shokaku*s were fitted with several longitudinal bulkheads. The first two and the watertight double bottom would absorb the energy of an exploding torpedo or mine. The space between the two internal bulkheads was filled with fuel, which could, once consumed, be replaced with seawater. This structure also included a double bulkhead that extended from the protection deck to the external edge of the hull plating and was made of two DS plates (an external one 18mm thick and an internal one of 12mm, thus totalling 30mm). In addition, vital spaces were protected by another 8mm anti-splinter bulkhead, placed behind the double bulkhead.

After the loss of *Taiho* and *Shokaku*, *Zuikaku*'s petrol tanks were reduced in capacity and shielded with concrete to further increase protection.

Artillery included eight Type 89 127/40 twin unshielded mounts, located in platforms also known as 'swallow's nests'. Four platforms were placed forward of the island, two on each side, and the other four at two-thirds of the ship's length, two on each side. The two platforms on the starboard side were immediately abaft the funnels and were fitted with anti-smoke screens.

The *Shokaku*s also had thirty-six Type 96 25/60 guns, grouped in twelve triple mounts placed on platforms. Six were located amidships on the port side, with a small space between the forward group of four and the other two. Two platforms were placed on the starboard side between the island and the funnels, while the other four, in pairs, were located abaft.

The aircraft carrier *Zuikaku* in November 1941. (NHHC)

Like almost all the most important Japanese warships, the anti-aircraft armament of the *Shokaku*s was strengthened with additional 25mm mounts after the Battle of Midway, notably:

June 1942 – installation of six triple mounts (one forward and one abaft the island and two immediately below the flight deck, two forward and two aft);

Autumn 1942 – addition of a third triple mount between those previously placed fore and aft;

June 1944 (before the Battle of the Philippine Sea) – installation of one triple and ten single mounts, giving a total of seventy 25mm guns (twenty triple and ten single mounts);

August 1944 (only in *Zuikaku*) – installation of additional twenty-six 25mm single mounts, sixteen in fixed positions and ten in pivoted mounts. These new mounts were placed on both sides, before the forward and the central elevators. Six Type 5 4.7in, twenty-eight-barrel rocket launchers were also installed.

To provide additional anti-mine and anti-submarine protection, the *Shokaku*s were also fitted with two paravanes (on both forward hull sides) and depth-charge throwers.

Although clear evidence is missing, presumably in the second half of 1942 the *Shokaku*s were provided with two Type 21 radars: one placed atop the island and the other in a retractable platform close to the flight deck. Furthermore, shortly before June 1944, both carriers had a Type 13 radar installed on a tripod mast abaft the island.

The *Shokaku*s were also equipped with a Type 91 forward sonar system, but this could only be used when they were alongside, at anchor or steaming at low speed.

COMPOSITION OF THE EMBARKED AIR WING

- **As designed**
18 (+ 2) A6M2, 27 (+ 5) D3A1, 27 (+ 5) B5N2

- **Pearl Harbor (December 1941)**
15 (*Zuikaku* 14) A6M2, 26 (*Zuikaku* 25) D3A1, 27 B5N2 (only as bombers)

- **Indian Ocean Raid (April 1942)**
18 A6M2, 27 D3A1, 27 B5N2

- **Coral Sea (May 1942)**
21 A6M2, 20 (*Zuikaku* 21) D3A1, 21 B5N2

- **Eastern Solomon Islands (August 1942)**
26 (*Zuikaku* 27) A6M2, 24 (*Zuikaku* 27) D3A1, 18 B5N2, 2 D4Y1-C (only *Shokaku*)

- **Santa Cruz Islands (October 1942)**
27 A6M2 and A6M3, 27 (*Zuikaku* 18) D3A2, 18 B5N2

- **Mariana Islands or Philippine Sea (June 1944)**
11 A6M2, 53 A6M5, 52 D4Y1 and D4Y2, 26 B6N2 (estimate)

- ***Zuikaku* during the Battle of Leyte Gulf (October 1944)**
42 A6M5 (16 as bombers), 14 B6N2, 7 D4Y2 (as reconnaissance planes)

October 1941: *Zuikaku* steaming in the Bungo Channel, the stretch of sea that divides the islands of Shikoku and Kyushu, in the Japanese metropolitan archipelago. (Kure Naval Museum – digitally coloured image, courtesy J Irotoko)

ZUIHO CLASS

***ZUIHO* Class**

	Shipyard	Laid down	Launched	Completed
***Zuiho* (ex-*Takasaki*)**	Yokosuka Arsenal	20 June 1935	19 June 1936	27 December 1940*
***Shoho* (ex-*Takasaki*)**	Yokosuka Arsenal	3 December 1934	1 June 193	15 January 1939**

Displacement	13,100t at trials; 14,200t full load
Dimensions	Length: 204.8m oa; 201.43m wl; 185m btwn pp. Beam: 18.2m wl. Draft: 6.64m
Flight deck	180 x 23m
Machinery	4 Kanpon boilers and 2 Kanpon geared turbines: 52,000shp, two shafts
Speed	28 knots
Fuel	Oil, 2,370 tons
Endurance	9,250 miles at 18 knots
Armament	8 Type 89 127/40 (4 twin mounts); 4 Type 96 25/60 (2 twin mounts) (*Shoho*, 4 triple mounts); 27 (+3) aircraft
Complement	785 officers and men

* Completed as aircraft carrier (works began in January 1940)

** Conversion carried out at the Yokosuka Arsenal. Works began on 20 December 1940 and were completed on 26 January 1942

The aircraft carrier *Shoho* on 20 December 1941. (Kure Naval Museum – digitally coloured image, courtesy J Irotoko)

The final configuration of the aircraft carrier *Zuiho* in autumn 1944; side and top views, machinery layout and A-A cross section. (Drawings by A Nani)

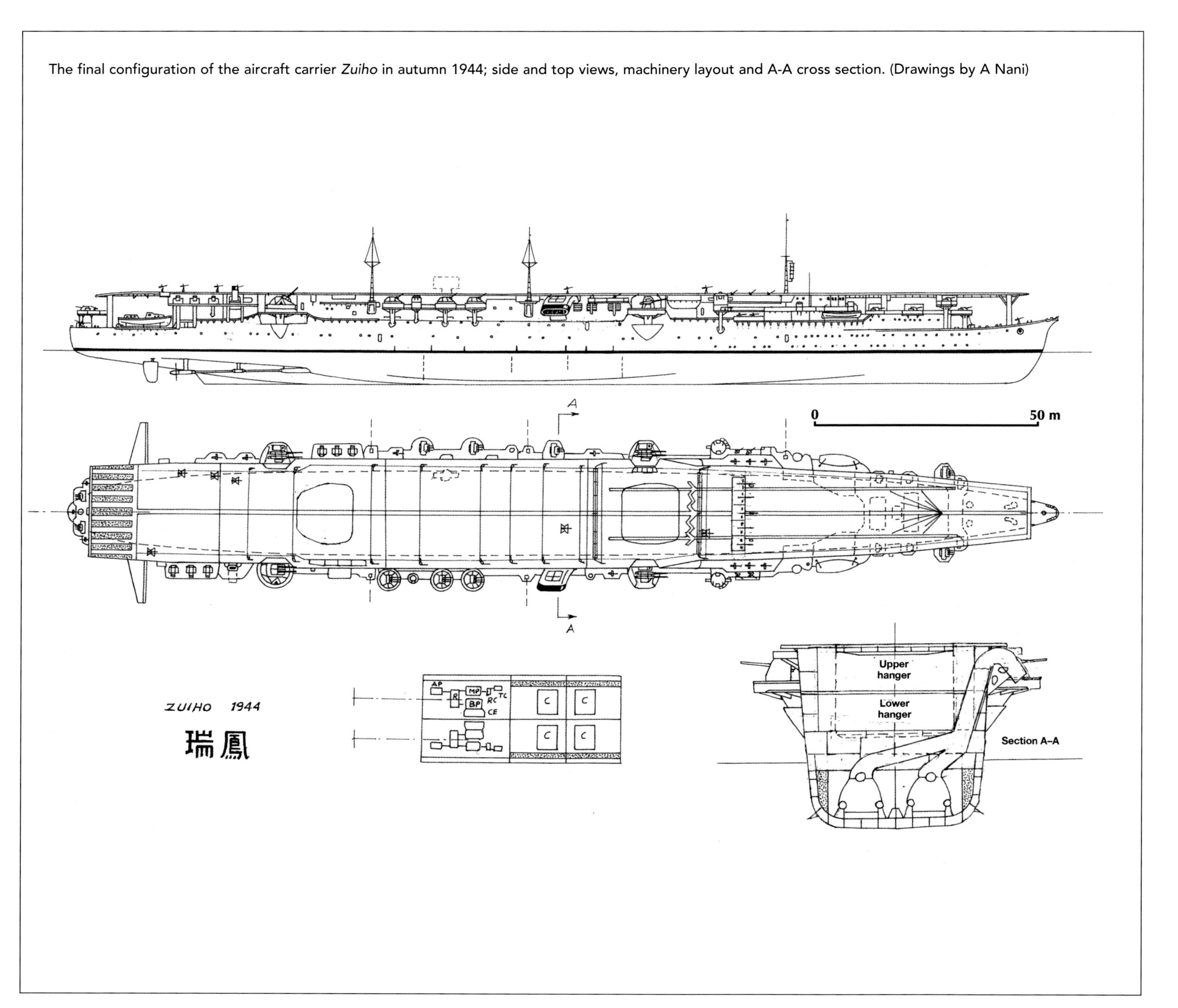

The aircraft carrier *Shoho* at the Yokosuka Arsenal in December 1941, her conversion work almost complete. Note, on the right, the large crane, a significant feature of the Arsenal, which appears in many photographs of Imperial Japanese Navy ships taken at that yard. (S Fukui collection)

Before defining the guidelines for the 1934 construction programme, the Imperial Japanese Navy had to assess whether or not the United States – with whom relations were progressively deteriorating – could launch important naval reinforcement plans. This assessment had to be made before the expiration of the 1930 London Treaty.

Given the requirement to operate an aircraft carrier force at least equal to that of the US Navy, it was necessary, in addition to the carriers themselves, to start building a number of auxiliary ships outside the treaty limits, possessing characteristics that, if necessary, would allow their conversion into aircraft carriers.

Among the vessels included in the '1934 Second Construction Replacement Programme', five[35] met this requirement. They were the seaplane support ships *Chitose*, *Chiyoda* and *Mizuho*[36] and the fast fleet tankers *Tsurugisaki* and *Takasaki*, the latter pair planned for completion as submarine support ships. However, while *Tsurugisaki* was completed as designed, *Takasaki* was launched but had her fitting-out work interrupted on 7 November 1938.

The decision to convert the fleet tankers into aircraft carriers, taken on 8 November 1939 for *Tsurugisaki* and one month later for *Takasaki*, required the immediate replacement of their machinery. In fact, the unreliability and poor performance of the Type 13 Mod 10 diesel engines, as emerged from the first months of *Tsurugisaki*'s activity as a submarine support ship, required their replacement with two geared turbines similar to those of the *Kagero*-class fleet destroyers. These turbines delivered 52,000shp, which allowed the ship to achieve the remarkable speed of 28 knots.

As *Takasaki* was still being fitted out, she was directly converted into an aircraft carrier and renamed *Zuiho*, followed one year later by *Tsurugisaki*, renamed *Shoho*.

Like *Ryujo*, these carriers were completed without the island, with command and control spaces located forward, under the flight deck. The side funnel was placed amidships on the starboard side; the exhaust of the auxiliary boiler was positioned on the starboard side towards the stern, with a small collapsible smokestack.

To ensure sufficient stability, an intermediate solution was adopted for the arrangement of the hangars, which did not fully embrace the traditional Japanese configuration of two superimposed structures with similar areas. The main hangar, built on the forecastle, was 124m long, 18m wide and 4.8m high. The lower hangar, 85m long, 13m wide and only 3.2m high, was certainly not conceived to allow aircraft rearmament and refuelling operations.

The flight deck was fitted with two elevators: the forward one measured 13 x 12m, that at the aft 12.5 x 12m. Flight deck equipment included seven Type Kure Mod 4 arresting gears, two

A clear view of the starboard side of *Zuiho* after her conversion into an aircraft carrier. (Kure Naval Museum)

Type Kusho Mod 3 safety barriers (one fixed and one mobile) and one windbreaker.

Armament included four Type 89 127/40 twin unshielded mounts and four Type 96 25/60 twin mounts (four triple mounts on *Shoho*). In September 1943, *Zuiho* had her flight deck lengthened to 192.6m, while the original 25mm twin mounts were replaced with sixteen triple mounts. One Type 21 radar was also installed. After the Battle of the Philippine Sea, the anti-aircraft battery was further enhanced with twenty-five 25mm single mounts and six 4.7in, twenty-eight-barrel rocket launchers.

COMPOSITION OF THE EMBARKED AIR WING

• ***Zuiho*, when commissioned (January 1939)**
16 A5M4, 12 B5N1

• ***Zuiho* (December 1941)**
12 A5M4, 12 B5N2

• ***Shoho*, when commissioned (January 1942)**
12 A5M4, 12 B5N2

• ***Shoho* at the Coral Sea (May 1942)**
6 A5M4, 6 A6M2, 9 B5N2

• ***Zuiho* at the Santa Cruz Islands (October 1942)**
21 A6M2 and A6M3, 8 B5N2

• ***Zuiho* at the Battle of Marianas/Philippine Sea (June 1944)**
A6M5, A6M2, B5N2, B6N2

• ***Zuiho* at Leyte Gulf (October 1944)**
12 A6M5 (four as bombers), 5 B6N2

The aircraft carrier *Zuiho* in a photo taken from *Zuikaku*, while steaming in the south-west Pacific after the Battle of the Eastern Solomon Islands, September 1942. (NHHC)

HIYO CLASS

HIYO Class

	Shipyard	Laid down	Launched	Completed
***Jumo* (ex-*Kashikawa Maru*)**	Mitsubishi, Nagasaki	20 March 1939	26 June 1941	3 May 1942
***Hiyo* (ex-*Izumo Maru*)**	Kawasaki, Kobe	30 November 1939	24 June 1941	31 July 1942

Displacement	27,500t at trials; 29,200t full load
Dimensions	Length: 219.32m oa; 215.3m wl; 206m btwn pp. Beam: 26.7m wl. Draft: 8.15m
Flight deck	210 x 30m (fore, 16m; aft, 25m)
Machinery	6 Mitsubishi (Kawasaki-La Mont in *Hiyo*) boilers and 2 Mitsubishi geared turbines; 56,000–57,000shp, two shafts
Speed	28 knots
Fuel	Oil, 4,100 tons
Endurance	10,000 miles at 18 knots
Armament	12 Type 89 127/40 (6 twin mounts); 24 Type 96 25/60 (8 triple mounts); 48 (+5) aircraft
Complement	1,187–1,224 officers and men

Between late 1940 and early 1941, the Japanese and American carrier fleets were on an equal footing. Nonetheless, the Imperial Japanese Navy staff was aware that this was a transitory circumstance, since intelligence and press sources were reporting that the United States were allocating funds for the construction of several more carriers.

As the Japanese shipbuilding industry was not considered capable of competing with America's, the Japanese Navy had long tried to remedy the situation by designing, or ordering the design of, certain types of auxiliary and/or merchant ships that could rapidly be converted to aircraft carriers.[37] However, when the US Navy programmes became evident, the Third (*Maru-San*) and Fourth (*Maru-Yon*) Replacement Construction Programmes envisaged only the construction of three fleet aircraft carriers. In an attempt to maintain a semblance of parity, the Imperial Japanese Navy decided to purchase two luxury ocean liners which had already been the subject of preliminarily negotiations between the government and the shipping company.

These ships were *Kashiwara Maru* and *Izumo Maru*, laid down in 1939 for NYK (Nippon Yusen Kaisha) for passenger service between Japan and the west coast of the United States and Canada. The two liners were intended to compete with those of the American and Canadian shipping companies, especially after the Olympic Committee had chosen Japan to host the 1940 Games.

In 1937, after negotiations between the government and NYK, the Ministry of Transportation decided to assume the burden of 80 per cent of the expected construction costs, considering that the final design met the requirements of both the shipping company and the Ministry of the Navy. However, the Ministry of Finance did not intend to exceed a state contribution of 50 per cent. The issue was resolved when the Ministry of the Navy decided to act as guarantor for a compromise formula that established the amount of state contribution at 60 per cent.

The design of the two ocean liners met the requirements of the Imperial Japanese Navy in various respects: a complete double hull; clearance between decks was much greater than that required in a passenger ship; additional tanks for machinery fuel and petrol; strengthened main decks; arrangement of the superstructures and passenger spaces[38] so as to allow the placement of hangars and elevators; and additional space available for electrical cables necessary for aircraft carrier operations.

A fire drill aboard the aircraft carrier *Hiyo* berthed in the Yokosuka Arsenal in October 1943. (Kure Naval Museum – digitally coloured image, courtesy J Irotoko)

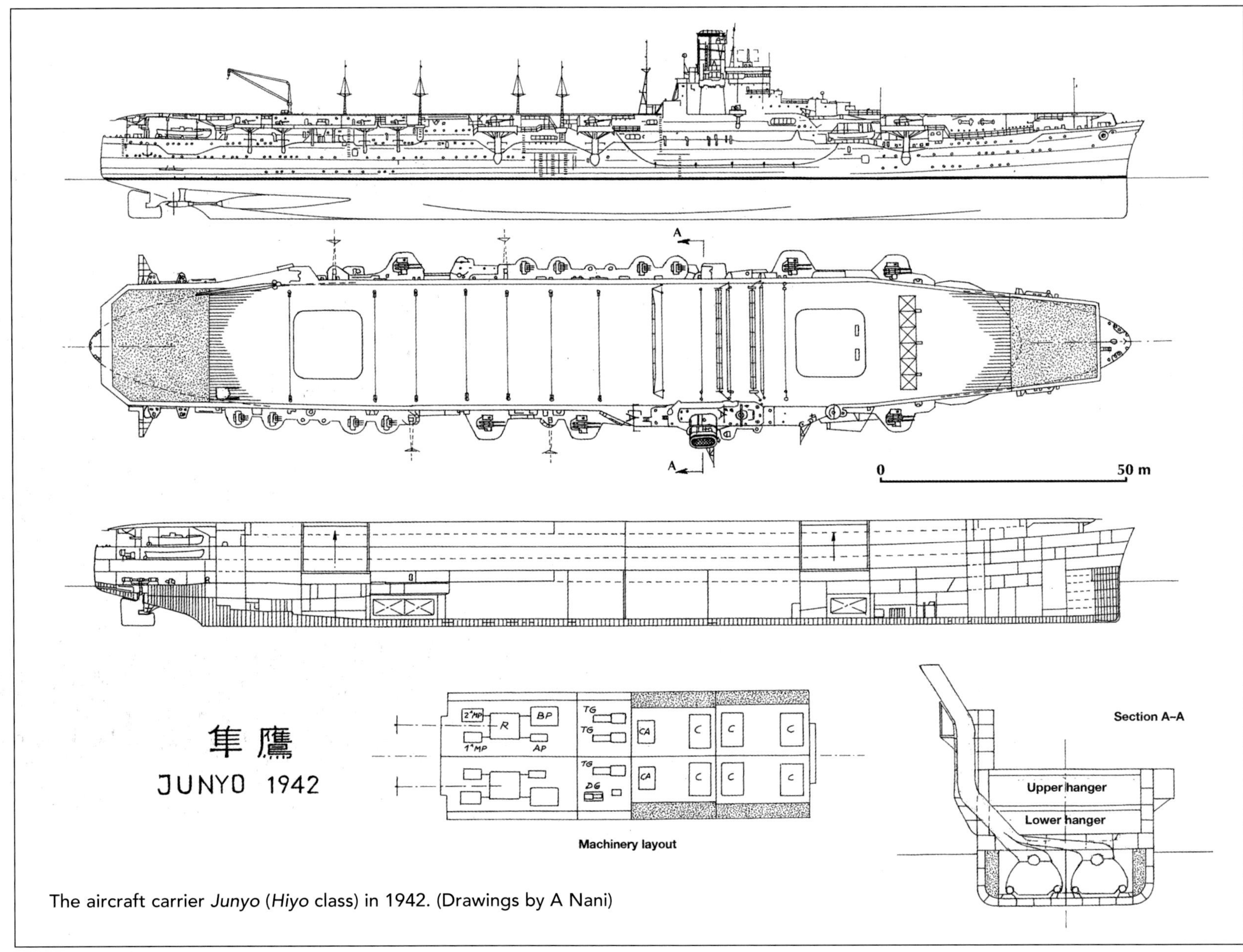

The aircraft carrier *Junyo* (*Hiyo* class) in 1942. (Drawings by A Nani)

After being laid down, however, work on the two ocean liners proceeded very slowly, priority being given to warships over merchant vessels. This also affected the allocation of materiel and manpower.

In October, after the approval of the new American aircraft carrier programme, the shipyards received, although still unofficially,[39] orders to convert *Kashiwara Maru* and *Izumo Maru*. For reasons of secrecy, they were cloaked under the anonymous designations of no. 1001 and no. 1002, later being named *Junyo* and *Hiyo*.[40]

Given the modifications to the original design requested by the Imperial Japanese Navy and the construction delay, the conversions were not particularly complex.

The hulls and machinery were only partially affected: the shapes of the bow and stern clearly reflected their merchant ship origins.

Adaptation of machinery proved more complicated. The two original geared turbines groups were maintained, but the boilers were replaced. Each carrier had six boilers: Mitsubishi type (operating at 40kg/cm^2 and 420°C) in *Junyo* and Kawasaki-La Mont type in *Hiyo*. However, this solution did not prove particularly successful, as the design power of 56,250shp did not allow the achievement of the expected operational speed of 25.5 knots at full load displacement. This type of machinery was subject to frequent breakdowns and provided an operational speed of no more than 23 knots, an inadequate performance for a fleet aircraft carrier, which also extended the time required for take-off of the embarked air wing.

Being former liners converted to aircraft carriers, the *Hiyo*s' armour protection was very poor. Machinery spaces had two overlapping plates of 25mm DS. Petrol tanks and magazines were shielded by DS plates, which would have barely been able to counter shrapnel or small-calibre projectiles.[41] Without longitudinal bulkheads, underwater protection was entrusted only to a compartmentation as similar as possible to that of a warship.

October 1945: the port side of *Junyo* at Sasebo, where she was scrapped between 1946 and 1947. (NHHC)

One of the few existing photographs, unfortunately of poor quality, of the aircraft carrier *Hiyo*. It was taken in late 1942, shortly after her commissioning.

Artillery included six Type 89 127/40 twin unshielded mounts, three on each side, on protruding platforms and distributed as follows: two athwartship, close to the forward elevator; two on the starboard side, abaft the island; and two on the port side, one behind the forward elevator and the other immediately before the aft one. Short-range anti-aircraft defence was provided by eight Type 96 Mod 2 25/60 triple mounts, with four on each side on platforms along the edges of the flight deck.

To counter the ever-increasing American air threat, the Japanese boosted the number of anti-aircraft guns in the *Hiyo*s as shown in the table below:

Like almost all major Japanese warships, the *Hiyo*s were fitted with radar. In the summer and autumn of 1942, both carriers received a Type 21 radar mounted atop the island, ahead of the funnel. An additional Type 21 radar was installed on the port side in March/August 1943, on a protruding platform at flight deck level, close to the aft elevator. In the spring of 1944, passive radar detection systems were installed in both carriers, while during the following summer, *Junyo* was equipped with a Type 13 air search radar mounted on a lattice mast abaft the island.

The flight deck, derived from the extension of the promenade deck originally planned for the two liners, was not fitted with expansion joints and was envisaged as a structural element of the hull strength. Being 210.3m long and with a maximum width of 30m, it ended just before bow and stern. The aft edge of the stern section, like in most Japanese aircraft carriers, was inclined downwards, in order to ease landing operations.

There were two 5-ton square-shaped elevators, with rounded corners, measuring about 14.07m per side and located a considerable distance from each other. Aircraft loading when the carriers were alongside was provided by a 4-ton collapsible crane placed on the port side.

The flight deck was fitted with nine Type Kure Mod 4 arresting cables (one in front of the forward elevator and the others between

	Hiyo	***Junyo***
Spring 1943	Four triple mounts	
July–August 1943		As *Hiyo*
Autumn 1943/Spring 1944	Four triple and twelve single mounts	As *Hiyo*
July/August 1944		Four triple, two twin and eighteen single mounts added
End August 1944		Four twin mounts replaced by six 4.7in twenty-eight-barrel rocket launchers

Between September and October 1945, *Junyo*, which survived the conflict relatively unscathed, was extensively examined at Sasebo by members of the US Naval Technical Mission to Japan, who took many photographs of the carrier. Note, in particular, the electronic equipment, including the Type 21 (top right) and Type 13 (bottom right) radars. (Clockwise from top left: NH-150350, 136995, 218542, 136998 and 150351)

Rear view of *Junyo*'s island at Sasebo in October 1945. Note the funnel inclined outwards, in order to emit smoke away from the island and the flight deck. A similar solution was adopted, about twenty years later, on the American aircraft carrier *John F Kennedy* (CV-67). (NHHC)

the two elevators), three Type Kusho Mod 3 safety barriers (two fixed and one mobile for emergency landings) and one windbreaker.

The *Hiyo*s had two closed hangars, one above the other. The upper one was 170m long, 24m wide and 4.8m high, while the lower hangar was 138m long, 24m wide and 3.2m high. Due to its lack of height, the lower hangar was only used for the storing of fighter planes; the space was also uncomfortable to work in, due to insufficient ventilation, the arrangement of boiler exhausts and consequent high temperatures.

Fire-fighting measures were based on the division of the hangars into separate sections through vertical armoured barriers. Due to the presence of aviation fuel supply stations, the hangars were fitted with devices capable of spraying these barriers with a foam solution.[42]

Another feature of the *Hiyo*s, compared to previous Japanese aircraft carriers, was the adoption of a completely new island which, apart from its unusual height and size, also included a funnel inclined 26° outwards.[43] This structure was supported by a large sponson, thus keeping the flight deck completely clear and, due to the funnel position, less subject to emissions from the boilers.

Considering that the *Hiyo*s were the only aircraft carriers of merchant origin to be employed in fleet operations – the other would have been the never-completed Italian *Aquila* – a brief analysis will be given of their performance in battle. Although they demonstrated an unexpected resistance to underwater attack, their Achilles heel was their lack of speed, which made them a real 'ball and chain' for the accompanying ships.

For example, during the Battle of the Philippine Sea in June 1944, the aircraft carriers of the 2nd and 3rd Division[44] and their 225 aircraft played only a secondary role, partly due to the inexperience of their captains in carrier operations. As the Japanese themselves reported: 'The six aircraft carriers of Joshima and Obayashi were too slow and limited by their narrow flight decks. Due to these circumstances, it was difficult to launch the new *Suisei* dive bombers that had entered service after Midway. Embarked in *Junyo*, the new bombers could not be used for training during the time spent at Tawi-Tawi, as the ship did not develop sufficient speed in that limited training area. The new *Tenzan* bombers also encountered difficulties in operating from these aircraft carriers.'[45]

COMPOSITION OF THE EMBARKED AIR WING

As originally designed
12 (+ 4) A5M4, 18 (+ 2) D3A1, 18 B5N1

Conversion design
12 (+ 3) A6M2, 18 (+ 2) D3A1 and D3A2, 18 B5N2

- ***Junyo* at Aleutian Islands** (June 1942)
6 (+ 2) A6M2, 15 (+ 4) D3A1 and D3A2

- ***Junyo* at Santa Cruz Islands** (October 1942)
18 A6M2, 18 D3A1 and D3A2, 9 B5N2

- **Guadalcanal (November 1942)**
23 (*Junyo* 27) A6M3, 15 (*Junyo* 12) D3A2, 9 B5N2

Marianas Islands/Philippine Sea (June 1944)
27 A6M2, 18 (*Junyo* 9) D3A2, 9 D4Y2 (only *Junyo*), 6 B6N2

TAIYO CLASS

***TAIYO* Class**

	Shipyard	Laid down	Launched	Completed
***Taiyo* (ex-*Kasuga Maru*)**	Mitsubishi, Nagasaki	6 January 1940	19 November 1940	*
***Unyo* (ex-*Yawata Maru*)**	Kawasaki, Kobe	14 December 1938	31 October 1939	31 July1940**
***Chuyo* (ex-*Nitta Maru*)**	Mitsubishi, Nagasaki	9 May 1938	20 May 1939	23 March 1940***

Displacement	20,000t at trials
Dimensions	Length: 180.24m oa; 173.7m wl; 168m btwn pp. Beam: 22.5m wl. Draft: abt 8.5m
Flight deck	172 x 23.5m
Machinery	4 Mitsubishi boilers and 2 Mitsubishi geared turbines; 25,200shp, 2 shafts
Speed	21 knots
Fuel	Oil, 2,500 tons
Endurance	8,500 miles at 18 knots
Armament	6 Type 10 127/45 single mounts (*Unyo* and *Chuyo*, 4 Type 10 127/45 single mounts); 8 Type 96 25/60 (4 twin mounts); 23 (+4) aircraft
Complement	747–850 officers and men

* Not completed as passenger liner. Converted at the Sasebo Arsenal. Works began on 1 May 1941 and ended on 5 November 1941

** Converted at the Kure Arsenal. Works began in January 1942 and ended on 31 May 1942

*** Converted at the Kure Arsenal. Works began on 27 May 1942 and ended on 25 November 1942

Initially intended for the ocean routes between Japan and Europe, three luxury liners of the NYK were later destined for conversion into aircraft carriers. However, while the decision to convert *Kasuga Maru* was taken when she was launched, that for *Nitta Maru* and *Yawata Maru* only came in 1942. The conversion work was quite limited, as shown by its short duration, because these carriers were initially envisaged for escort missions and/or as aircraft ferries.

Machinery remained as originally installed, with two Mitsubishi geared turbines fed by four Mitsubishi boilers. Power was 25,200shp, with a top speed of 21 knots. As usual, exhaust was emitted through a funnel located on the starboard side of the hull.

The flight deck, 172m long and 23.5m wide, was fitted with two axial elevators measuring 13 x 12m, eight Type Kure Mod 4 arresting gears and three Type Kusho Mod 10 safety barriers (one fixed and two mobile). A windbreaker was probably also installed. As in almost all converted Japanese aircraft carriers, the command and control post was located in the forward area, below the flight deck.

There were differences in the main anti-aircraft armament between *Taiyo* and the other two carriers. The choice of these weapons reflected the issues encountered by the Japanese, being forced to rely on the 'old' 120/45 Mod 10 guns dating back to 1926. *Taiyo* received six single mounts, *Unyo* and *Chuyo* four. All three carriers relied on four Type 96 25/60 twin mounts for short-range defence.

The *Taiyo*s' anti-aircraft armament was later strengthened, taking into account differences in the sources, as follows:

Unyo – in June 1944, two 4.7in mounts were replaced by fourteen 25mm guns, augmented the following month by another forty-two (two triple and thirty-six single), for a total of sixty-four barrels. At the time, ten Type 93 13.2/76 mounts were also installed.

Taiyo – six 25mm triple mounts were installed in 1944. It is unclear whether, by July 1944, short-range anti-aircraft armament had been brought to roughly the same level as *Unyo*'s.

Chuyo – in July 1943, six 25mm triple and five 13.2mm single mounts were installed.

The embarked air wing relied on a single hangar which could house twenty-three aircraft, with four in reserve. All three carriers had a Type 21 radar.

COMPOSITION OF THE EMBARKED AIR WING

• **When commissioned**
Mix of A6M2 and B5N2

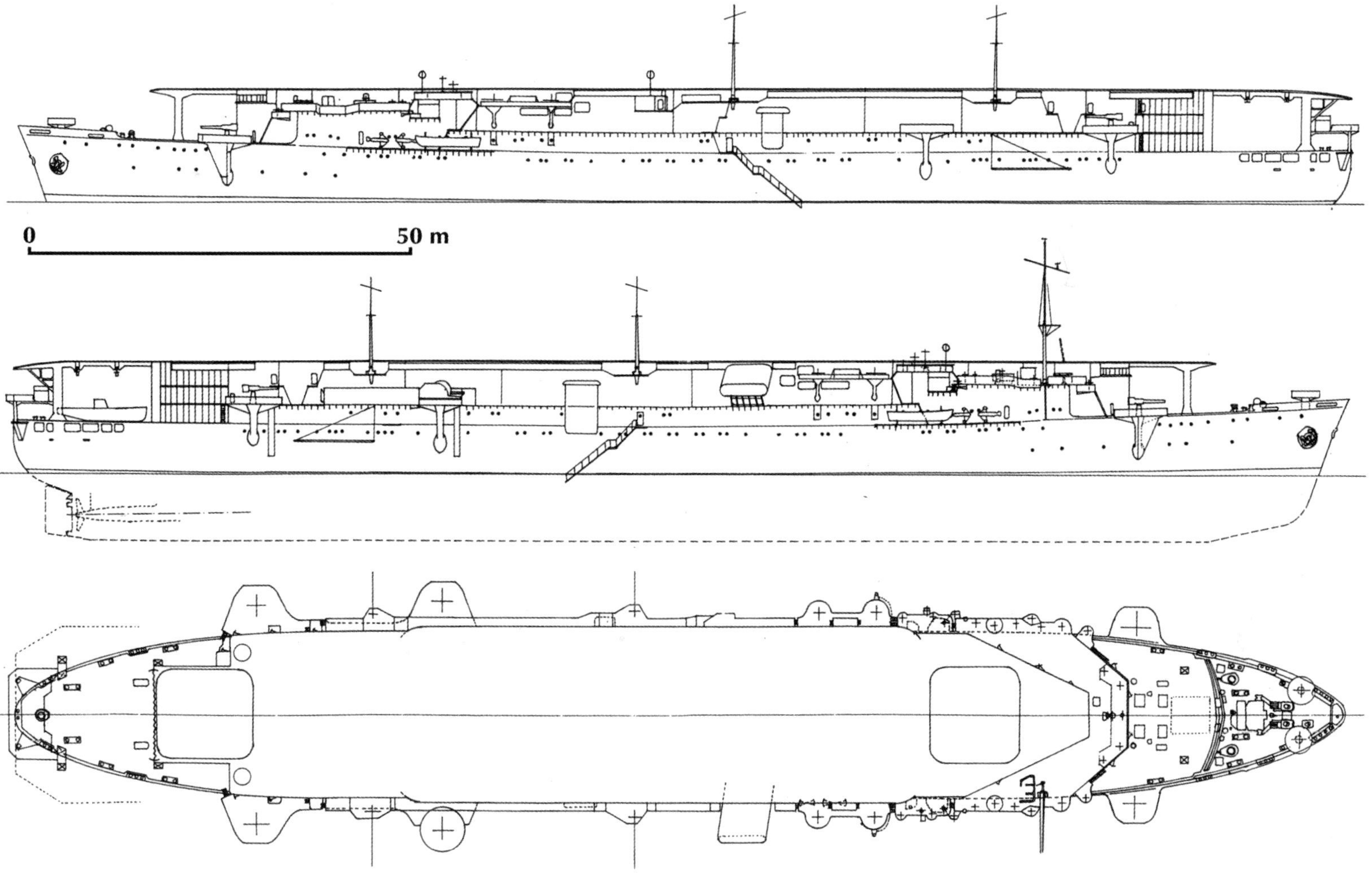

The escort carrier *Taiyo* in 1942: port and starboard side views and top view of the hangar deck. (From M Ledet, *Samourai sur porte-avions*)

The escort carrier *Chuyo* at anchor in Truk Lagoon in May 1943. (S Fukui collection)

The passenger liner *Nitta Maru*, later converted into the aircraft carrier *Chuyo*. (NHHC, NH-111623)

Taiyo at anchor in the Yokosuka Arsenal on 30 September 1943. Note the typical hull lines of a merchant vessel. (Kure Naval Museum – digitally coloured image, courtesy J Irotoko)

SHINYO

SHINYO

	Shipyard	Laid down	Launched	Completed
***Shinyo* (ex-*Scharnhorst*)**	Weser, Bremen	?	14 December 1934	1935*

Displacement	20,900t at trials
Dimensions	Length: 198.34m oa; 189.36m wl; 185m btwn pp. Beam: 25.6m wl. Draft: 8m
Flight deck	180 x 24.5m
Machinery	4 Kanpon boilers and 2 AEG turboelectric systems; 26,000shp, 2 shafts
Speed	21 knots
Fuel	Unknown
Endurance	8,500 miles at 18 knots
Armament	8 Type 89 127/40 (4 twin mounts); 30 Type 96 25/60 (10 triple mounts); 27 (+6) aircraft
Complement	834 officers and men

* Converted at the Kure Arsenal. Works began on 21 September 1942 and were completed on 15 December 1943

At the outbreak of the Second World War, the German ocean liner *Scharnhorst* of the Norddeustcher Lloyd shipping company was caught in the port of Kobe. She was formally acquired by Japan for use as a troop transport. However, after the Battle of Midway, it was decided to convert her into an escort aircraft carrier. She was renamed *Shinyo*.

Conversion works, carried out at the Kure Arsenal, followed those already ongoing on four other vessels originally conceived as passenger ships. This meant a single-level hangar, a flight deck of relatively small size, and petrol tanks and magazines protected by a light layer of concrete. However, unlike other similar contemporary units, *Shinyo* was equipped with bulges to improve her transversal stability and ensure minimal underwater protection.

After removing the superstructures, a 180m-long and 24.5m-wide flight deck was installed. It was equipped with two 13 x 12m elevators, eight Type 3 Mod 3 arresting gears and three Type 3

Shinyo during machinery trials off Iyonada on 1 November 1943. (Kure Naval Museum – digitally coloured image, courtesy J Irotoko)

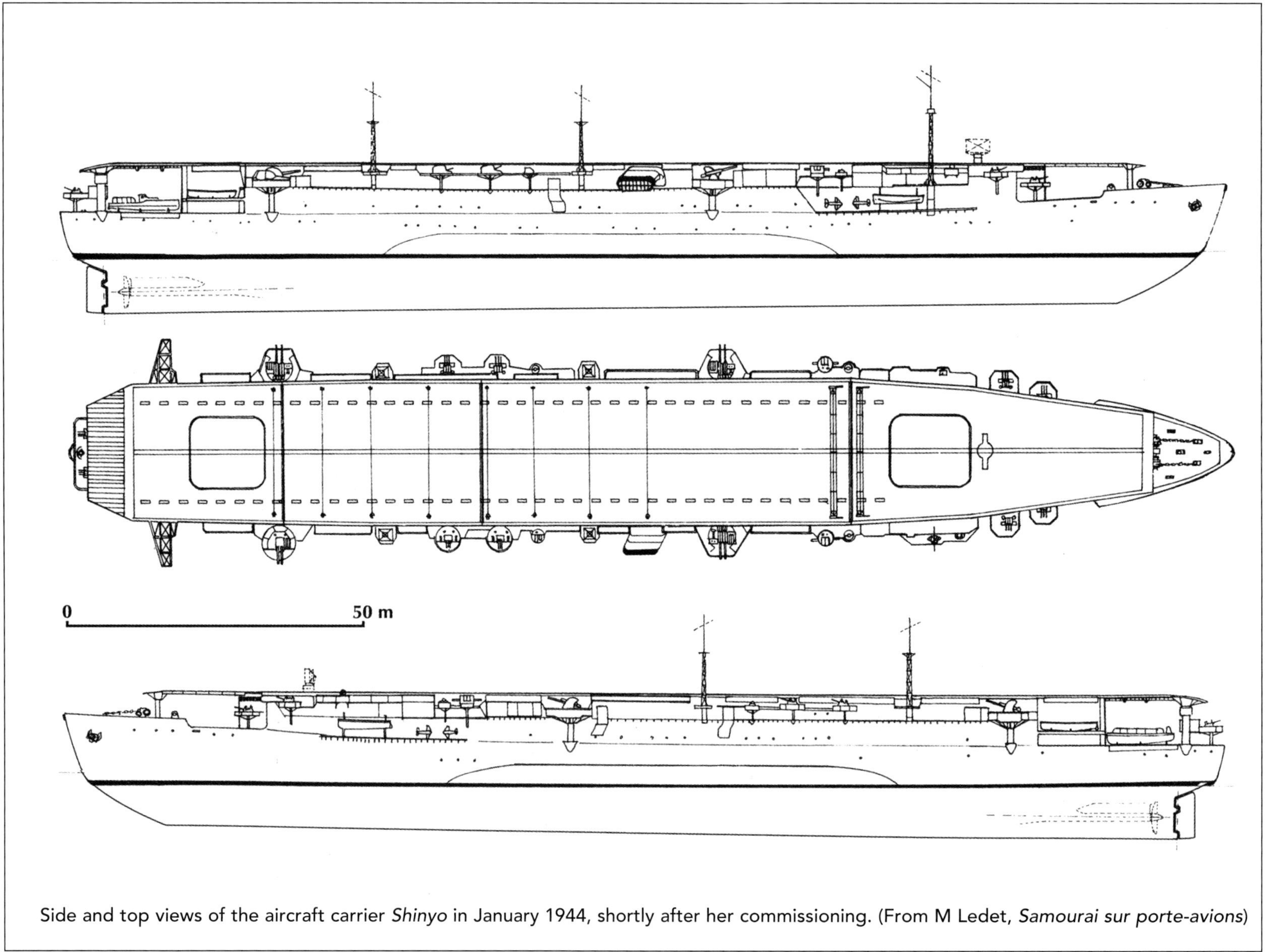

Side and top views of the aircraft carrier *Shinyo* in January 1944, shortly after her commissioning. (From M Ledet, *Samourai sur porte-avions*)

Mod 10 safety barriers (two fixed and one mobile); the windbreak barrier was probably not adopted. As usual, the command and control post was placed towards the bow, below the flight deck.

Uniquely in Japanese aircraft carriers, machinery (two AEG turboelectric systems) remained unchanged. Conversely, due to the unavailability of spare parts and to their complex operation, the four original Wagner boilers were replaced with four Kanpons. However, lack of availability of the latter caused a four-month delay in completing the conversion. As usual, the funnel was placed on the starboard side of the hull.

Artillery included four Type 89 127/40 twin unshielded mounts and ten Type 96 25/60 triple mounts; at the beginning of 1944 and during the following summer, these were added to by, respectively, twelve and eight mounts. The embarked air wing included thirty-three aircraft, plus six in reserve.

A Type 21 radar was also fitted, supported by a platform located in the forward port side of the hull.

COMPOSITION OF THE EMBARKED AIR WING

- **When commissioned**

Mix of A6M2 and B5N2

KAIYO

KAIYO

	Shipyard	Laid down	Launched	Completed
(ex-*Argentina Maru*)	Mitsubishi, Nagasaki	2 February 1938	9 December 1938	31 May 1939*
Displacement	16,700t at trials			
Dimensions	Length: 166.36m oa; 159.6m wl; 155m btwn pp. Beam: 21.9m wl. Draft: 8.25m			
Flight deck	160 x 23m			
Machinery	4 Kanpon boilers and 2 Kanpon geared turbines; 52,000shp, 2 shafts			
Speed	23 knots			
Fuel	Unknown			
Endurance	7,000 miles at 18 knots			
Armament	8 Type 89 127/40 (4 twin mounts); 24 Type 96 (8 25/60 triple mounts); 24 aircraft			
Complement	587 officers and men			

* Converted at Mitsubishi Kawasaki. Works began on 10 December 1942 and were completed on 23 November 1943

The passenger ship *Argentina Maru*, owned by the OSK (Osaka Shosen Kaisha) Shipping Company, was requisitioned by the Imperial Japanese Navy on 1 May 1942 to be used as a troop transport. However, after Midway it was decided to purchase the vessel (20 December 1942) and convert her into an escort carrier, later named *Kaiyo*.

Transformation work began in December 1942 at the Mitsubishi shipyard in Nagasaki and was intended to be completed in seven months by the end of July 1943. However, difficulties in supplying materiel and a shortage of specialised manpower[46] caused completion of the work to be postponed by four months.

Conversion works were as a result rather limited. After the removal of all superstructures, a 160m-long and 23m-wide flight deck was built, covered with a wooden floor and fitted with two elevators measuring 13 x 12m. The flight deck equipment included eight Type Kure Mod 4 arresting gears and three Type Kusho Mod 3 safety barriers (two fixed and one mobile). A windbreaker was probably not fitted.

As was the case for other Japanese aircraft carriers converted from merchant ships, the command and control post was placed forward, below the flight deck.

In order to gain more speed, the original diesel engines were replaced by two geared turbines of the same type as those installed on the fleet destroyers (probably the *Kageros*). Fed by steam produced by four boilers, they developed 52,000shp on two shafts, giving a top speed of 23 knots.

Smoke was emitted through the usual side funnel placed on the starboard side, approximately amidships. It is noteworthy that, in order to balance the lightening resulting from the removal of the original superstructures, approximately 2,000 tons of ballast was embarked, including seawater, fuel and gravel.

The half-sunken and stranded wreck of the aircraft carrier *Kaiyo* in Beppu Bay (Kyushu), sometime in 1946/47. (NHHC, NH-85386)

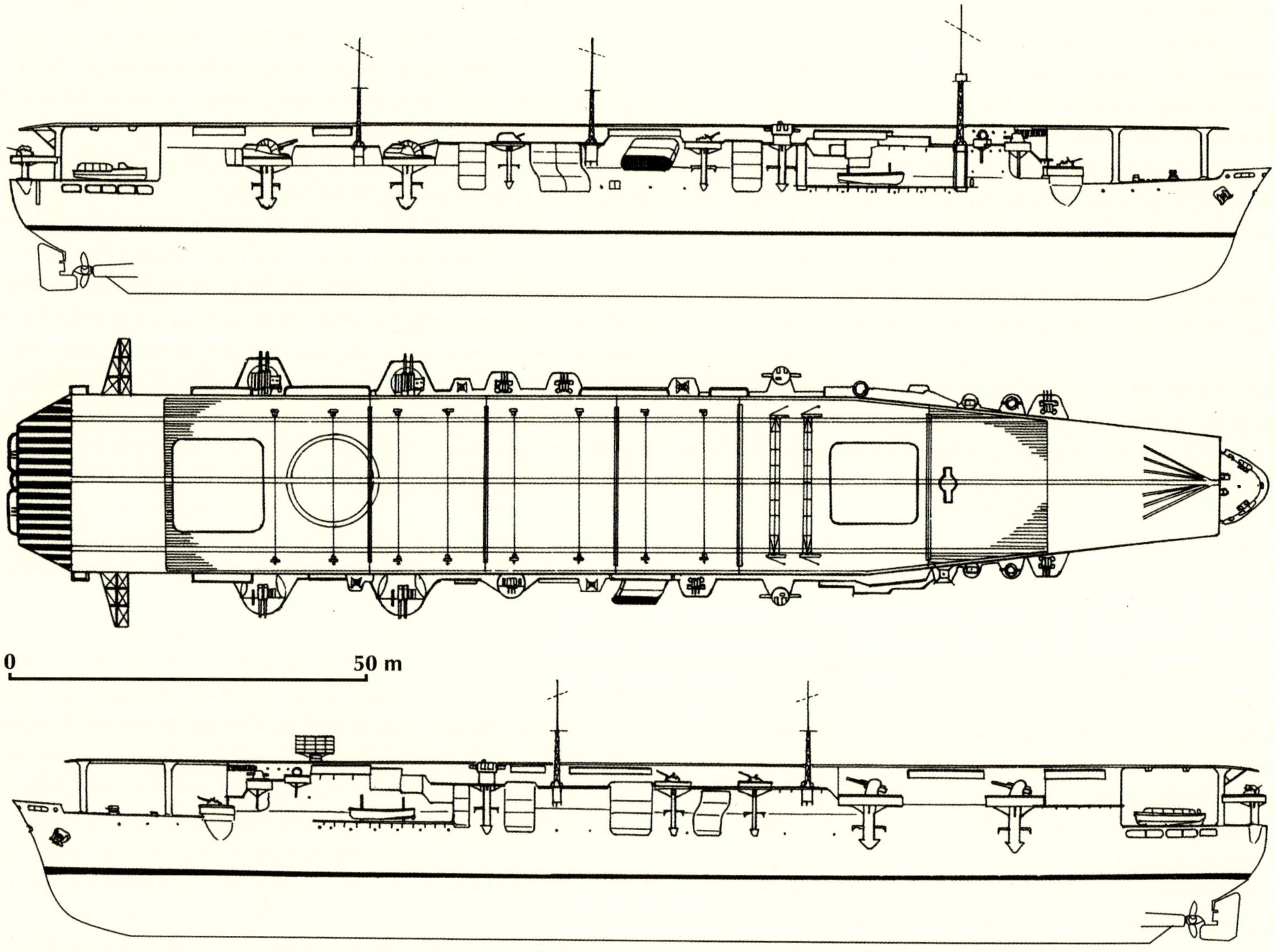

Side and top views of the aircraft carrier *Kaiyo* when commissioned in late 1943. (From M Ledet, *Samourai sur porte-avions*)

Armament included four Type 89 127/40 twin mounts and eight Type 96 25/60 triple mounts, these being increased in July 1944 with an additional six triple and two single mounts of the same type.

Kaiyo had a single hangar. The embarked air wing included sixteen fighters and eight torpedo-bombers. A Type 21 radar was placed forward, on the port side of the hull.

COMPOSITION OF THE EMBARKED AIR WING

- **When commissioned**

16 A6M2, 8 B5N2

Kaiyo at trials off Tokuyama on 15 November 1943. Note the mattress antenna of the Type 21 radar.

CHIYODA CLASS

***CHIYODA* Class**

	Shipyard	Laid down	Launched	Completed
Chiyoda	Kure Arsenal	14 December 1936	19 November 1937	15 December 1938*
Chitose	Kure Arsenal	26 November 1934	29 November 1936	25 July 1938**
Displacement	13,650t at trials; 15,200t full load			
Dimensions	Length: 192.5m oa; 184.6m wl. Beam: 20.8m wl. Draft: 7.5m			
Flight deck	180 x 23m			
Machinery	4 Kanpon boilers, 2 Kanpon geared turbines and 2 diesel engines; 56,800shp, 2 shafts			
Fuel	2,680 tons			
Endurance	11,810 miles at 18 knots			
Armament	8 Type 89 127/40 (4 twin mounts); 30 Type 96 25/60 (10 triple mounts); 30 aircraft			
Complement	785 officers and men			

* Converted at the Yokosuka Arsenal. Works began on 16 January 1943 and were completed on 31 October 1943

** Converted at the Sasebo Arsenal. Works began on 26 January 1943 and were completed on 1 January 1944

The '1934 Second Replacement Construction Programme' included two seaplane carriers which, provisionally known as transport ship No 1 and No 2, were later named *Chitose* and *Chiyoda*.[47]

Because of the different roles envisaged for these ships, the designers faced many problems. Indeed, although they were planned as seaplane carriers (with twenty-four aircraft in total, twelve on the deck and as many in the hangar), they also had to meet additional requirements.

When needed, they were expected to be able to operate as midget submarine carriers (in Japanese, *kohyoteki*),[48] fast oilers or aircraft carriers, as was later the case. Taking these factors into account, the designers were forced to introduce several changes, especially to the hangar, elevators, power plant and machinery spaces, some of the latter initially being intended for fuel storage.

After their completion, and while peace was maintained, these ships operated as seaplane carriers, their ability to carry midget submarines being kept secret. Just before the outbreak of hostilities, they were converted to carry twelve midget submarines inside the hangar originally intended for aircraft. The submarines were to be launched through large stern doors. Cranes fixed to the four sides of the central structure, with a hatch underneath, would be used for recovering and lowering the midget submarines into the hangar.

After the conversion into midget carriers (1940/1), the two *Chiyoda*s carried out a series of trials, during which, with calm seas

Chitose at trials in Tokyo Bay on 1 December 1943, after her conversion into an aircraft carrier. (Kure Naval Museum – digitally coloured image, courtesy J Irotoko)

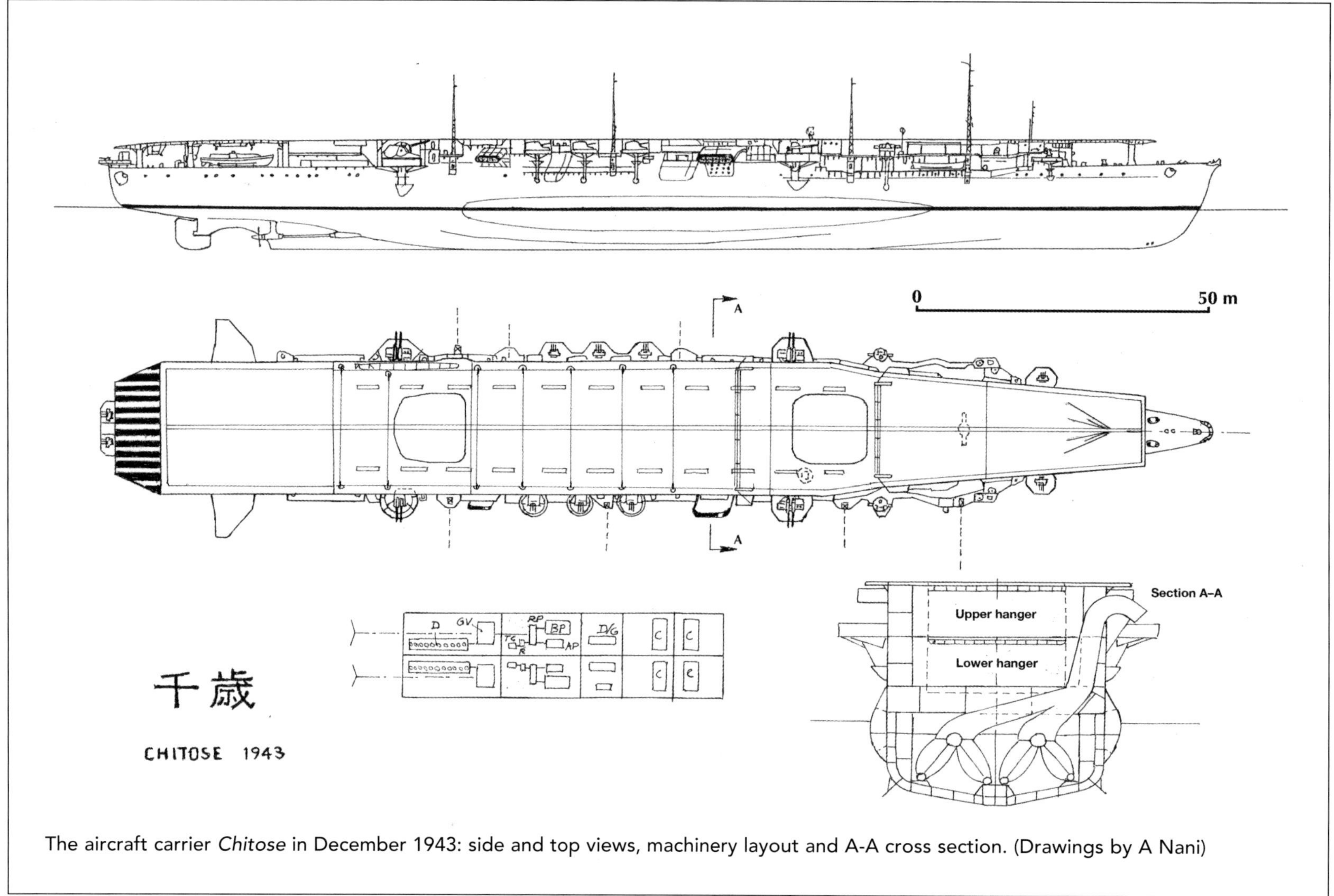

The aircraft carrier *Chitose* in December 1943: side and top views, machinery layout and A-A cross section. (Drawings by A Nani)

and well-trained personnel, they launched twelve submarines through the rear door in about twenty minutes, at a rate of two roughly every three minutes. However, both *Chiyoda* and *Chitose* had little opportunity to operate as midget carriers, as the boats they had transported to the Aleutian Islands were destroyed or damaged by the US Air Force.

In an attempt to recover from the consequences of the Japanese defeat at Midway, it was decided to convert the *Chiyoda*s into aircraft carriers. Work to achieve this lasted about a year. The lower aft half-hangar, 60m long and 13m wide, was maintained.

Above, in correspondence with the forecastle deck, a new 100m-long and 18m wide hangar was built. Due to the increased displacement and in order to keep the flight deck high enough above sea level and improve transverse stability, the *Chiyoda*s were fitted with two large bulges, which increased their width by about two metres.[49]

The original machinery was preserved as, after initial problems due to its complexity, a sufficient degree of reliability was achieved. Fumes were emitted through the usual lateral funnel, placed on the starboard side. Command and control spaces were positioned in a forward structure below the flight deck.

The flight deck was equipped with two square-shaped elevators measuring 14 x 14m, eight Type Kure Mod 4 arresting gears, two Type Kusho Mod 3 safety barriers and a windbreaker.

Armament initially included four Type 89 127/40 twin mounts and ten Type 96 25/60 triple mounts. After June 1944, these were augmented with six additional triple mounts.

COMPOSITION OF THE EMBARKED AIR WING

- **When commissioned**
15 A6M2, 6 A6M5, 9 B5N2

- **Marianas Islands/Philippine Sea (June 1944)**
mix of A6M5, A6M2, B5N2, B6N2

- **Leyte Gulf (October 1944)**
8 A6M5, 4 A6M5 (used as fighter bombers), 4 B5N2 (6 in *Chitose*)

The seaplane tender *Chitose* in 1941 before her conversion into an aircraft carrier. The same occurred to her sister, *Chiyoda*. (S Fukui collection)

Port view of the carrier *Chitose*, shortly after her commissioning. (Kure Naval Museum)

TAIHO

TAIHO

	Shipyard	Laid down	Launched	Completed
	Kawasaki, Kobe	10 July 1941	7 April 1943	7 March 1944
Displacement	34,200t at trials; abt 37,100t full load			
Dimensions	Length: 260.6m oa; 253m wl. Beam: 27.7m wl. Draught: 9.67m			
Flight deck	257.5 x 30m (forward 18m; aft 27m)			
Machinery	8 Kanpon boilers and 4 Kanpon geared turbines; 160,000shp, 4 shafts			
Speed	33.3 knots			
Fuel	5,700t			
Endurance	10,000 miles at 18 knots			
Protection	Vertical, 165mm; deck, 75 + 20mm			
Armament	12 Type 98 100/54 (6 twin mounts); 51 Type 96 25/60 (17 triple mounts); 52 (+1) aircraft			
Complement	1,570 officers and men			

The decision to build an aircraft carrier, later named *Taiho*, was included in the '1939 Fourth Replacement Construction Programme' (*Maru-Yon*). This was discussed during the 74th Imperial Conference on 26 December 1938 and finally approved on 5 March 1939, but the project initially encountered two major obstacles. After the outbreak of the war against China, the Japanese Army had the lion's share in the funds allocated, while a number of senior admirals of the Imperial Jaoanese Navy continued to make no secret of their distrust towards aircraft carriers. However, since the US Navy's plans to strengthen the fleet could not be ignored, *Taiho*'s construction went ahead.

Unlike the *Shokaku*s, conceived for a predominantly offensive role, *Taiho* was envisaged under a completely opposite concept, with a stronger emphasis on the capability to absorb damage. This peculiarity would allow her to operate closer to enemy forces and consequently to increase the range of its embarked air wing.

To pursue this new carrier concept, the designers had to reconcile the preliminary requirements of the Imperial Navy Staff, namely: an armoured flight deck; a general increase in protection against bombs and torpedoes; the adoption of a single island/funnel structure; and a closed bow ('Hurricane bow' type) similar to that implemented on the contemporary British *Illustrious*-class aircraft carriers, the first of the type in the world with an armoured flight deck.

Rendering of the aircraft carrier *Taiho* at sea in its likely appearance.

As the armoured flight deck meant a considerable increase in weight, in order not to raise the ship's centre of gravity *Taiho* had one deck fewer than the *Shokaku*s. Another peculiarity that fuelled heated debate was the planned adoption of a new type of island that incorporated a large funnel inclined outwards by 26°. However, its location on the starboard side, about one-third of the way along the ship's length, sparked additional discussions. It was argued that a funnel placed 17m over the flight deck would hinder air operations at night, not to mention the increase in turbulence caused by gas exhaustion. However, a series of tests in the wind tunnel at the Yokosuka Arsenal helped to dispel any doubts regarding this issue.

Protection represented the distinctive feature of *Taiho* not only with the armoured flight deck,[50] but also the protection of the vessel's sensitive spaces. However, this approach followed a different path from that adopted by the British on *Illustrious*.[51]

The flight deck had no expansion joints, as it was part of the hull structure and was covered by a wooden floor.[52] There were two elevators[53] spaced approximately 150m apart and of almost equal size: 14 x 13.6m the forward one and 14 x 14m the aft one. Horizontal protection consisted of 75mm CNC steel plates, joined together by armoured bolts and placed on 20mm DS plates, which theoretically should have withstood the effects of a 500kg armour-piercing bomb dropped by a dive bomber. The entire structure was supported by an underlying box-shaped construction reinforced on its lower side by DS plates acting as splinters.

Considering the significant amount of weight already taken up by the armoured flight deck, the vertical protection of the hull,

The aircraft carrier *Taiho* in 1944: side and top views, layout of machinery, cross section (armour thickness in mm). (Drawings by A Nani, coloured by M Brescia)

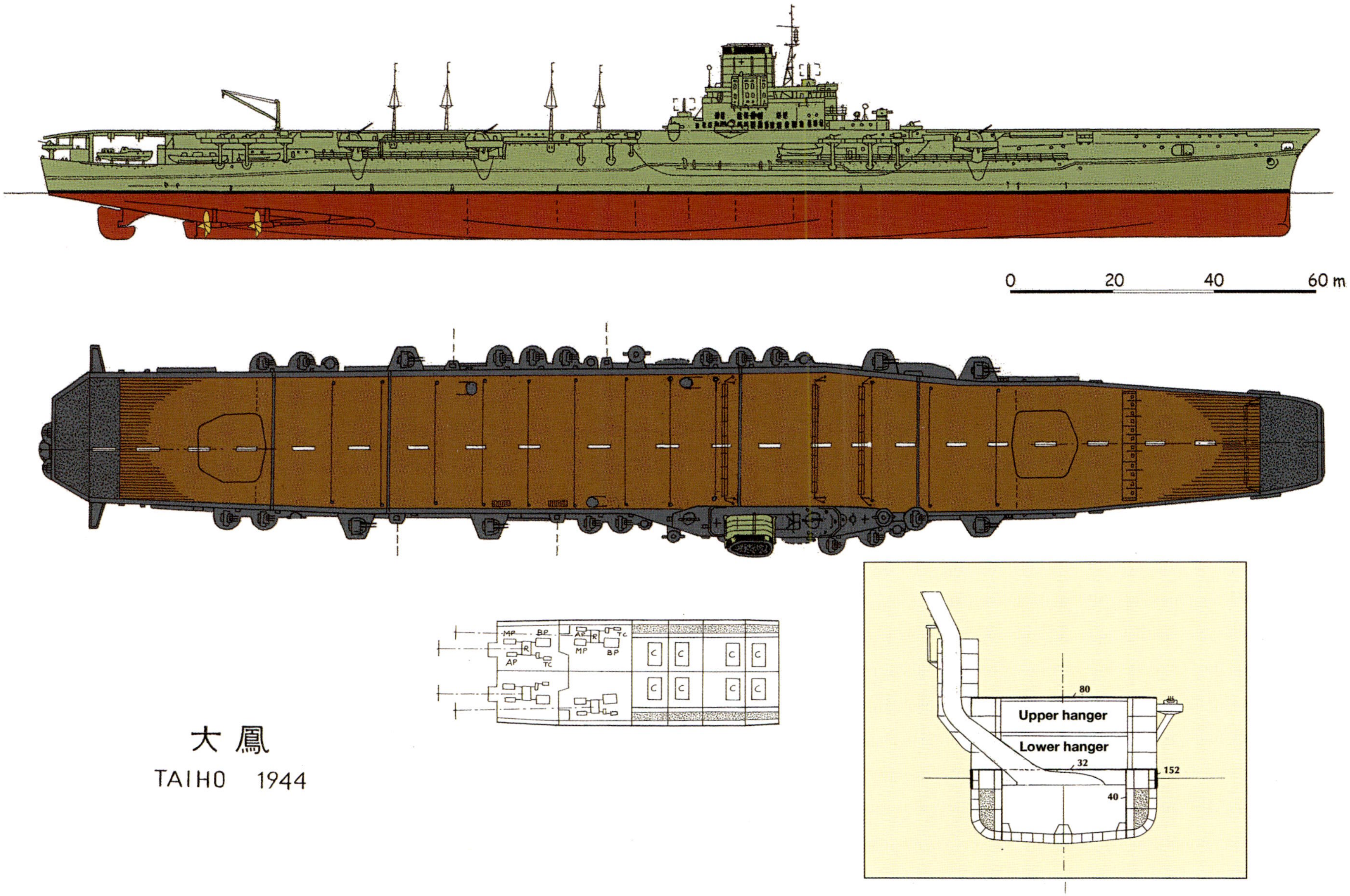

0 20 40 60 m

大鳳
TAIHO 1944

MP BP AP R TC

Upper hanger
Lower hanger
80
32
40
152

around machinery spaces and magazines, was provided by a 55mm CNC steel belt which was reinforced abaft, at a distance of about 2.5m, by a 25mm DS splinter bulkhead. In the unlikely event of operation within the range of enemy artillery, protection of particular vulnerable spaces could not be neglected.

Consequently, the forward and aft magazines were respectively protected by 165–80mm and 130–70mm of NVNC steel plates, while the extremely dangerous petrol tanks were provided with 50–60mm of CNC steel.

The bridge was protected by 25mm DS plates, while the wheelhouse was enclosed in a steel cylinder, theoretically capable of withstanding 5.9in shell hits.[54] The main steering gear room was protected on the sides and top by 125mm of NVNC steel; the auxiliary steering gear room had 35mm of CNC steel on the sides and 100mm of NVNC steel on top.

The main armoured deck was the lower hangar deck, which had different thicknesses: the aft section (machinery and magazines) had 32mm of CNC steel and 16mm of DS, totalling 48mm; the forward section (machinery and magazines) was protected by 40mm CNC steel. Petrol tanks, located abaft and forward of magazines, were protected by 50mm CNC steel plates at the stern and 90mm at the bow.[55]

Underwater protection was conceptually similar to that of the *Shokaku*s, but simplified and perhaps less effective. It consisted of a 22mm DS double bulkhead about 3m from both hull sides. Below the machinery spaces there was the traditional double bottom; a triple bottom was placed below magazines and petrol tanks. To withstand explosions of mines and/or torpedoes, the keel was also armoured around the most vulnerable spaces (steering gear rooms, magazines, petrol tanks, etc).

The two hangars had the same height (5m), but were slightly different in width: 18m the upper one, 17m the lower one. The upper hangar sides were armoured with 25mm DS plates, essentially for shrapnel protection. Like on the *Shokaku*s, there were also 1.5 x 0.7m side openings closed by 25mm DS doors so as to vent externally the excess pressure caused by vapours from damaged petrol tanks.

The upper and lower hangars could be split into five and four sections respectively by movable fire bulkheads. Bulkheads around the elevators were made of 7mm-thick DS steel plates.

Specific safety measures were provided against fires inside the hangars, these being closed and thus having limited possibilities of venting externally. In the event of fire, each section of the two hangars – that enclosed between two fire bulkheads – was equipped on both sides with two sets of nozzles at heights of 1.5m and 2m. The lower nozzles were to spray the hangar deck with a foam-based solution, while the upper ones were to project the same solution towards the upper part of the hangar or towards any uncovered part of it. The lower hangar was also equipped, in case of damage caused by bombs and/or torpedoes, with a CO_2 emission system controlled by stations protected by DS, with tempered glass windows. The upper hangar had five stations: two in the forward section, two in the middle sections (between the two elevators) and one in the aft section.

One of the few known pictures of *Taiho*, likely taken when she was at anchor in the waters of the Lingga archipelago (Indonesia), before the Battle of the Philippine Sea on 19 June 1944.

To counterbalance the imposing island/funnel structure, the flight deck was 2m offset in its aft section area. Although the deck's width provided large parking areas for aircraft, their movement was difficult due to both the overlapping hangars and the location of the two elevators, protected by 25mm DS plates but far from each other at the two ends of the flight deck.

For take-off operations, the installation of two forward catapults had been planned, in anticipation of the introduction of new types of aircraft that would have required a longer take-off run. Due to the absence of a reliable catapult, however, this plan was later abandoned, as was the location of a windbreaker before the forward elevator. Landing operations were aided by fourteen Kusho Type Mod. 4 arresting gears and three Type Mod. 3 safety barriers (two fixed and one mobile).

Machinery, although with some differences, was similar to that of the *Shokaku*s. Due to the increased displacement, the ship's speed was slightly lower. On the other hand, thanks to the greater provision of fuel, range was increased.

Instead of the Type 89 127/40 gun, armament included the brand-new Type 98 100/65, considered by the Japanese as the most successful anti-aircraft gun that the Imperial Navy had ever had. Short-range defence was provided by seventeen Type 96 25/60 triple mounts. Some sources report that before the Battle of the Marianas, these were augmented by about twenty single mounts.

When completed, *Taiho* had three radars: one Type 13 and one Type 21 mounted atop the island, and one Type 21 abaft of it.

COMPOSITION OF THE EMBARKED AIR WING

- **Original design**
  18 (+ 6) A6M2, 18 (+ 6) D3A2, 27 (+ 3) B5N2
- **Revised design**
  18 (+ 1) A7M1, 36 B7A1, 6 C6N1
- **Marianas Islands/Philippine Sea (June 1944)**
  27 A6M5, 18 B6N2, 18 D4Y1 and D4Y2, 9 D3A2, 3 D4Y1-C

RYUHO

RYUHO

	Shipyard	Laid down	Launched	Completed
(ex-*Taigei*)	Yokosuka Arsenal	12 April 1933	16 November 1933	31 March 1934*
Displacement	15,300t at trials; 16,700t full load			
Dimensions	Length: 215.65m oa; 210m wl; 197.3m btwn pp. Beam: 19.6m wl. Draught: 6.64m			
Flight deck	185 x 23m			
Machinery	4 Kanpon boilers and 2 Kanpon geared turbines; 52,000shp, 2 shafts			
Speed	26.2 knots			
Fuel	Oil, 2,400 tons			
Endurance	8,000 miles at 18 knots			
Armament	8 Type 89 127/40 (4 twin mounts); 30 Type 96 25/60 (10 triple mounts); 31 aircraft			
Complement	990 officers and men			

* Converted at Yokosuka Arsenal. Works began on 18 December 1941 and were completed on 28 November 1942

The aircraft carrier *Ryuho* in late 1942: side and top views, machinery layout and A-A cross section. (Drawings by A Nani)

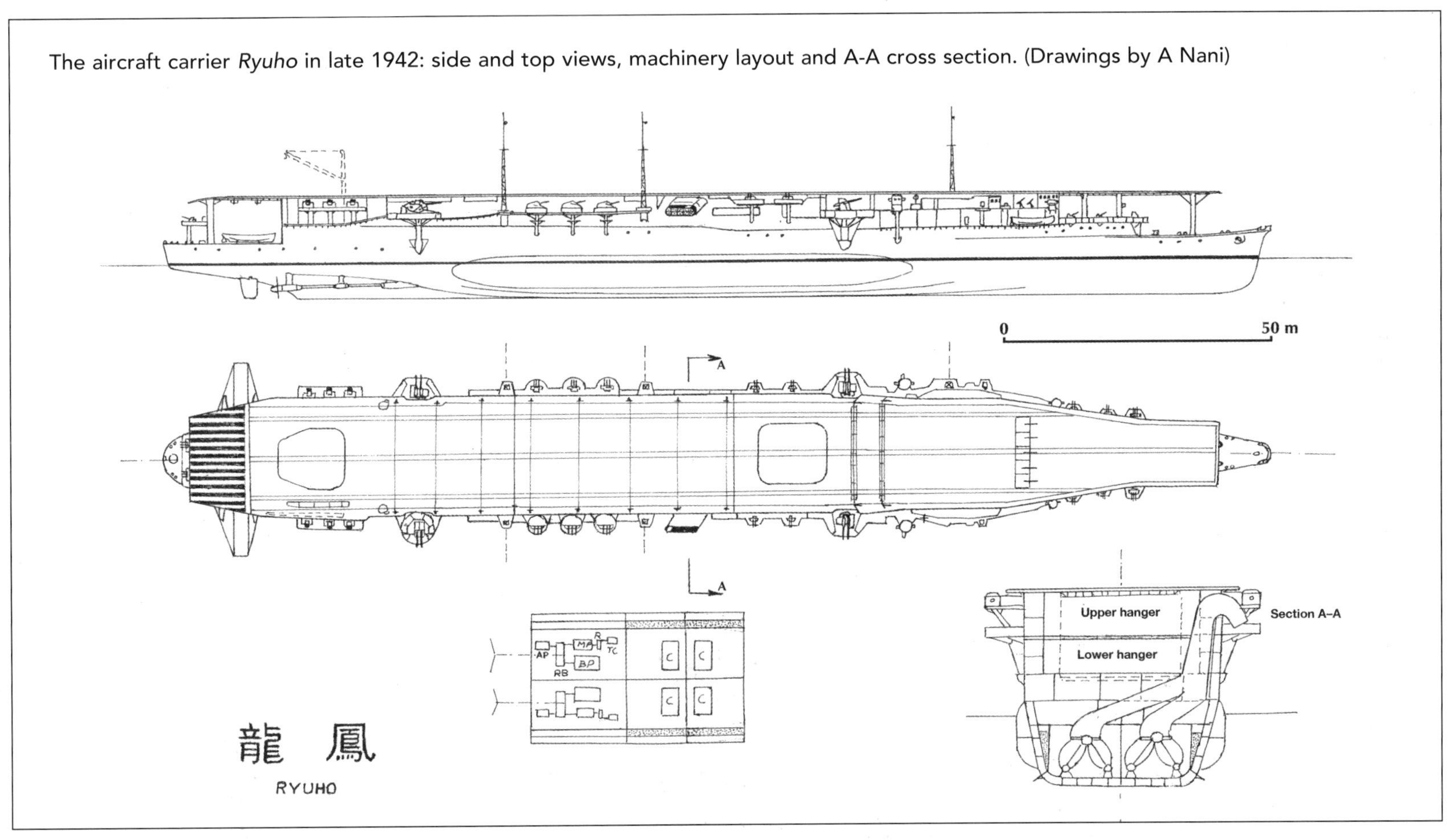

Built in the early 1930s as the submarine support vessel *Taigei*, *Ryuho* featured a fully welded hull and non-overlapping joints; all frames were also welded. However, this construction method had already highlighted a series of problems on the slipway, the sizeable overall length of the ship causing buckling that affected both the bow and stern sections. Consequently, both of them were cut, repositioned and fixed to the hull middle section by means of tear-proof rivets.

Despite these modifications, *Taigei* continued to have poor stability, so much so that between spring 1936 and summer 1937 she had to undergo a further round of work involving the

The submarine tender *Taigei* underway in 1935. (S Fukui collection)

The carrier *Ryuho* during machinery trials off Yokosuka in early November 1942. (Kure Naval Museum)

installation of bulges and new hull structural reinforcements.

Additional problems stemmed from the original diesel engines,[56] which proved unreliable and underperforming.

Taigei had several defects that would emerge again after the decision to convert her into an aircraft carrier.

On the eve of the war, to address a perceived economic and industrial inferiority, Japan decided to transform three submarine support ships into aircraft carriers: the two *Takasaki*s, which became the *Zuiho*s, and *Taigei*, renamed as *Ryuho*.

Conversion works, assigned to the Yokosuka Arsenal, began just ten days after the attack on Pearl Harbor.

As in the *Zuiho*s, the original diesel machinery was replaced by two Kanpon geared turbines – probably of the same type already adopted in the *Kagero*-class destroyers – which, fed by four Kanpon boilers, were able to deliver 52,000shp for a top speed of 26 knots.[57] The usual side funnel emitted fumes downwards.

Without an island and with the command spaces located below the flight deck, *Ryuho* was equipped with two hangars. The upper one was approximately 124m long, 18m wide and 4.8m high. The lower hangar had a length of 85m, a beam of 13m and was 3.2m high. Overall, the two hangars had a surface of 3,337m^2 and a volume of 14,249m^3.

The flight deck was equipped with two axial 13 x 12m elevators and was originally 185m long and 23m wide. In 1944, in order to operate new types of aircraft, the length was increased to 200m, as was done in *Zuiho*. Other features included eight Type Kure Mod 4 arresting gears, two Type Kusho Mod 3 safety barriers and a windbreaker.

The original anti-aircraft armament included the usual Type 89 127/40 guns (four twin mounts) and ten Type 96 25/60 machine guns in triple mounts. However, since the latter proved inadequate to deal with new types of Allied aircraft, the Japanese increased their number in an attempt to somehow mask their technical and functional shortcomings.

Starting from August 1943, four new 25mm twin and four single mounts were installed, as well as three new Type 93 13.2/76 twin mounts. Later, during the lengthening of the flight deck, the number of single 25mm guns was increased to twenty-three, and six 4.7in twenty-eight-barrel rocket launchers were also installed. However, these figures are only indicative since, as reported by Shizuo Fukui, another thirteen single mounts were also temporarily mounted (one 25mm and twelve 13.2mm).

Considered the least successful of the converted Japanese aircraft carriers, *Ryuho* displayed stability issues to the extent that, once completed, seven months of trials were necessary before she could be considered fully operational.

The upper hangar structure of *Ryuho* in an image taken in October 1945 after the US occupation of Etajima, where the wreck was located in the summer of 1945. (NHHC)

The aircraft carrier *Ryuho*, badly damaged by US bombers in the final stages of the conflict, at anchor near the coast of Higasinoumi's island on 9 October 1945. (NHHC, digitally coloured image, courtesy J Irotoko)

COMPOSITION OF THE EMBARKED AIR WING

- **June 1943**
  21 A6M2, 9 B5N2
- **Philippine Sea/Marianas Islands (June 1944)**
  9 A6M2, 15 A6M5, 9 B6N2

SHINANO

SHINANO

	Shipyard	Laid down	Launched	Completed
	Yokosuka Arsenal	4 May 1940	8 October 1944	19 November 1944
Displacement	68,059t at trials; 71,890t full load			
Dimensions	Length: 265m oa; 256m wl; 244m btwn pp. Beam: 36.3m wl. Draught: 10.31m			
Flight deck	256 x 40m			
Machinery	12 Kanpon boilers and 4 Kanpon geared turbines; 150,000shp, 4 shafts			
Speed	27 knots			
Fuel	Oil, 8,900 tons			
Endurance	10,000 miles at 18 knots			
Armament	16 Type 89 127/40 (8 twin mounts); 35 Type 96 25/60 triple and the same number of single mounts, totalling 140 machine guns; 6 4.7in 28-barrel rocket launchers; 42 (+5) aircraft			
Complement	2,400 officers and men			

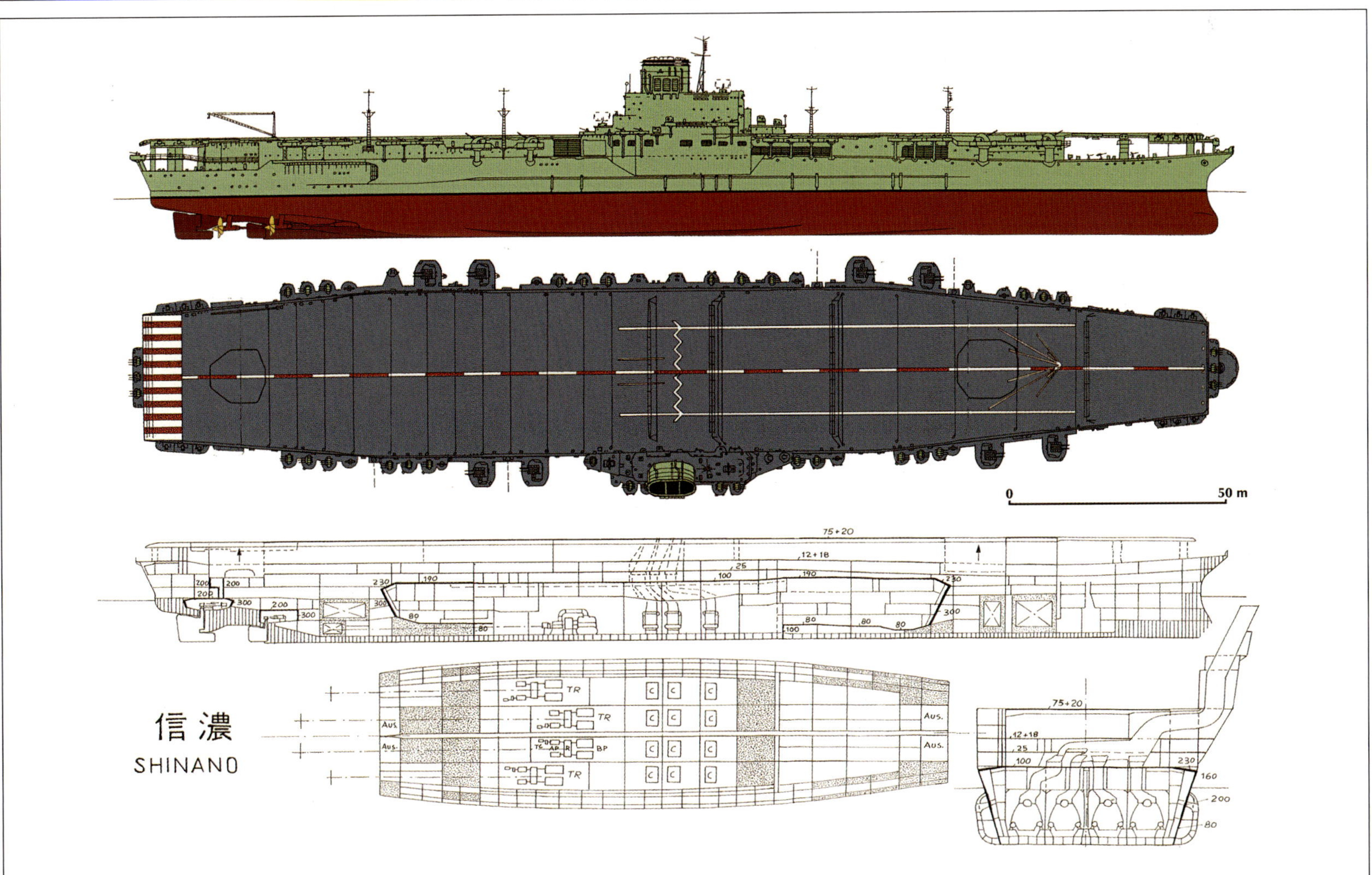

The aircraft carrier *Shinano* when commissioned (November 1944): side and top views, inboard profile, machinery layout and cross section (armour thickness in mm). (Drawings by A Nani, digitally coloured by M Brescia)

The two *Yamato*-class battleships planned in the *Maru-Yon* Programme, initially known as ship No 110 and ship No 111, had their work suspended after the completion of their double bottom because the delivery of armour plates was delayed. Later, as the political situation became increasingly complicated, the order of priority for warship construction also changed, battleships being delayed to advance other types of fighting vessels.

Two other factors also contributed to slowing down the construction process: assessing the opportunity of switching from double to triple bottoms around machinery spaces and magazines, and installing new armour plates for underwater protection. This highlighted a certain vulnerability of battleships to air and underwater attacks, as had been learned from the first combat operations. Furthermore, a month before the attack on Pearl Harbor, the Imperial Navy Staff had drawn up a memorandum, according to which battleships and heavy cruisers had to give way to aircraft carriers, submarines and escort units.

At the outbreak of war, it was decided that work on No 110, later named *Shinano*, should continue only as long as necessary to make the ship buoyant and thus clear the slipway. This decision was maintained until October 1942, when conversion works began. However, full-scale work commenced only in the following spring. Ship No 111 was laid down at Kure on 7 November 1940 and unofficially named *Kii*. In March 1942, the dismantling of her double bottom began, with the recovered materiel being used to build pontoons and cargo ships.

After the Battle of Midway, when *Shinano* was about 45 per cent built, it was decided to complete her as an aircraft carrier, in part due to the limited progress of the works and the possibility of keeping her hull, machinery, electrical network and other auxiliary components identical to *Yamato*'s.

Various disputes emerged about the characteristics that the ship should assume. Some officers, tied to 'classic' concepts, favoured an aircraft carrier that, with a protection similar to the *Yamato*s, would not only have offensive capabilities much greater than *Taiho*'s, but also the possibility of operating a much larger air wing. Other officers, still shocked by what had happened at Midway, favoured an aircraft-less ship, capable of operating as a floating base which, protected by a deck almost invulnerable to air attacks, could carry out refuelling, rearmament and maintenance operations in her hangar for aircraft embarked on frontline aircraft carriers.

After long discussions, a compromise was reached, abandoning the concept of the floating base[58] in favour of a traditional aircraft carrier. However, the possibility of supporting the air wings of other aircraft carriers would remain, thanks to a greater supply of aviation fuel than the *Shokaku*s and *Taiho*s.

Engineer Vice Admiral Keiji Fukuda was responsible for the conversion project. He had already supervised the *Yamato* design and, like his entire staff, had now to ensure that the future aircraft carrier was fitted with a protection scheme focused on the following parameters: underwater protection identical to the *Yamato*s; vertical protection capable of resisting a 7.9in shell fired from 10,000m; vital components capable of withstanding the effects of 800kg armour-piercing bombs dropped from a height of 4,000m; and a flight deck immune to 500kg bombs dropped from a dive bomber.

Vertical protection, which in the battleship *Shinano* was to be 400mm VH steel, was rearranged both in thickness (200mm) and material (NVNC). The thickness of the protective deck, whose purpose was to preserve the most vulnerable internal spaces should a bomb pierce both the flight deck and then the hangar floor, was reduced to 100mm from the planned 190mm. However, since some MNC plates had been completed, a 'mixed' solution was decided upon. Barbettes and openings for the planned 18.1in and 6.1in turrets were closed with the 190mm plates already available, while 100mm NVNC steel plates would protect machinery spaces. Furthermore, to ensure the best protection for magazines, the protective deck edges had NVNC steel plates 320mm thick.

Underwater defence was provided, in addition to compartmentalisation, by the same type of bulkheads already adopted on *Yamato* and *Musashi*. As a further defensive measure, a triple bottom ran below machinery spaces and magazines.

The flight deck above the hangar was treated with a compound of rubber, sawdust and concrete to absorb the effects of a 500kg bomb, similar to the situation on *Taiho*. Armour in this area included 75mm NVNC steel plates. In order to reduce installation times, they were connected to each other by 25mm DS joint covers. This entire structure was laid on a framework of 800mm box beams protected by 20mm and 14mm DS plates, respectively at its upper and lower parts. The upper plates were connected to the deck above, while the lower ones acted as shrapnel protection inside the hangar.

Measures were also taken to eliminate, or at least reduce, any internal damage that could lead to the ship's loss. At Midway, for example, the sinking of four aircraft carriers was caused not only by bomb hits, but what happened internally. Fires had developed not only inside the hangars but also through ventilation ducts damaged by shrapnel and explosions. This had caused the deaths of many engineering personnel and left the ships immobilised, without steering and electrical power.

Shinano's hangar, 208m long and 29m wide, was split into two sections. The 125m-long forward section was partially open due to the presence of large windows, 10m long, to be closed with sturdy tarpaulins when aircraft rearming and refuelling took place during daylight. The 83m-long aft section of the hangar was closed, like in all other Japanese aircraft carriers. However, before the ship was completed, a 12m-long emergency opening was created. Internal protection was provided by a double plate (25mm + 25mm) of DS. The open section, which housed a lot of sensitive equipment (machinery, ventilation ducts, bomb elevators, torpedoes and ammunition, etc), was protected, depending on the area, by 25–38mm DS plates.

Continuing to follow the lessons learned at Midway, fire-fighting equipment was carefully planned. The two elevators (15 x 14m forward and 13 x 13m aft) were separated from the rest of the hangar by a 7mm DS bulkhead. Additionally, the central part of the hangar was divided into four sections by three fire-proof barriers made of raw wool covered with asbestos.

Since the hangar was the largest of all Japanese aircraft carriers, a foam system was installed that, starting from the middle, was able to spray over almost 15m on both sides. A remarkable novelty, this system consisted of a soapy water solution stored in special tanks and sprayed by two seawater pumps each with a capacity of 200 tons per hour, positioned so that even the most distant pump could intervene on the other side of the hangar.

Petrol tanks were located in the second hold deck, forward and aft of the armoured citadel. In its central part, the first platform deck above these tanks had 70–80mm NVNC steel plates supported by 25mm DS plates, tapered to 50mm (25mm + 25mm) DS. This structure, theoretically, should have been able to withstand the explosion of a 500kg bomb dropped by a dive bomber or a 5.9in shell. As additional protection, these tanks were enveloped by about 2,000 tons of seawater, in order to contain ruptures or fires.

The island, approximately 15m long and 7m wide, was positioned amidships on the starboard side, and housed some important spaces (wheelhouse, bridge, etc) protected by CNC steel plates.

Machinery was identical to the two previous *Yamato*s. It included four Kanpon geared turbines which, fed by twelve Kanpon boilers (working at 25kg/cm^2 and 325°C), delivered a total of 150,000shp on four shafts, allowing a maximum speed of 27 knots. Again based on what happened at Midway, escape routes from machinery spaces and on both sides of the lower deck were provided for engineering personnel.

Having rejected the proposals to install 7.9in or even 12in guns, arranged as in the American *Lexington*s at their commissioning, armament included eight Type 89 127/40 twin mounts. Originally, it had been planned to install the same number of Type 98 100/65 twin mounts, but this proposal was later dropped due to production difficulties. Short-range defence was provided by twenty-three Type 96 25/60 triple mounts, later augmented with an additional twelve and finally, after the Marianas combat, by thirty-five single mounts, thus totalling 140 barrels. Six twenty-eight-barrel 4.7in rocket launchers were also installed in this last period.

The planned air wing was rather limited. Landings were supported by fifteen Type 3 Mod 10 arresting gears (twelve for normal aft landings and three for emergency bow landings) and three Type 3 safety barriers.

As for radars, some drawing plans highlight three air search systems: a Type 13 and a Type 21 atop the island and a Type 13 on a mast close to the forward elevator.

The displacement of *Shinano* at trials and at full load were 68,059 tons and 71,890 tons, respectively. This was therefore slightly lower than those of the previous *Yamato*s, as the lack of 18.1in turrets had been somewhat compensated by the armoured flight deck. The summary of weights regarding the displacement at trials is shown above.[59]

Components	Weight, t	%
Hull	23,346	34.3
Fitting out	2,629	3.86
Armour	17,694	26
Additional protection	6,550	9.62
Machinery	4,957	7.28
Ballast	1,077	1.58
Artillery/torpedoes	1,106	1.63
Aircraft	1,000	1.47
Fuel	5,935	8.73
Other weights	3,764	5.53

COMPOSITION OF THE EMBARKED AIR WING

- **Original design**

18 (+ 2) A7M1, 18 (+ 2) B7A1, 6 (+ 1) C6N1

Rendering of the aircraft carrier *Shinano* when commissioned. (S Fukui collection)

UNRYU CLASS

***UNRYU* Class**

	Shipyard	Laid down	Launched	Completed
Unryu	Yokosuka Arsenal	1 August 1942	25 November 1943	6 August 1944
Amagi	Mitsubishi, Nagasaki	1 October 1942	15 October 1943	10 August 1944
No 5002*	Yokosuka Arsenal	–	–	–
Katsuragi	Kure Arsenal	8 December 1942	19 January 1944	15 October 1944
Kasagi	Mitsubishi, Nagasaki	14 April 1943	19 October 1944	–
No 5005*	Yokosuka Arsenal	–	–	–
Aso	Kure Arsenal	8 June 1943	1 November 1944	–
Ikoma	Kawasaki, Kobe	5 July 1943	17 November 1944	–
***Kurama* (tbc)**	Mitsubishi, Nagasaki	November 1943	–	December 1945**
No 5009	Yokosuka Arsenal	July 1943**	–	March 1946**
No 5010	Mitsubishi, Nagasaki	April 1944**	–	June 1946**
No 5011	Yokosuka Arsenal	June 1944**	–	September 1946**
No 5012	Kure Arsenal	June 1944**	–	September 1946**
No 5013	Yokosuka Arsenal	June 1944**	–	March 1947**
No 5014	Yokosuka Arsenal	October 1944**	–	September 1947**
No 5015	Yokosuka Arsenal	January 1945**	–	March 1948**
Displacement	20,400t at trials (*Unryu, Amagi*), 20.899t (*Katsuragi*); 22,700t full load (*Unryu, Amagi*), 22,534t (*Katsuragi*)			
Dimensions	Length: 227.35m oa; 223m wl; 206.52m btwn pp. Beam: 26.8m max, 22m wl. Draught: 7.9m			
Flight deck	216.9 x 27m			
Machinery	8 Kanpon boilers and 4 Kanpon geared turbines; 152,000shp (*Unryu, Amagi*), 104,000shp (*Katsuragi, Aso*), 4 shafts			
Speed	34 knots (*Unryu, Amagi*), 32 knots (*Katsuragi, Aso*)			
Fuel	Oil, 3,670 tons			
Endurance	8,000 miles at 18 knots			
Protection	Vertical 140mm, deck 56mm			
Armament	12 Type 89 127/40 (6 twin mounts); 93 Type 96 25/60 (21 triple and 30 single mounts); 6 4.7in, 28-barrel rocket launchers; 48 aircraft			
Complement	990 officers and men (1,600 as flagship)			

* Construction cancelled and replaced by the conversion of the battleship *Shinano* as an aircraft carrier. Additionally, it was planned that from *Ikoma* onwards the design would be improved.

** Planned

Following the approval of the *Maru-Kyu* Plan,[60] several meetings between the political authorities and Imperial Navy representatives led to the decision to standardise the construction of new warships, adopting designs of ships already in service, with the aim of reducing construction times as much as possible. Regarding aircraft carriers, it was decided to focus on a modified *Hiryu*-type because it was considered, compared to the large fleet carriers, cheaper and quicker to build and therefore easier to replicate.

The ill-fated clash at Midway had reversed the order of construction priorities. The aircraft carrier now assumed the role of capital ship, paving the way for the construction of the carrier foreseen in the *Maru-Kyu* Plan, which was given the name *Unryu*. It was also decided to build five additional carriers between 1942 and 1943, which were to be followed by another eight.

Unryu at anchor off Yokosuka on 16 July 1944. (Kure Naval Museum – digitally coloured image, courtesy J Irotoko)

Although considered a direct derivation of the *Hiryus*, the *Unryus* differed in some aspects, primarily the relocation of the island to the starboard side. In comparison with the *Hiryus*, this island had only four levels, the first of which was level with the flight deck. However, a greater island length ensured a better centralisation of command and control for the anti-aircraft armament, as well as for radar and communication equipment.

To speed up construction times, while avoiding weakening the amidships hull section, the number of elevators was reduced to two, both measuring 14 x 14m. However, their lifting capability was increased to 7 tons, in order to operate new and heavier types of aircraft already in service or being planned. Two auxiliary elevators, one at the bow and another at the stern, were also fitted in order to move bombs and torpedoes from magazines to the flight deck.

In reality, while the aft elevator was suitable for moving both bombs and torpedoes, the forward one was limited to bombs.[61]

The flight deck had the same size as the *Hiryus*', but different equipment: nine Type 3 Mod 10-11-12 arresting gears and three Type 3 Mod 10 emergency barriers (two fixed and one mobile). Initially, it was envisaged to also install a catapult as well as to use rockets for assisted take-off, but these concepts were soon abandoned.

One problem that had to be addressed was machinery, because of the limited availability of suitable equipment. Thus, while *Unryu* and *Amagi* had geared turbines similar to those used on the *Suzuya*-class heavy cruisers, capable of developing 162,000shp for a speed of 34 knots, *Katsuragi* and *Aso* were fitted with geared turbines of a type already installed on destroyers,[62] capable of only 104,000shp and 32 knots. Steam was provided by eight Kanpon boilers operating as follows: 30kg/cm^2 and 350°C in *Katsuragi* and *Aso*; 22kg/cm^2 and 300°C in *Unryu* and *Amagi*.

Like almost all Japanese aircraft carriers, the *Unryus* had two hangars, the upper hangar being split into four compartments and the lower one into three. Both sides of the hangars were equipped with a new type of fire extinguisher which, using a 2 per cent soapy solution in water as a stabiliser, guaranteed a better performance than the CO_2-type that proved almost useless at Midway.

Other measures stemming from lessons learned in war were implemented to improve firefighting, including doubling the ventilation capacity to counter the accumulation of aviation fuel vapours. This was achieved by increasing the number of ducts so as to guarantee a number of hourly air changes significantly higher than in previous carriers. As a further measure, air intakes for machinery spaces, which were previously present only on the opposite side to the funnels,[63] were now located on both sides of the hull. Improved fireproof paint was also used, eliminating much materiel considered potentially flammable.

To improve stability in the event of damage, the number of portholes and side openings was reduced. Furthermore, it was deemed appropriate to install two balanced rudders as in *Soryu*,

This photograph of *Kasagi*, taken by US occupation forces in Sasebo in October 1945, highlights the structure of the two superimposed hangars. (USN – digitally coloured image, courtesy J Irotoko)

The aircraft carrier *Unryu* when commissioned (August 1944): side and top views, inboard profile, machinery layout and cross section (armour thickness in mm). (Drawings by A Nani)

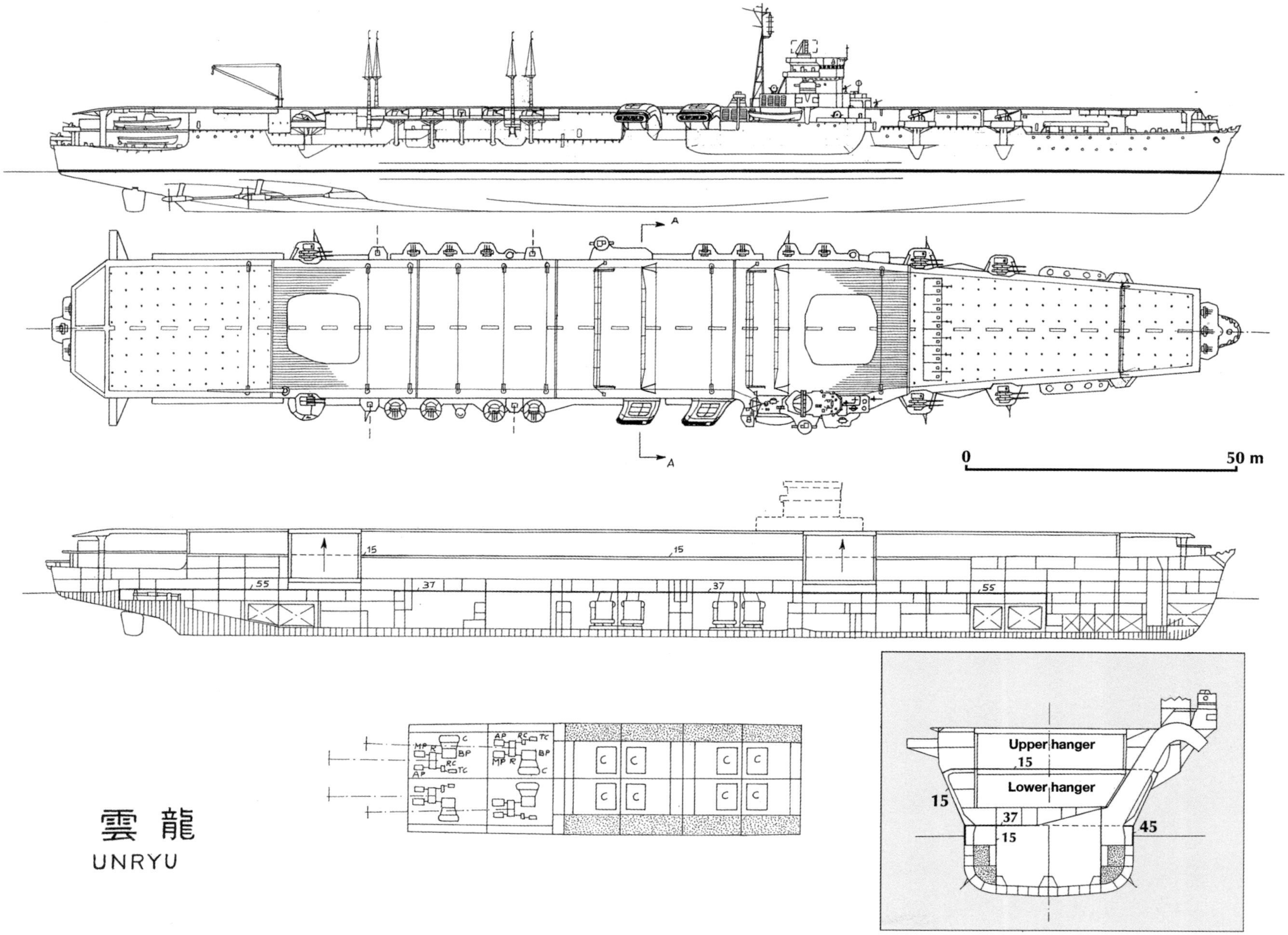

The aircraft carrier *Amagi* in November or December 1944. (S Fukui collection)

These two pictures, taken from US reconnaissance aircraft, show the aircraft carrier *Katsuragi* moored along the coast of the small island of Mitsuko Jima (Kure) in spring 194, before extensive camouflage works were carried out, as described in Appendix 4. (USAF)

Inside *Katsuragi*'s upper hangar in October 1945, after the occupation of Kure by US forces. Note the damaged flight deck. (NHHC)

The funnels of *Kasagi* being inspected by US Navy personnel on 19 October 1945. (USN)

The incomplete aircraft carrier *Kasagi* along with three Japanese submarines in Sasebo on 5 November 1945. A *Sen Taka*-class boat is moored on her port side. (USN)

Hiryu's semi-compensated type having proved unsatisfactory. The protection scheme was similar to that on *Hiryu*, but with improvements derived from combat experience. For example, machinery and auxiliary spaces were protected by a 25mm DS double longitudinal bulkhead.

The upper hangar deck, which was the strength deck, was fitted with three DS plates of different thicknesses: 20+25+25mm.

The main anti-aircraft armament, identical to *Hiryu*'s, included six 127/40 twin mounts. Four – two per side – were located forward of the island, and two (one per side, with that on the starboard side without an anti-smoke screen) close to the aft elevator. According to the design, short-range defence was to include thirty-one 25/60 machine guns (nine triple and two twin mounts), later increased to thirty-nine (thirteen triple mounts) and finally increased again to sixty-three/sixty-six, still in triple mounts. Six 4.7in twenty-eight-barrel rocket launchers were later installed in the three completed carriers, while the number of 25/60 single mounts remains uncertain, varying between twenty-one and thirty.

The incomplete aircraft carrier *Aso* in Kure on 20 December 1946. Her demolition would officially begin the following day. (USN)

Construction of the aircraft carrier *Ikoma* at the Kawasaki shipyard in Kobe was suspended on 9 November 1944. The vessel was later moored in Kobe Bay and camouflaged to blend in with the surrounding coast, as shown in this 1946 image. (USN)

Katsuragi's electronic equipment included two Type 21 radars, one atop the island and the other in a niche located on the port side of the aft section of the flight deck, and two Type 13 radars, one on a lattice mast abaft the island and one on a side platform on the starboard side of the flight deck. Underwater surveillance was provided by a Type 0 passive array and a Type 93 active sonar. Electronic warfare relied on three radar countermeasures systems: two Type E-27 operating on metric-wave band and one Mod 3 operating on centimetric-wave band.

COMPOSITION OF THE EMBARKED AIR WING

- **Original design**
12 (+ 3) A6M2, 27 (+ 3) D3A2, 18 (+ 2) B5N2

- **Following design**
18 (+ 2) A7M, 27 D4Y1, 6 C6N1

- **Final configuration of the three completed carriers**
27 A6M, 9 D4Y1, 9 B6N2, 3 D4Y1-C

TAIHO MOD CLASS

***TAIHIO* Mod Class**

	Shipyard	Laid down	Launched	Completed/Planned
No 5021	Kure Arsenal	February 1944	–	January 1947
No 5022	Kawasaki, Kobe	August 1944	–	July 1947
No 5023	Mitsubishi, Nagasaki	April 1945	–	March 1948
No 5024	Yokosuka Arsenal	November 1945	–	August 1948
No 5025	Kure Arsenal	November 1945	–	September 1948
Displacement	35,800t at trials; 38,500t full load			
Dimensions	Length: 265.7m oa. Beam: 27.8m wl. Draught: 9.7m			
Flight deck	261.5 x 31m			
Machinery	8 Kanpon boilers and 4 Kanpon geared turbines; 160,000shp, 4 shafts			
Speed	33 knots			
Fuel	n/a			
Endurance	10,000 miles at 18 knots			
Protection	Vertical, 152mm; deck, 80mm (hypothetical figures)			
Armament	8 Type 98 100/65 twin mounts; 22 Type 96 25/60 triple mounts; 51 (+2) aircraft			
Complement	1,800 officers and men			

Among the twenty-nine aircraft carriers to be built from scratch or converted as part of the 'Fifth Replacement Construction Programme' (*Kai-Maru-Go*), and whose commissioning was planned between 1942 and 1948, the five modified *Taiho*s would surely have been the most important.

These were to be an enlarged and updated version of *Taiho* as regards displacement and dimensions, with a very slender hull, a high length/beam ratio and a small bulbous bow, allowing the vessels to achieve high speeds. Armament would also be improved, with two additional 100/65 mounts and five 25/60 triple mounts, as had been suggested by *Taiho*'s officers.

As for protection, *Taiho*'s scheme would probably have been maintained. However, significant improvements were foreseen for underwater protection, taking into account the increased potential of the new American torpedoes. Furthermore, given the lessons of Midway, bomb and torpedo elevators would have been directly connected from magazines to the flight deck, thus avoiding refuelling or rearming aircraft in the hangars.

Fuel tank arrangements would have been further improved compared to *Taiho* by providing additional fire-fighting and anti-explosion safety equipment. The loss of *Taiho*, which exploded after torpedoes hit her petrol tanks, had already demonstrated the importance of carefully managing this aspect of safety.

Machinery included four geared turbines fed by eight boilers and was to be the same as in *Taiho*. Each steam turbine would consist of an HP stage, an MP stage and an LP stage, the latter with a built-in reverse stage, in addition to a cruising turbine. All turbines would have been connected, by means of a single reduction gear, to the relevant shaft/propeller.

Although power was equal to *Taiho*'s, the ships would be slightly slower due to the increased displacement. Two rudders were planned: a larger main one, semi-compensated, and a smaller auxiliary one.

Two superimposed hangars were planned, with an armoured flight deck fitted with two axial elevators; a second armoured deck, the lower hangar deck, would increase the protection of fuel tanks and magazines. The island, similar to *Taiho*'s, would have been located on the starboard side about one-third of the way along the ship's length, with a built-in funnel inclined outwards.

Landing operations would have been aided by fourteen Type 3 Mod 10 arresting gears, three Type 3 emergency barriers and one windbreak barrier.

COMPOSITION OF THE EMBARKED AIR WING

- **As planned**

18 (+ 2) A7M1, 27 B7A1, 6 C6N1

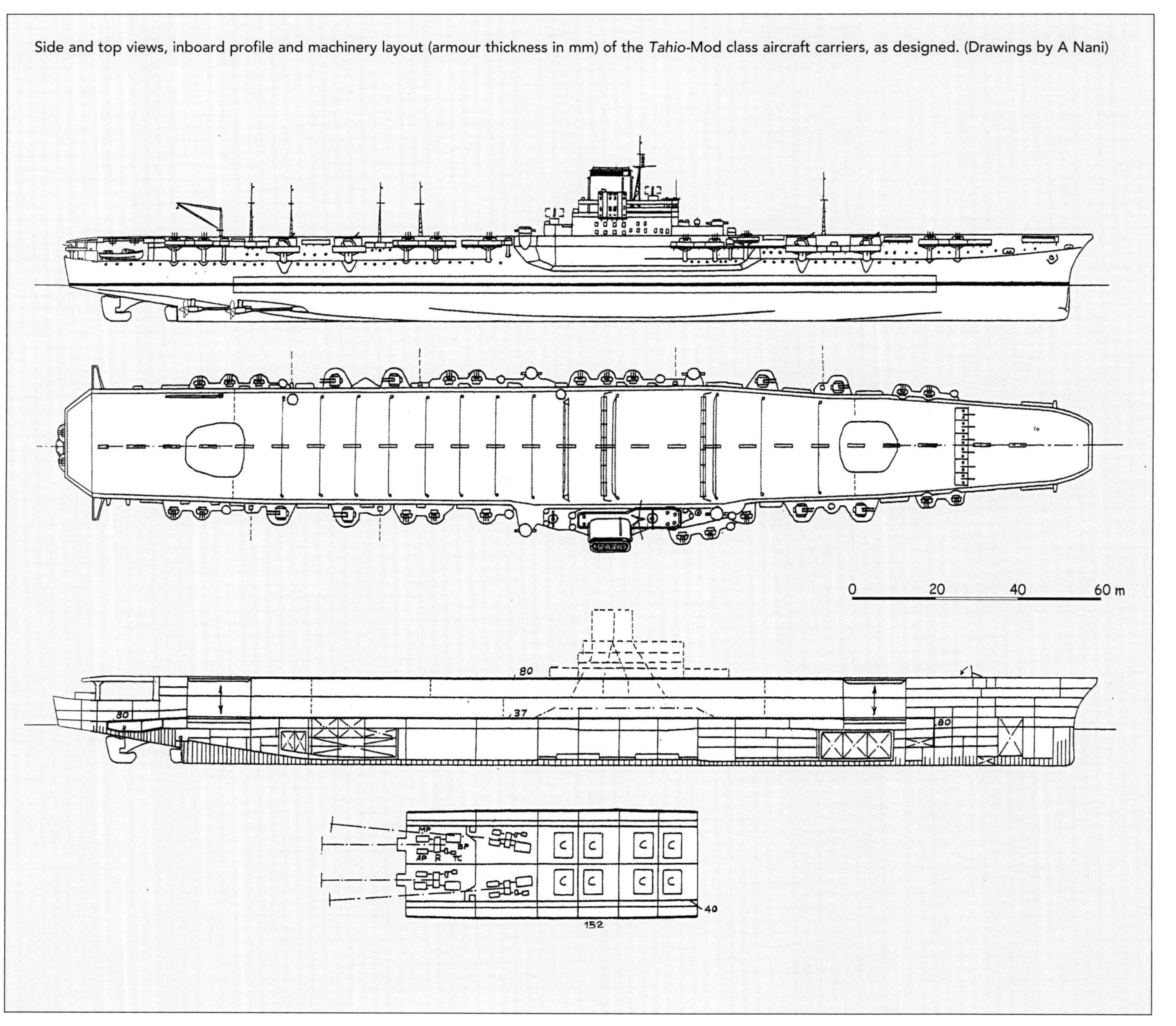

Side and top views, inboard profile and machinery layout (armour thickness in mm) of the *Tahio*-Mod class aircraft carriers, as designed. (Drawings by A Nani)

IBUKI

IBUKI

	Shipyard	Laid down	Launched	Completed
	Kure Arsenal	24 April 1942	21 May 1943	*
Displacement	14,800t at trials; 16,071t full load			
Dimensions	Length: 200.6m oa; 198.3m wl; 187.2m btwn pp. Beam: 21.2m wl. Draught: 6.04m			
Flight deck	205 x 23m			
Machinery	4 Kanpon boilers and 2 Kanpon geared turbines; 72,000shp, 2 shafts			
Speed	29 knots			
Fuel	Oil, 3,060 tons			
Endurance	7,500 miles at 18 knots			
Armament	8 Type 98 76.2/60 (4 twin mounts); 48 Type 96 25/60 (16 triple mounts); 4 4.7in, 28-barrel rocket launchers, twenty-seven aircraft			
Complement	989–1,105 officers and men			

* Towed to the Kure Arsenal for conversion into an aircraft carrier. Works began at the end of 1943 and were interrupted on 16 March 1945

Ship No 300 and her twin[64] were planned as part of the July 1941 *Maru-Kyu* Plan and laid down at Kure in April 1942. Both ships were heavy cruisers featuring, with some improvements, the characteristics of the two *Suzuya*s.[65] The Imperial Navy Staff, certain that war was inevitable, had decided to adopt the design of warships already in service, both for economic reasons and to keep construction times as short as possible.

Both cruisers were still in the initial construction stage when the disastrous clash at Midway forced a radical rethinking of new-construction priorities. Consequently, the few keel elements placed on the slipway for the cruiser being built in Nagasaki were demolished to free it up and allow the construction of the aircraft carrier *Amagi*. The cruiser being built in Kure was more advanced, so it was decided to continue her construction, launching the hull in May 1943. She had officially been named *Ibuki* on 5 April.

Ibuki's hull remained in Kure for some time, waiting for the Imperial Navy Staff to decide on her use. Initially, they considered transforming her into a fast fleet oiler – a naval component that the Japanese were rather lacking – but the idea of conversion into an aircraft carrier prevailed because Japan had been left with so few of them after Midway.

Probably aware of the American decision to transform some *Cleveland*-class cruisers into light aircraft carriers (the future *Independence* class),[66] the Japanese decided to follow the same path, considering that *Ibuki*'s small size did not allow her transformation into a fleet carrier. On the other hand, since her hull was equipped with sufficient armour and she was capable of reaching a high speed, it would have been unreasonable to use her just for escort purposes. Thus, based on the specifications provided by the Imperial Navy, a conversion design was drawn up in autumn 1943, entrusting its execution to the Sasebo Arsenal, to where the submarine support ship *Jingei* towed *Ibuki*'s hull.

Dismantling the magazines initially planned for the 7.9in guns allowed the housing of aircraft bombs and torpedoes, as well as ammunition intended for the ship's defence. Despite some opposition, it was also decided to halve the original machinery planned, with maximum power of 152,000shp allowing 35 knots, thereby eliminating two pairs of boilers and the aft geared turbines driving the external propellers. Spaces thus gained were allocated to new oil and petrol tanks, the latter being located – uniquely on Japanese aircraft carriers – inside the armoured citadel.

In view of the extreme danger posed by petrol vapours, the loss of the then-brand new *Taiho* to this cause resulted in some rethinking on this matter during the reconstruction of *Ibuki*. Consequently, as an additional protective measure, it was decided that, regardless of their location inside or outside the armoured citadel, these tanks would be shielded with pre-stressed concrete panels.

As for hull protection, it was decided to adopt the configuration originally planned for the *Suzuya*-class cruisers. This included a compound armoured belt (NVNC and CNC steel plates) with a maximum thickness of 100mm (25mm at the edges). Horizontal protection would be provided by a 35mm CNC steel armoured deck, tapering to 60mm.

Underwater protection was to be provided by two small bulges, running almost the entire length of the machinery spaces. These also aimed to improve transverse stability. However, this would be to the detriment of speed, which was to be around 29 knots. Machinery included two Kanpon geared turbines which, fed by four Kanpon boilers (working at 22kg/cm^2 and 300°C), would develop 72,000shp.

A small island located on the starboard side would house command and control spaces. The usual downward-inclined funnel was to be placed abaft the island.

Twenty-seven aircraft were to be housed in a single hangar connected to the flight deck by two 13 x 11.6m axial elevators. The flight deck would be fitted with two Type 3 Mod 10 safety barriers and nine Type 3 Mod 10 arresting gears. While the safety barriers were to be placed abeam the island, the arresting gears, regularly spaced from each other, would have been positioned between the middle and aft sections of the flight deck. Due to the limited width of the flight deck, a windbreaker was not planned.

Regarding armament, the Japanese had initially envisaged only twenty-two Type 96 25/60 triple mounts.

Later, due to the new types of Allied aircraft being able to survive 25mm hits, it was decided to replace six 25mm mounts with two new Type 98 76.2/60 twin mounts, already installed in the *Agano*-class cruisers. Four 4.7in twenty-eight-barrel rocket launchers were also added, two forward on the port side and two aft on the starboard side.

With regard to electronic equipment, Shizuo Fukui in his *Japanese Naval Vessels at the End of World War II* reports two Type 13 radars (one atop the island and one on an aft tripod mast), one Type 22 and one Type 21 radars, respectively positioned atop the island and in a pop-up position on the starboard side of the flight deck. A sonar room connected to twelve passive hydrophones (six on each side) would be located at the bow.

COMPOSITION OF THE EMBARKED AIR WING

- **As planned**

15 A7M1, 12 B7A

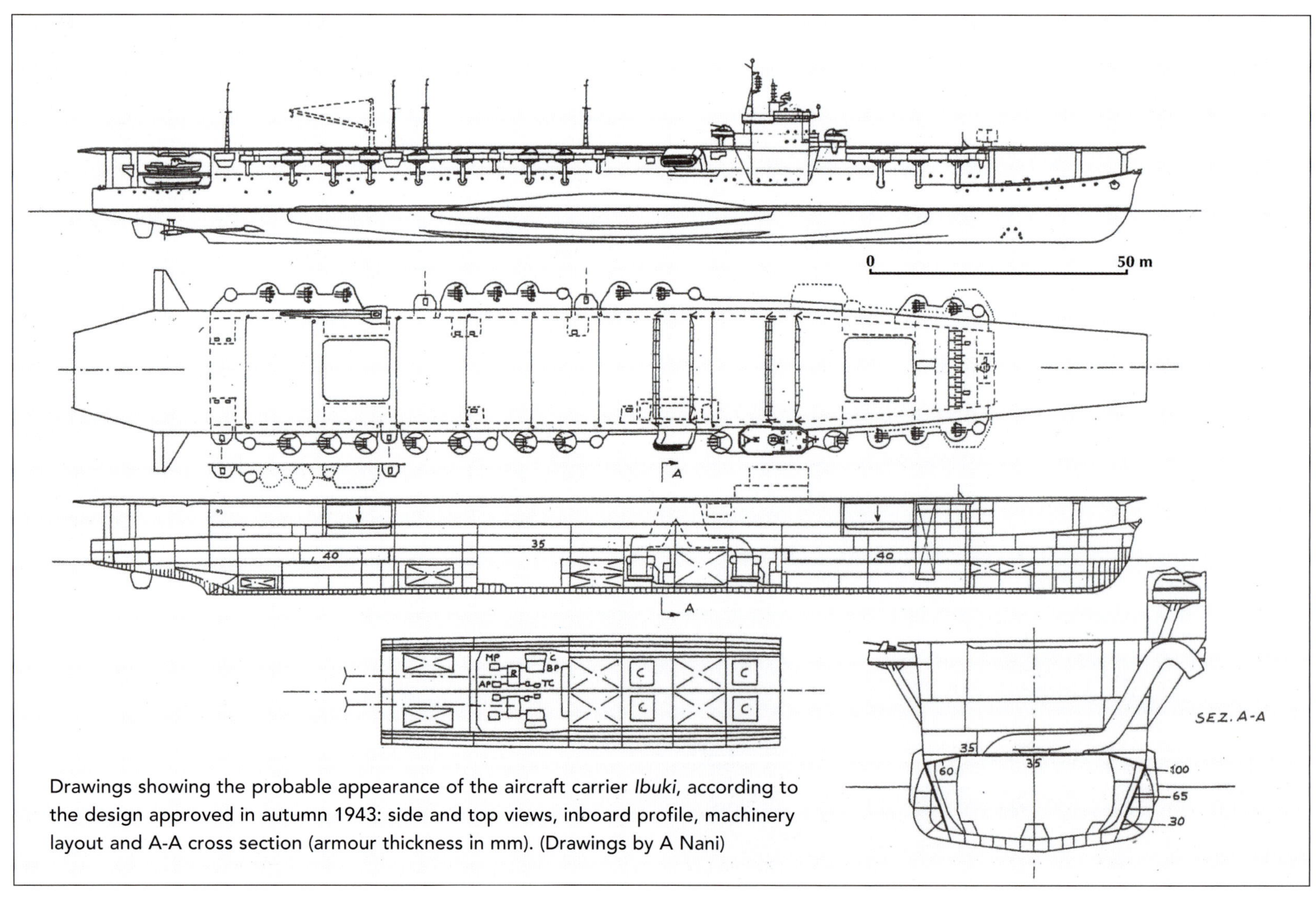

Drawings showing the probable appearance of the aircraft carrier *Ibuki*, according to the design approved in autumn 1943: side and top views, inboard profile, machinery layout and A-A cross section (armour thickness in mm). (Drawings by A Nani)

Three pictures of the uncompleted aircraft carrier *Ibuki* at Sasebo in September 1945. (S Fukui collection)

The carrier *Ibuki* in a picture taken after her launch at Kure Arsenal on 21 May 1943. (Kure Naval Museum)

OPERATIONS

Only Japanese aircraft carrier actions during the China campaign and the Second World War are covered here. Due to the fact that the Japanese Navy was accustomed to grouping ships with similar characteristics into homogeneous divisions, the following details contain some repetitions or overlaps which were impossible to eliminate completely. The same applies to operations of the mixed groups created after the Battle of Midway.

Hosho

In January 1932, *Hosho* formed, together with *Kaga*, the 1st Aircraft Carrier Division that, following the 'Mukden Incident', was mobilised to support Japanese troops stationed in the Shanghai area. Between 5 and 26 February, the aircraft of *Hosho* and *Kaga* provided direct support to Japanese Army operations, as well as countering the effectiveness of the Chinese air force. These operations ended on 1 March 1932 when the Japanese Army forced the Chinese to sign a ceasefire and accept the puppet government of Manchukuo.

Upon its return to Japan, *Hosho* underwent work to repair damage suffered during the 4th Fleet Incident and upgrade her features. After the 'Marco Polo Bridge Incident' of 7 July 1937, tensions between China and Japan, which had been quiet for some time, exploded into open conflict. The three aircraft carriers available at that time (*Ryujo* and *Hosho* of the 1st Division and *Kaga* of the 2nd Division) were consequently committed to the Chinese front, where *Hosho* was involved in operations between July and October 1937.

During the attack on Pearl Harbor, *Hosho* and *Zuiho* were assigned to support the bulk of the Combined Fleet (eight battleships, seven cruisers and twenty-eight destroyers), protecting the return home of Admiral Nagumo's Attack Force. In April 1942, after the Doolittle raid on Tokyo, *Hosho* took part in the Imperial Navy's attempt to engage the American formation as it was returning home. During operation MI (the attack on Midway), *Hosho* was part of the Main Corps (1st Fleet), under the direct orders of the commander-in-chief of the Combined Fleet, Admiral Isoroku Yamamoto.

Hosho undergoing trials in December 1922. (Kure Naval Museum)

Hosho steaming in Chinese waters in late 1937.

After the Midway disaster, *Hosho* was moved from the 1st to the 3rd Fleet, where she was involved in several aircraft landing trials. In January 1943, she was definitively assigned to training duties, including testing the feasibility of adopting new types of aircraft, such as the Judy and Tenzan. On 19 March 1945, during an air attack on Kure by the US Navy's Task Force 58, the flight deck of *Hosho* was slightly damaged by small-calibre bombs. Two days later, *Hosho* was classified as a 'fourth rank reserve vessel', with most of her crew assigned to other duties. At end of the war, the still-unscathed flight deck section was removed, while the hangar was modified to accommodate passengers. *Hosho* was then employed until August 1946 in repatriating Japanese personnel (military and civilian) who still were overseas at the end of the war. Transferred to the Ministry of the Interior, *Hosho* was eventually scrapped in Osaka between September 1946 and May 1947.

After the end of the Second World War, *Hosho* was employed to repatriate Japanese personnel (military and civilian). Note the aft section of the flight deck extended towards the stern, as well as the naval flag (*Hinomaru*) replaced by the national one. (NHHC)

Akagi

After major reconstruction and modernisation works from 1935–8, *Akagi* and the seaplane carrier *Chiyoda* provided air cover to the landing forces that invaded and occupied the Chinese island of Hainan in February 1939.

In November, *Akagi* and the 2nd Aircraft Carrier Division (consisting of *Soryu* and *Hiryu*) supported landings in various locations on the coast of the South China Sea. From 27 March to 2 April 1940, *Akagi* took part in operations against Chinese forces before returning to Japan, where she remained for a long period, except for a brief mission in support of operations the Japanese Army was conducting in the South Pacific area.

Members of the crew and aircraft on the flight deck of *Akagi* in the days immediately preceding the attack on Pearl Harbor. (NHHC)

On 10 April 1941, *Akagi* became the flagship of the 1st Air Fleet and was assigned, with *Kaga*, to the 1st Aircraft Carrier Division. She was the flagship of the Attack Force (*Kido Butai*) involved in Operation Z (the attack on Pearl Harbor) on 7 December 1941. *Akagi*, *Kaga* and the 5th Aircraft Carrier Division then took part in Operation R, during which the Allied positions in Rabaul (New Guinea) and Kavieng (New Ireland) were attacked. Both Rabaul and Kavieng were occupied on 22 and 23 March 1942. On 19 February 1942, *Akagi*, *Kaga* and the 2nd Aircraft Carrier Division attacked the port at Darwin in northern Australia, sinking two ships and damaging nine more.

Between the end of February and the beginning of March 1942, *Akagi*, *Kaga* and the 2nd Aircraft Carrier Division supported the conquest of Java. *Akagi* then served as flagship of Vice Admiral Nagumo during Operation A (the Indian Ocean raid), which while having a positive outcome on a tactical level, proved disappointing strategically.

Right and below: two well-known pictures taken on board *Akagi* during the attack on Pearl Harbor. (NHHC)

The aircraft carrier *Akagi* heads west into the Indian Ocean during Operation A on 26 March 1942, together with other warships visible in the background. Note the characteristic *futons* (mattresses) positioned on the bridge and auxiliary bridge as splinter protection.

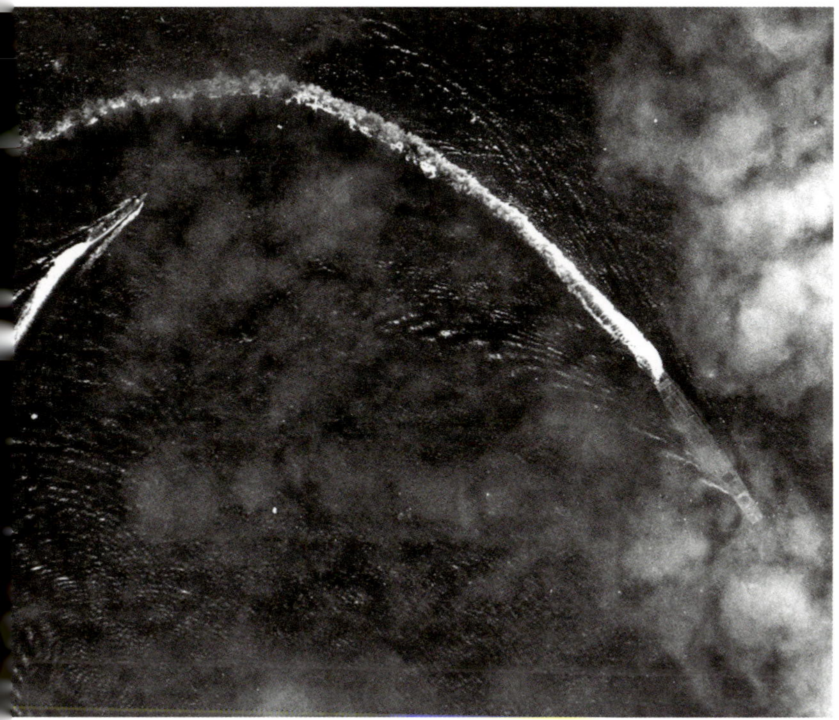

Akagi manoeuvres to avoid being hit by bombs from USAAF B-17s. The ship on the left is the destroyer *Nowaki*. (USAF 57576)

While bound for the Hawaiian Islands in early December 1941, the flight deck personnel of *Kaga* are briefed on the details of the attack plan and the position of the American ships in Pearl Harbor. (Kure Naval Museum – digitally coloured image, courtesy J Irotoko)

The aircraft carrier *Kaga* underway during Operation MI, which culminated in the Battle of Midway, were she was sunk.

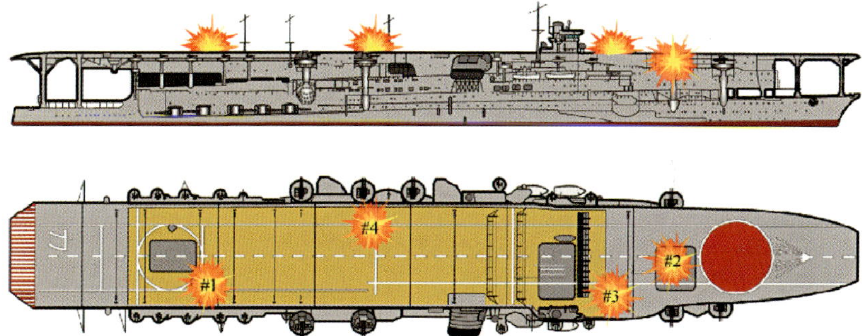

Drawings showing the impact points of bombs dropped by Dauntless dive bombers from the American carrier *Enterprise* that led to the sinking of *Kaga* at 0520hrs on 5 June 1942.

The aircraft carrier *Kaga* in flames and devastated by explosions off the Midway Islands on 4 June 1942. She sank the following day. (NHHC)

The carrier *Ryujo* underway at high speed in late autumn 1941. (Kure Naval Museum)

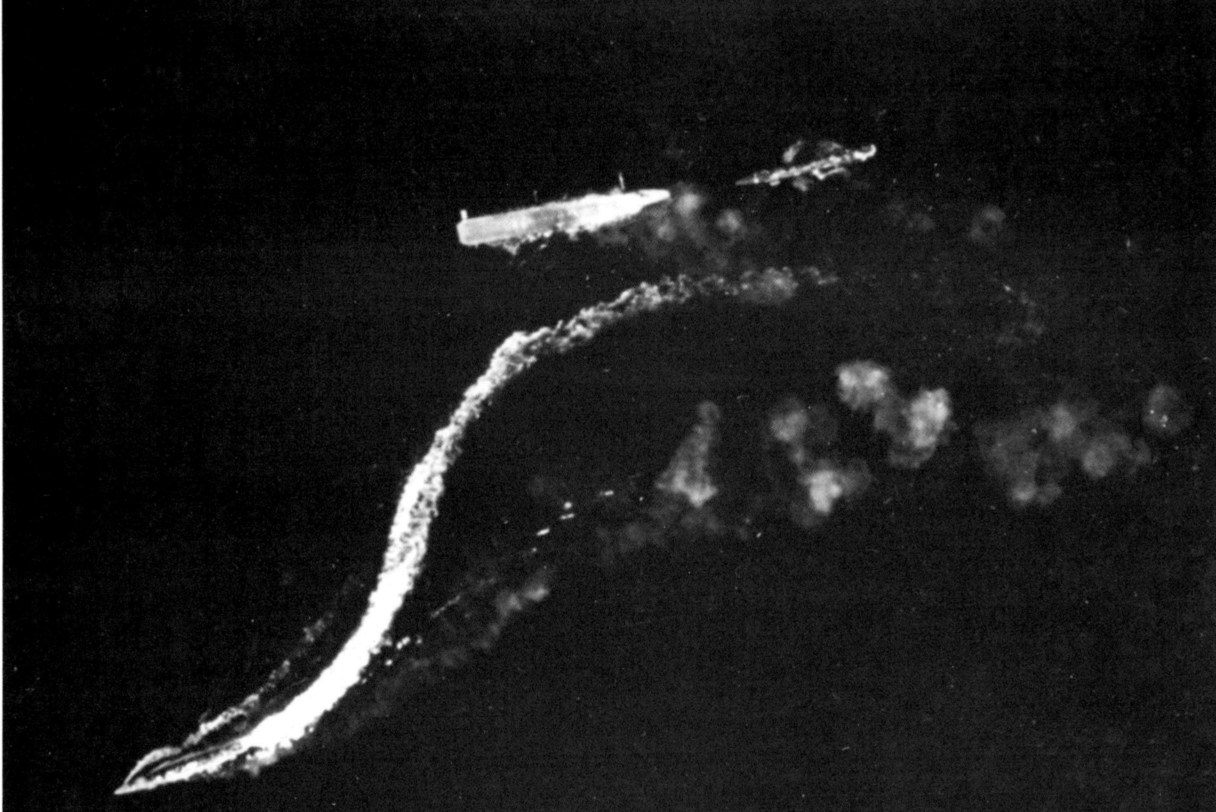

The aircraft carrier *Ryuho* (top centre) photographed from a USAAF B-17 bomber, immobilised after being hit by dive bombers and torpedo bombers from the American carrier *Saratoga* during the Battle of the Eastern Solomon Islands on 24 August 1942. The destroyer *Amatsukaze* (bottom left) is fleeing from the area to escape the B-17s' bombs, while the destroyer *Tokituskaze* (top right) is moving away from the *Ryuho* (whose crew she was rescuing) for the same reason. (NHHC NH 80-G-88018)

The aircraft carrier *Soryu* at anchor in the Kurile Islands in November 1941. (S Fukui collection)

Val dive bombers on the flight deck of *Hiryu* en route to Pearl Harbor, with the carrier *Soryu* visible in the background. (NHHC NH 80-G-182559)

Akagi was then involved, again with *Kaga*, in Operation MI (the attack on Midway Island). At 1026hrs on 4 June 1942, *Akagi* was attacked by three SBD Dauntless dive bombers from the aircraft carrier USS *Enterprise*, which hit her with two bombs. The first pierced the central elevator and penetrated the hangar, causing the explosion of ammunition carelessly piled beside the aircraft. The second bomb, which also hit *Akagi* in the central area, transformed the carrier into a flaming wreck.

At 0450hrs on 5 June, since saving her proved impossible, Admiral Yamamoto ordered her sunk. The destroyers *Arashio*, *Hagikaze*, *Maikaze* and *Nowaki* each fired one torpedo into *Akagi*, which sank at 0520hrs. The death toll was fortunately limited, 263 men lost their lives, while there were 1,070 survivors.

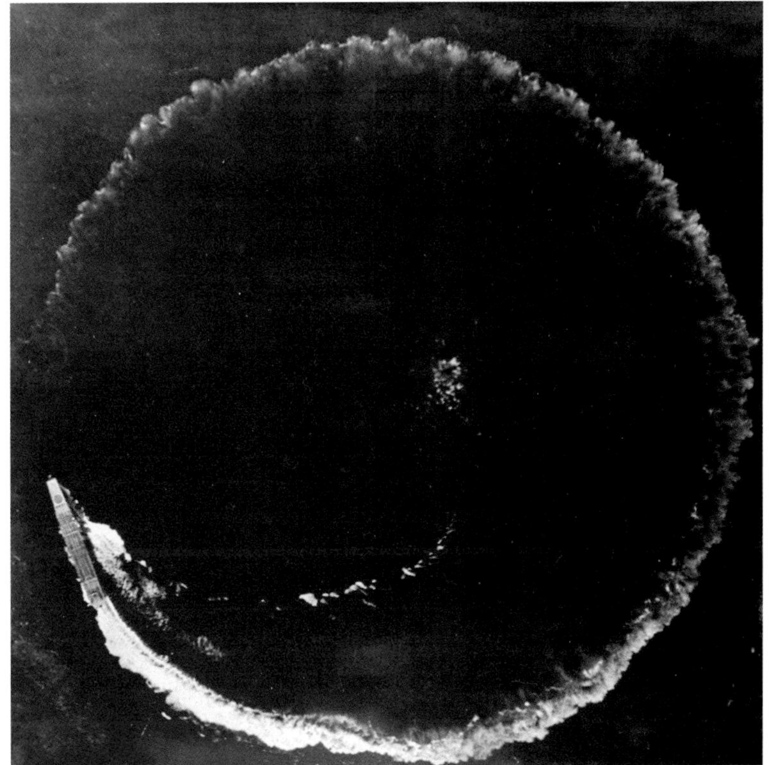

Soryu, under attack by a group of USAAF B-17 bombers, effects a 360° turn at 0800hrs on 4 June 1942 during the Battle of Midway (see also the similar picture of *Ryuho* on page 84). (Library of Congress, Prints and Photographs Division, lsa.8e00397)

Kaga

In February 1932, *Kaga* and *Hosho*, as part of the 1st Aircraft Carrier Division, were deployed at the mouth of the Yangtze River to support Japanese Army units operating in the Shanghai area. The intervention by Japanese forces, which occurred from 3–26 February and forced the Chinese to accept a ceasefire, was motivated by an anti-Japanese popular uprising. The Japanese, intending to take over the city of Shanghai, took advantage of the insurrection to dictate conditions deemed unacceptable by the Chinese. The Marco Polo Bridge Incident, a minor event leading nevertheless to war against China, saw *Kaga* involved on several occasions between August 1937 and December 1938, after the Japanese conquest of Canton.

The aircraft carrier *Hiryu* turns to port during an attack carried out by USAAF B-17 bombers off Midway early on the morning of 4 June 1942. (USAF)

Kaga remained in Japan for refitting and air–naval training until the start of Operation Z (the attack on Pearl Harbor), to which she contributed with *Akagi* as part of the 1st Aircraft Carrier Division. Once again with *Akagi* and the 5th Aircraft Carrier Division, *Kaga* took part in Operation R, leading to the conquest of Rabaul and Kavieng in January 1942. On 19 February, *Kaga* was involved in the attack on Darwin. Between the end of February and the beginning of March, she provided air support during the conquest of the island of Java.

Kaga did not participate in Operation A, as at the time of the Indian Ocean raid she was undergoing repairs in Sasebo to damage caused by a collision with rocks off Darwin. In early June, *Kaga* was sunk during Operation MI, the attack on Midway. At 1022hrs on 4 June, she was attacked by dive bombers from the American aircraft carrier *Enterprise* and hit by four bombs: in the bow elevator area, near the aft elevator, on the left side of the island and on the port aft side.

The first bomb exploded in the upper hangar, causing a series of fires that were fuelled by the explosion of bombs and torpedoes, as well as by leaking petrol· Many fire pumps were unserviceable and *Kaga* was soon reduced to a flaming wreck. At 1359hrs, she was attacked by the American submarine *Nautilus*, but all four torpedoes fired missed their target. At 1925hrs, once the survivors were recovered and the portrait of the Emperor from the ship had been brought to safety, *Kaga* was sunk by two torpedoes fired by the destroyer *Hagikaze*. Although 814 crew members were killed, some 1,300 survived the sinking.

Hiryu, severely damaged and about to sink, 5 June 1942. (NHHC)

Hiryu, burning and sinking, in a picture taken from a Yokosuka B4Y torpedo bomber from the aircraft carrier *Hosho*.

Ryujo

The first action involving *Ryujo* dates back to 1937 when her aircraft, together with those from *Kaga* and *Hosho*, hit several Chinese targets in the Shanghai area between 15 and 31 August. In October that year, *Ryujo* and *Hosho* provided tactical support to Japanese Army units operating near Shanghai and Nanjing. In January 1938, *Ryujo* and the brand-new *Soryu* were assigned to the 2nd Aircraft Carrier Division. In March, the aircraft of the 2nd Division supported the Japanese offensive against Canton, which fell on 12 October. *Ryujo* then returned to Japan, where she was downgraded to a reserve ship before returning to active service in November 1940 as flagship of the 3rd Aircraft Carrier Division.

At the outbreak of the Second World War, *Ryujo* was assigned to Operation M (the conquest of the Philippines) in order to support the landings in Legapsi and Davao. She took part in operations against Singapore, which surrendered on 15 February 1942, and was then involved in the conquest of Java, which was completed on 7 March. After operating in Burmese waters, *Ryujo* was assigned to Operation C on 1 April as part of the force tasked with attacking British merchant traffic in the Bay of Bengal. Between 5 and 7 April, her torpedo bombers sunk or damaged a number of merchant ships in the Indian ports of Coconada and Vizigapatam.

In early May, *Ryujo* and *Junyo* joined the 4th Aircraft Carrier Division, part of the Northern Force tasked to attack and seize the Aleutian archipelago. She remained in the area until 7 July, then returned to Kure. After the American landing on Guadalcanal (7 August 1942), *Ryujo* departed for Truk on 16 August and was involved in the Battle of the Eastern Solomons Islands, where she was sunk. Shortly before 1400hrs on 24 August, *Ryujo* was attacked by thirty-one dive bombers and eight torpedo bombers from USS *Saratoga*.

She was hit by three bombs and one torpedo on the starboard side. The latter caused the most serious damage, putting the rudder and machinery out of action. *Ryujo* was forced to stop and the fires were extinguished. However, the flooding caused by the torpedo increased her list, until she capsized in the late afternoon. Losses amounted to 120 crewmen, the destroyers *Amatsukaze* and *Tokitsukaze* rescuing many survivors.

A Zero fighter taking off from *Shokaku*, part of the first wave of aircraft preparing to attack Pearl Harbor early on the morning of 7 December 1941. (NHHC)

Three sequential images showing the aircraft carrier *Shokaku* being hit by a bomb dropped by a US Navy Dauntless dive bomber during the Battle of the Coral Sea on the morning of 8 May 1942. (NHHC 80-G-17027, 17028 and 17029)

Crewmen on *Shokaku* try to extinguish fires caused by several bombs dropped by American Dauntless dive bombers during the Battle of the Santa Cruz Islands on 26 October 1942. (NHHC)

A Nakajima B5N1 Kate torpedo bomber lands on *Shokaku*, underway in the south-west Pacific on 18 March 1943. (Kure Naval Museum)

The aircraft carrier *Zuikaku* at anchor in Kobe on 25 September 1941, the day she entered service with the Imperial Japanese Navy. (Kure Naval Museum)

Soryu

When commissioned, *Soryu* was assigned, like *Ryujo*, to the 2nd Aircraft Carrier Division. After operating against China in the Canton and Nanjing areas, *Soryu* returned to Japan to continue training pilots who needed familiarisation with the new types of aircraft gradually entering service. In April 1941, *Soryu* formed, with sister ship *Hiryu*, the new 2nd Aircraft Carrier Division, now part of the 1st Air Fleet. In July and August, she joined *Hiryu* in operations leading to the conquest of French Indochina, then took part in the attack on Pearl Harbor (Operation Z). Between 16 and 23 December, *Soryu* joined *Hiryu* in operations during the conquest of Wake Island.

In January 1942, again supported by *Hiryu*, *Soryu* attacked the island of Ambon in the Moluccas archipelago, then contributed to the conquest of Kendari airport (Celebes island). On 19 February, together with *Hiryu*, *Akagi* and *Kaga*, she attacked the port at Darwin, where a dozen ships were sunk, including the American seaplane support ship *William B. Preston* (AVD-7) and the destroyer *Peary* (DD-226). Between the end of February and early March, *Soryu* joined *Hiryu* and the 1st Aircraft Carrier Division in the conquest of Java, then took part in the raid in the Indian Ocean (Operation A) between 1 and 10 April. *Soryu* joined *Hiryu* as part of the Attack Force in Operation MI aimed at the conquest of Midway.

The *Zuikaku* under attack by aircraft from the American carrier *Hornet*. The dive bombers scored a hit, damaging her flight deck during the Battle of the Philippine Sea on 20 June 1944. (NHHC NH 80-G-238026)

Zero fighters taking off from *Zuikaku* in the early morning of 7 December 1941, in a well-known image from Japanese sources of the first attack wave against Pearl Harbor. (NHHC)

At 1025hrs on 4 June, while facing a torpedo attack, *Soryu* was attacked by thirteen dive bombers from the American carrier *Yorktown*: between three and five bombs hit the flight deck, where a number of armed and fuelled aircraft were ready to be launched for an upcoming strike.

The flames spread to the hangar below, reaching bombs and torpedo spaces and causing secondary explosions that sealed the carrier's fate. Within a short time, fires were out of control, the *Soryu* stopped and the order was given to abandon ship. The destroyers *Hamakaze* and *Isokaze* rescued survivors, completing the operation around 1800hrs. About an hour later, *Soryu* sank. More than 700 crewmen were lost.

This sequence, taken from a US Navy aircraft, shows different phases of the attack on *Zuikaku* during the Battle of Cape Engaño that led to her sinking. (NHHC – digitally coloured images, courtesy J Irotoko)

The light cruiser *Oyodo* comes alongside the sinking carrier *Zuikaku* to embark her crew. (Kure Naval Museum)

Although of poor quality, this picture documents the dramatic moment when the crew salute the flag of the *Zuikaku*, heavily listing to port and about to sink. (NHHC NH-73069)

Hiryu

Once commissioned, *Hiryu* remained in Japan, allowing pilots to be familiarised with new types of aircraft. In April 1941, *Hiryu* and sister ship *Soryu* were established as the 2nd Aircraft Carrier Division, part of the 1st Air Fleet. In July and August she took part in operations leading to the conquest of French Indochina, then attacked Pearl Harbor on 7 December as part of Operation Z. While returning to Japan after the attack, *Hiryu* and *Soryu* were detached to attack Wake Island, whose garrison surrendered on 23 December.

In January 1942, again supported by *Soryu*, *Hiryu* attacked the island of Ambon in the Moluccas archipelago, then participated in the seizing of the airport of Kendari (Celebes island). On 19 February, together with *Kaga*, *Akagi* and *Soryu*, she launched aircraft to attack Darwin. Between the end of February and early March, *Hiryu* and other carriers supported the invasion of Java.

Between 1 and 10 April, she took part in Operation A (the Indian Ocean raid), bombing the harbour of Colombo in Ceylon and sinking a freighter and her escort corvette at sea. On 25 May 1942, *Hiryu* sailed with *Kaga*, *Akagi* and *Soryu*, which constituted the 1st and 2nd Aircraft Carrier Divisions, for the invasion of Midway (Operation MI). On 4 June, *Hiryu*'s aircraft contributed to the attack on ground targets, providing air defence for the Japanese strike force and attacking the US aircraft carriers, until four bombs dropped by SBD Dauntless dive bombers from USS *Enterprise* hit *Hiryu* in the bow area at 1750hrs. The resulting explosions caused the flight deck to collapse and hurl the forward elevator against the ship's island.

The resultant fires could not be brought under control. During the night, machinery stopped and additional explosions rocked *Hiryu*, until the order to abandon ship was given. After the destroyers *Kazagumo* and *Makigumo* recovered her survivors, the carrier was torpedoed by *Makigumo* at around 0500hrs on 5 June, but did not sink immediately. Around 0700hrs, an aircraft from the carrier *Hosho* reported that *Hiryu* was still afloat and there were still survivors on board. The destroyer *Tanikaze* was immediately sent to the area but was unable to locate her, probably because *Hiryu* had sunk in the meantime.

The aircraft carrier *Zuiho* (bottom middle) is attacked by aircraft from the American carriers *Essex*, *Lexington* and *Langley* at the Battle of Cape Engaño on 25 October 1944. (NHHC NH-95786)

Shokaku

When commissioned, *Shokaku* was assigned to the brand-new 5th Aircraft Carrier Division with her sister ship, *Zuikaku*. She took part in Operation Z (the attack on Pearl Harbor) on 7 December 1941.

Zuiho in the process of sinking on the afternoon of 25 October 1944. (NHHC NH 80-G-272552)

A torpedo launched by a Devastator torpedo bomber from USS *Lexington* hits *Shoho* during the Battle of the Coral Sea on 7 May 1942. (NHHC NH 80-G-17026)

In January 1942, she joined *Zuikaku*, *Akagi* and *Kaga* for a raid on eastern New Guinea (north-western sector of the Solomon Islands), but the attacks against Rabaul (20 January) and Lae (21 January) proved ineffective due to the absence of valuable targets.

In February, after the raids carried out by the American aircraft carriers *Enterprise* and *Yorktown* against the Marshall Islands, *Shokaku* was assigned, together with *Zuikaku*, to carry out surveillance cruises in home waters in the Yokosuka–Mikawa–Kure area. In March and April 1942, *Shokaku* took part in the Indian Ocean raid, during which her aircraft attacked Colombo on 5 April.

Shokaku was then deployed to Truk to support Operation MO, the attempt to capture Port Moresby in New Guinea, and took part in the Battle of the Coral Sea (7–8 May), where she was damaged by three bomb hits: one on the port bow, one on the starboard side that damaged the forward elevator and one at the stern, near the aircraft engine repair shop. *Shokaku* managed to reach Kure on 17 May, and on 16 June entered dry dock for repairs. While steaming back to Kure, she had risked capsizing in heavy seas due to the large amount of seawater entering the hull through the damaged bow.

The time required for repairs prevented *Shokaku* from participating in the Battle of Midway. Following her return to frontline duty, *Shokaku*, sister-ship *Zuikaku* and *Zuiho* were redesignated as the 1st Aircraft Carrier Division, established after the Midway disaster. After the American landing on Guadalcanal, she took part in the Battle of the East Solomon Islands (24 August), where she was slightly damaged in near misses by dive bombers from USS *Enterprise*.

After a stop in Truk from 23 September to 11 October, *Shokaku* took part, again with her sister ship, in the Battle of the Santa Cruz Islands (26 October), during which she was seriously damaged and risked sinking after being hit by six bombs, two on the bow and four near the aft elevator.

Shoho is hit by a 500kg bomb during the Battle of the Coral Sea on 7 May 1942. The carrier sank shortly after being hit a second time. (NHHC).

The aircraft carriers of the 2nd Division: *Junyo* (middle), *Hiyo* (left) and *Ryuho* (second on the left). This picture was taken from the heavy cruiser *Maya* during the Battle of the Philippine Sea. (Kure Naval Museum)

On 20 June 1944, *Junyo* was hit by American aircraft that damaged the island, destroying the funnel. Although the damage was not particularly serious, *Junyo* did not participate further in the Battle of the Philippine Sea. (NHHC)

Nonetheless, she managed to return to Japan for repairs, which were carried out at the Yokosuka Arsenal, keeping her out of action for several months until 19 March 1943. In May, together with *Zuikaku* and *Zuiho*, she was assigned to guarantee the 'absolute line of defence' which included the Aleutian, Wake, Marshall, Gilbert and Bismarck Islands. From July 1943 to May 1944, *Shokaku* remained mostly in Truk, where the bulk of the fleet was concentrated, without directly clashing with American forces.

Shokaku participated in Operation A (the defence of the Mariana Islands), together with *Taiho* and *Zuikaku*, in the 1st Aircraft Carrier Division of the Mobile Force. The Battle of the Philippine (or Mariana) Sea (18–21 June) represented her last mission.

At 1048hrs on 19 June, the American submarine *Cavalla* hit *Shokaku* with torpedoes on the starboard side. She was in a very vulnerable condition because several aircraft, just having landed, were being refuelled and rearmed. Several explosions followed, causing the ship to list, despite attempts to balance her. The torpedoes put part of the machinery out of action and interrupted power supply, preventing the timely activation of fire-fighting pumps.

The crew initially managed to contain the fire, but petrol vapours continued to spread through the ship, fuelling fires and explosions inside the closed hangar. By 1430hrs, the situation was out of control and worsening. At 1508hrs, the explosion of a bomb ignited the petrol vapours accumulated inside the hangar. The order to abandon ship was given, but *Shokaku* sank a few minutes later, taking with her over 1,200 men (887 crew members and 376 aviation personnel). The light cruiser *Yahagi* and three destroyers rescued 570 men.

Zuikaku

When commissioned, *Zuikaku*, like sister-ship *Shokaku*, was assigned to the 5th Aircraft Carrier Division. She took part in the

Many details of the port side of the island can be appreciated in this image showing a signalman on the flight deck of the carrier *Junyo*. (Kure Naval Museum)

Junyo at anchor in Sasebo on 26 September 1945. The carrier was scrapped between 1946 and 1947. (NHHC – digitally coloured image, courtesy J Irotoko)

Unyo at anchor in Truk lagoon in May 1943. (S Fukui collection)

Operation Z attack on Pearl Harbor on 7 December 1941. The following January, she joined *Shokaku*, *Akagi* and *Kaga* to raid eastern New Guinea (north-western sector of Solomon Islands), but the attacks against Rabaul (on 20 January) and Lae (on 21 January) achieved poor results due to the absence of valuable targets. In February, after the raids carried out by the American aircraft carriers *Yorktown* and *Enterprise* against the Marshall Islands, *Zuikaku* was tasked, together with *Shokaku*, with carrying out surveillance cruises in the Yokosuka–Mikawa–Kure area. *Zuikaku* took part in Operation A (the Indian Ocean raid) from 1–10 April 1942, then she and her sister ship, *Shokaku*, joined Operation MO, the attempted capture of Port Moresby in New Guinea. *Zuikaku* emerged unscathed from the ensuing Battle of the Coral Sea (7–8 May). Later, she was assigned, together with *Junyo*, *Zuiho* and

The aircraft carrier *Chiyoda* burning during the Battle of Cape Engaño in the late evening of 25 October 1944. She and the destroyer *Hatsuzuki* were sunk by gunfire from the American cruisers *Wichita*, *New Orleans*, *Santa Fe* and *Mobile*. (USN)

Ryuho, to escorting the convoy tasked with the occupation of the Aleutian Islands (June–July 1942).

After the Midway disaster, *Zuikaku,* together with *Shokaku* and *Zuiho*, became part of the 1st Aircraft Carrier Division.

After the American landing on Guadalcanal, *Zuikaku* and *Shokaku* were engaged in the Battle of the Eastern Solomon Islands (24 August), where her aircraft severely damaged the American

The carrier *Taiho* at anchor at Tawi-Tawi (Mindanao) in late May 1944. (Kure Naval Museum – digitally coloured image, courtesy J Irotoko)

One of the few existing images – unfortunately of poor quality – depicting the aircraft carrier *Taiho* in late May 1944. (NHHC)

carrier *Enterprise*. She was then based at Truk for the next few months. On 26 October 1942, in the Battle of the Santa Cruz Islands, her aircraft again damaged the repaired *Enterprise*, as well as *Hornet*, which was later sunk by Japanese destroyers. *Zuikaku* then returned to the home islands via Truk for training duties and ferrying aircraft tasked with the defence of Rabaul (March 1943), a role not particularly suited to a frontline warship.

In May, *Zuikaku* was assigned, together with *Shokaku* and *Zuiho*, to Operation Z, aimed at guaranteeing the 'absolute line of defence' which included the Aleutian, Wake, Marshall, Gilbert and Bismarck Islands. From July 1943 to May 1944, she largely remained in Truk, where the bulk of the Japanese fleet was concentrated to defend the area. Operation A (the defence of the Marianas) saw *Zuikaku* back in action, with *Taiho* and *Shokaku*, as part of the 1st Aircraft Carrier Division of the First Mobile Fleet, engaged in the Battle of the Philippine Sea (18–21 June).

On 20 June, *Zuikaku* was attacked by dive bombers from USS *Hornet* (CV-12). One bomb (three according to US sources) pierced *Zuikaku*'s flight deck, igniting several fires in the hangar. At first, the damage seemed irreparable, so much so that the order to abandon ship was given. However, *Zuikaku*'s experienced damage-control teams managed to get the fires under control, allowing the carrier to reach the port of Kure under her own power with the survivors of *Taiho* and *Hiyo*, both of which had been sunk during the battle.

Once the repairs were completed, *Zuikaku* was grouped together with *Zuiho*, *Chitose* and *Chiyoda*, these being the surviving aircraft carriers the Japanese Fleet could still operate. In October 1944, she was the flagship of the decoy Northern Force (including *Zuiho*, *Chitose* and *Chiyoda*), intended to act as bait for the American aircraft carriers. On 25 October, *Zuikaku* was operating east-north-east of Cape Engaño in the Philippines, when aircraft from the American carriers *Intrepid*, *Lexington*, *San Jacinto* and *Cowpens* hit her with seventeen bombs and seven torpedoes.

With *Zuikaku* listing heavily to port, the order was issued to abandon ship. She capsized and sank at 1414hrs with almost half the crew still on board, officers having forced the men to gather on the flight deck to sing the national anthem. The destroyers *Wakatsuki* and *Kuwa* rescued over 850 survivors.

Zuiho

In September 1941, *Zuiho* was the flagship of the 3rd Aircraft Carrier Division, which also included *Hosho*. During the attack on Pearl Harbor, she was part of the naval group, led by Admiral Yamamoto, tasked with covering the return of the Attack Force. In June 1942, she participated in the Battle of Midway as part of the main body of the Invasion Force. Once the planned conquest of the island was cancelled, *Zuiho* was diverted to support the invasion of the Aleutian Islands. After Midway, as part of the reorganisation of the Japanese aircraft carrier force, she was assigned to the 2nd Aircraft Carrier Division, which also included the two *Hiyo*s. *Zuiho* sailed to Truk on 1 October 1942, taking part in the Battle of the Santa Cruz Islands on the 26th, during which two dive bombers from USS *Enterprise* hit her in the aft section of the flight deck. The damage was limited but put *Zuiho* out of action, forcing her to withdraw from the battle and return to Truk, together with *Shokaku*, which was also damaged. Both carriers returned to Japan on 7 November for repairs, which were completed in mid-December. From 31 January to 9 February 1943, *Zuiho* took part in Operation K, the evacuation of Guadalcanal, then for the rest of the year she operated between Japanese home waters and the advanced base of Truk, without being involved in any significant events.

In January 1944, *Zuiho* was assigned, together with *Chitose* and *Chiyoda*, to the 3rd Aircraft Carrier Division of the 1st Mobile Fleet. From 18–21 June, she took part in the Battle of the Philippine Sea, from which she emerged unscathed. *Zuiho* was later attached to the newly formed 3rd Aircraft Carrier Division, which brought together almost all the surviving Japanese carriers. In October, after the Japanese received reports of American landings on Leyte in the Philippines, *Zuiho* and her consorts were ordered to approach the Gulf of Leyte from the north as a diversion, so as to attract the US carriers towards them and away from their landing area. This, it was hoped, would allow the Japanese battle force to attack the American transport ships and destroy them.

The carrier *Ryuho* in a picture taken in Kure by an aircraft from the American escort carrier *Siboney* in October 1945. *Ryuho* survived the war, but was scrapped in 1946. (NHHC NH 80-G-351386)

The aircraft carrier *Shinano* during sea trials. She sank on 19 November 1944, having been torpedoed by the American submarine *Archerfish* the previous day. As is the case for *Taiho*, there are very few photographs of *Shinano*. (Kure Naval Museum)

At 1317hrs on 25 October, *Zuiho* was attacked off Cape Engaño by aircraft from the American carriers *Essex*, *Lexington* and *Langley*. *Zuiho* was hit by a torpedo on the starboard side and a bomb near the aft elevator; other bombs exploded nearby, damaging the hull in several places. Fifteen minutes later, she was hit by another torpedo and a small bomb, while several narrow misses cut steam pipes and caused flooding of the engine rooms and one boiler room. Speed dropped to 12 knots while the crew tried in vain to deal with the flooding. At 1445hrs, the last working engine stopped, leaving the ship dead in the water with an increasing list to starboard. *Zuiho* sank stern-first and capsized at 1526hrs, with the loss of seven officers and 208 men. The battleship *Ise* and destroyer *Kuwa* managed to rescue 759 survivors.

Shoho

After commissioning on 30 November 1941, *Shoho* was assigned, together with *Ryujo*, to the 4th Aircraft Carrier Division. Her first mission was to transport six dismantled A6M2 fighters to Truk, where she arrived on 10 February 1942.

After the Doolittle raid (18 April 1942), she was put on alert, together with the cruisers of the 4th Division (*Atago*, *Takao* and *Maya*) and the 5th Division (*Myoko* and *Haguro*), to intercept the American force, but the mission was later cancelled. In late April, *Shoho* was assigned, together with the 6th Cruiser Division (*Aoba*, *Kinugasa*, *Furutaka* and *Kako*) to protect the invasion force taking part in Operation MO, which aimed to capture Tulagi (Solomon Islands) and Port Moresby (New Guinea).

Drawing showing the impact points of the four torpedoes, fired by the American submarine *Archerfish*, that sank *Shinano*. The coloured areas indicate the flooded compartments.

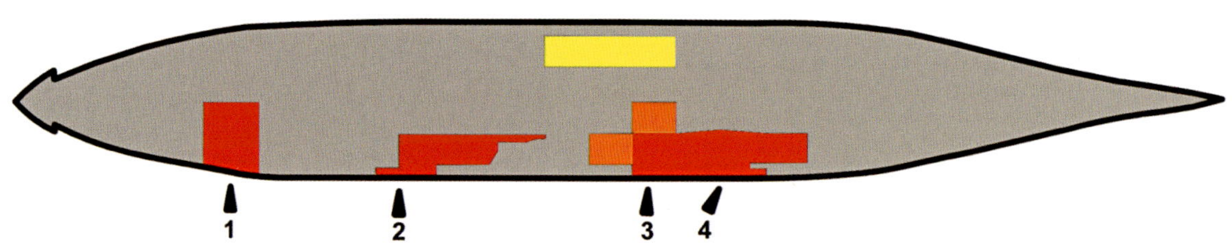

On the afternoon of 19 December 1944, the American submarine *Redfish* (from whose periscope this image was taken) torpedoed and sank the aircraft carrier *Unryu* some 200 miles south-east of Shanghai. (L D MacGregor collection).

The wreck of the carrier *Amagi*, half-sunken and listing to port, in the Bay of Kure on 1 June 1946. *Amagi* had been in this condition since the end of March 1945, after being repeatedly hit by carrier-based aircraft from Task Force 38 and USAAF B-24 bombers. (NHHC)

After the successful landing at Tulagi on 3 May, *Shoho* took part, together with *Shokaku* and *Zuikaku*, in the Battle of the Coral Sea. At 1117hrs on 7 May, *Shoho* was attacked by fifteen dive bombers from USS *Lexington*, which hit her with two 1,000lb bombs in the aft elevator area. The bombs exploded inside the hangar, setting on fire several fully fuelled and armed aircraft. A few minutes later, during an attack carried out by Devastator torpedo bombers, *Shoho* was hit on both sides by five torpedoes that knocked out power and flooded engine and boiler rooms. Reduced to a flaming wreck, she sank at 1131hrs. Some 300 men managed to abandon ship, but had to wait for hours in the water before being picked up by the destroyer *Sazanami*, which found only 203 survivors.

Junyo

Upon commissioning on 3 May 1942, *Junyo* was assigned to the 4th Aircraft Carrier Division, together with *Ryujo*. A month later, she was tasked to support Operation AL, which planned to seize several of the Aleutian Islands in order to provide an early warning in case of an American attack from the north. On 3 and 4 June, the American installations in Dutch Harbor were bombed by aircraft from *Junyo*, while the islands of Attu, Kiska and Adak were occupied between 7 and 10 June. In July 1942, after the Midway disaster, *Junyo* – initially designated as an auxiliary carrier – was assigned, together with sister-ship *Hiyo*, to the 2nd Aircraft Carrier Division to operate against American forces in the Guadalcanal area.

On 26 October, *Junyo* took part in the Battle of the Santa Cruz Islands, from which she emerged unscathed. Later, as part of the last attempt of the Japanese to resolve the struggle in this crucial sector in their favour, she took part, together with *Hiyo*, in the Battle of Guadalcanal (12–13 November), marking the beginning of the end of the Japanese presence in the area. Until early February 1943, *Junyo* provided cover to several convoys during the evacuation from Guadalcanal.

In April, *Junyo* detached her air group to Rabaul to participate in Operation I-Go, an offensive against Allied forces in the Solomon Islands and New Guinea. From August until October, she was tasked to ferry aircraft, personnel and equipment to the Caroline Islands. On 5 November, en route from Truk to Kure, *Junyo* was torpedoed by the American submarine *Halibut*, which launched all six of her bow torpedoes but achieved only one hit, killing four men and damaging the carrier's propellers and rudder.

Junyo, unable to manoeuvre, was taken in tow by the cruiser *Tone* and reached Kure on 19 November. She remained in Kure for repairs until the end of February 1944, before being assigned to the 2nd Aircraft Carrier Division, together with *Hiyo* and *Ryuho*. *Junyo* was involved in aircraft training until 11 May, when she sailed for the Philippines.

In June 1944, she took part in the Battle of the Philippine Sea, where she was slightly damaged by two bombs on the 19th. After repairs in Kure, *Junyo* remained in the Inland Sea until the end of

October, when she was tasked to transport equipment to Borneo. In November, she was attacked several times, but unsuccessfully, by American submarines. However, early in the morning of 9 December 1944, off the coast of Nomosaki, the submarines *Redfish* (SS-339) and *Sea Devil* (SS-400) hit her on the starboard side with two torpedoes that flooded several compartments and killed nineteen crewmen.

Despite the flooding and consequent list to starboard, *Junyo* managed to sail with one shaft and, assisted by the escort destroyer *Machi*, reached Sasebo, where repair works began on 18 December. These were soon abandoned due to lack of materiel and the priority given to the production of pocket submarines. *Junyo* was then classified as a reserve ship, and her armament and other equipment were removed in August 1945. The ship was surrendered to the Allies on 2 September, stricken from the Japanese Navy List and scrapped in Sasebo between June 1946 and August 1947.

Hiyo

Hiyo was commissioned on 31 July 1942, and on 12 August became the flagship of the 2nd Aircraft Carrier Division. On 9 October, *Hiyo* arrived at Truk with sister-ship *Junyo* and was assigned to the 3rd Fleet, which also included two battleships, three heavy cruisers and their escorts. They were then ordered to attack the American supply convoys supporting the landings on Guadalcanal. A fire that broke out in the generator room on 21 October reduced her speed to 16 knots, compelling *Hiyo* to return to Truk for repairs and preventing her participation in the Battle of the Santa Cruz Islands (26 October). *Hiyo* returned to Kure on 11 December, underwent a brief refit and spent a couple of months training in the Inland Sea, before sailing for Truk on 22 March 1943.

In April, she took part, together with *Junyo* and *Zuikaku*, in Operation I-Go, which targeted Allied bases in the Solomon Islands and New Guinea, with the purpose of strengthening the Japanese base on Rabaul. On 11 May, *Hiyo*, the 2nd Carrier Division and two battleships departed Truk to defend the occupied Aleutian Islands, but the Americans recaptured Attu before the Japanese could intervene. On 7 June, *Hiyo* departed Yokosuka, bound for Truk. While en route, she was torpedoed by the American submarine *Trigger* off Miyaka Island.

The submarine fired six torpedoes; the first exploded prematurely and two others missed, but three hit *Hiyo* on the starboard side. Two of them exploded, one at the bow and the other near a boiler room, knocking out all power. The carrier managed to return to Tateyama around midnight the following day. She was repaired in Yokosuka until 15 September, then re-embarked her air wing, which in the meantime had been assigned first to *Ryuho* and then to *Junyo*. Between October 1943 and May 1944, *Hiyo* carried out only limited activity, mainly operating as an aircraft ferry in missions to Singapore, Palau and Manila.

On 11 May, *Hiyo*, together with *Junyo, Ryuho* and other ships, including the super-battleship *Musashi*, left Japan for Tawi-Tawi, 35nm east of North Borneo, where the remainder of the Combined Fleet was concentrated. The Japanese fleet was en route to the Sulu Sea in the central Philippines on 13 June to practise carrier operations when it learnt of the American attack on the Mariana Islands the previous day. The ensuing Battle of the Philippine Sea (18–21 June) marked the end of *Hiyo*.

At dusk on 20 June, *Hiyo* was attacked by four torpedo bombers from the American light carrier *Belleau Wood*, which scored two torpedo hits – one on each side – knocking out her engines. Quickly engulfed in flames, fuelled by leaking petrol vapours – as was also the case for *Taiho* and *Shokaku* – *Hiyo* began to list to starboard and sank stern-first at 1932hrs, dragging 250 crewmen to their deaths. Some 1,300 survivors were rescued by the escorting destroyers.

The *Unryu*-class aircraft carrier *Kasagi* still incomplete at Sasebo on 27 September 1945. She was scrapped there between 1946 and 1947. (NHHC – digitally coloured image, courtesy J Irotoko)

The aircraft carrier *Katsuragi* stops at Rabaul for refuelling en route from the Solomon Islands to Japan on 31 January 1946. In the post-war period, she was used for the repatriation of Japanese Army and Navy personnel. (USN)

Taiyo

The converted passenger ship *Kasuga Maru* was completed as an escort carrier on 15 September 1941. Before the start of the war in the Pacific, she was engaged in training and transport missions, and on the eve of the attack on Pearl Harbor had just arrived in Palau, ferrying fighter aircraft. On 14 July 1942, *Taiyo* was assigned to the Combined Fleet, but was soon detached from the main body and mainly used to resupply Truk, Rabaul and the Marshall Islands. In the early afternoon of 28 September, when en route 40 miles south of Truk, *Taiyo* was torpedoed on the starboard side by the American submarine *Trout* (SS-202), causing the death of thirteen crewmen. She was able to reach Rabaul for emergency repairs, then left for Kure on 4 October for permanent repairs that were completed on the 26th.

Once operational, *Taiyo* resumed her escort and aircraft ferrying duties from Japan to Truk and Kavieng. While en route to Truk on 9 April 1943, she was once again torpedoed, this time by the American submarine *Tunny*, but thanks to the premature explosion of all four torpedoes the damage caused was only limited. On 24 May she was torpedoed for a third time by the American submarine *Cabrilla*, again without serious consequence. *Taiyo*'s last mission began on 10 August 1944 when, with a dozen B5N2 torpedo bombers on board, she was tasked to escort a convoy to Singapore via Manila. On the evening of 18 August, she was torpedoed and sunk off Cape Bolinao (Luzon) by the American submarine *Rasher*, with an estimated loss of 400 crewmen.

Unyo

Until November 1943, *Unyo* was mainly tasked with ferrying aircraft from Japan to Truk, Saipan, Rabaul, the Philippines and the Dutch East Indies. On 19 January 1944, while en route to Yokosuka, she was torpedoed by USS *Haddock*, which scored a couple of hits that severely damaged the carrier's bow. *Unyo* managed to reach Saipan for emergency repairs and later departed for Yokosuka, where permanent repairs were completed on 28 June. *Unyo* was then assigned to the 1st Surface Escort Force. On 25 August, she departed Japan, together with the cruiser *Kashii*, to escort a convoy headed to Singapore, where she arrived on 5 September. On the night of 16/17 September, while on the return route, *Unyo* was struck by two torpedoes from USS *Barb* south-east of Hong Kong. A storm developed during the night and caused further damage, leading to the interior bulkheads collapsing and *Unyo* developing a heavy list to starboard. She capsized and sank around 0800hrs on 17 September. Sources disagree on the losses among the crew, but according to some they were only limited.

Chuyo

Chuyo was the first Japanese escort aircraft carrier to enter service. She spent most of her service life ferrying aircraft, cargo, supplies and passengers between Japan and Truk. She made the first of her thirteen trips (about one per month) on 12 December 1942, and was back in Yokosuka two weeks later. On 12 September 1943, on the way back from her twelfth voyage, she was torpedoed by the American submarine *Cabrilla*, which scored a hit on her starboard side. However, damage was only superficial and *Chuyo* was able to reach Yokosuka two days later. Once repairs were completed, she departed on 16 November with a convoy heading for Truk, together with the heavy cruiser *Maya* and four destroyers (*Akebono*, *Ushio*, *Sazanami* and *Urakaze*). On 30 November, *Chuyo* departed for Japan in company with the carriers *Zuiho* and *Unyo*, *Maya* and four destroyers. Shortly after midnight on 4 December, approximately 260 miles south-east of Yokosuka, she was hit in the bow by a torpedo fired by USS *Sailfish*. The explosion blew off the carrier's bow and caused the flight deck to collapse. To reduce pressure on the interior bulkheads, *Chuyo* began steaming astern at half speed towards Yokosuka, but at 0555hrs she was again torpedoed by *Sailfish*, this time in the port engine room. These second hits caused the engines to stop. *Maya* and the destroyer *Urakaze* came alongside to assist the carrier, but *Sailfish* attacked again at 0842hrs, hitting *Chuyo* with one or two more torpedoes on the port side. This caused massive flooding and the carrier capsized, sinking so quickly that there were few survivors. Only 161 crewmen and passengers were saved, including one American prisoner of war. Losses amounted to 737 passengers and 513 crewmen.

Shinyo

Once commissioned on 15 November 1943, *Shinyo* was assigned to the Escort Force, under the command of the Combined Fleet. She spent the first six months of 1944 in the Inland Sea on training missions. From 6 July to 15 August 1944, she provided air cover to two convoys (Hi-69, also including *Taiyo* and *Kaiyo*, and Hi-70) transporting vehicles and aircraft to Manila and Singapore. On 8 September, *Shinyo* left Kure escorting another convoy, consisting of nine cargo ships, bound for Singapore, where she arrived on 22 September. On 9 November, *Shinyo* was assigned to convoy Hi-81, which was to be joined off the coast of Korea by other ships and then split into two sections, bound for Manila and Singapore respectively. The carrier left Japan on 14 November. At 2305hrs on 17 November, while in the East China Sea some 140nm north-east of Shanghai, she was hit on the starboard side by at least three torpedoes from the American submarine *Spadefish*. This caused the fuel tanks to explode, starting a massive fire. Deprived of power and heavily listing to starboard, *Shinyo* sank stern-first around 2340hrs. Only seventy of 1,200 crewmen survived.

Kaiyo

After completion on 23 November 1943, *Kaiyo* was tasked to transport aircraft to Japanese overseas bases. On the night of 10 February 1944, while en route to Truk, she was attacked by USS *Permit*, but the torpedoes missed. On 17 March she was assigned to the 1st Surface Escort Division, and from 29 March to 16 April 1944 provided anti-submarine protection to nine transports bound for Singapore. In late May, *Kaiyo* was tasked to accompany convoy Hi-65 (including five oil tankers, four cargo ships and a troop transport), heading for Takao (Formosa) and then Singapore, where it arrived on 12 June. After a short refit in Kure, *Kaiyo* was loaded with sixty-five dismantled Zero fighters, fifty-five Judy bombers and ten transport aircraft, and joined – together with *Shinyo*, *Taiyo* and the light cruiser *Kashii* – convoy Hi-69, sailing for Manila on 13 July.

On 21 October, *Kaiyo* departed Kure, joining *Ryuho* and the escort destroyers *Momi*, *Ume* and *Momo* to ferry aircraft to Keelung (Formosa), where they arrived on the 27th. As the only available escort aircraft carrier, *Kaiyo* was assigned on 13 December to the 1st Escort Fleet and completed her last mission in the Philippines before returning to Japan at the end of December. In January 1945, she was transferred to Kure and assigned to pilot training duties in the Inland Sea. On 19 March, while at Kure, she was attacked by American aircraft from Task Force 58, which hit her twice. One bomb pierced the flight deck on the left side, before exploding in the water. More bombs exploded near the ship, causing flooding in the port engine room. *Kaiyo* was repaired and on 20 April was assigned to serve as a target ship for kamikaze and manned torpedo (*Kaiten*) crews.

She resumed her pilot training duties a month later and hit a magnetic mine on 18 July, suffering only minor damage. On 24 July, she was attacked by aircraft from the American Task Force 38 and the British Task Force 37 (including the aircraft carriers *Formidable*, *Victorious*, *Implacable* and *Indefatigable*). *Kaiyo* did not suffer any significant damage, but in an attempt to avoid the attack she struck a mine, which damaged the rudder and ruptured several steam pipes. Severe flooding meant she had to be assisted by the former destroyer *Yukikaze* and towed to Beppu Bay, where she was attacked again on 28 and 29 July by American aircraft. On 9 August, air strikes by B-25J bombers of the USAAF 38th Bombing Group further damaged the carrier, despite extensive camouflage being used to mask her. The end of the war found *Kaiyo* listing on her port side and half-submerged. She was seized by the American occupation forces and scrapped between September 1946 and January 1948.

Chiyoda

On 1 February 1944, upon conversion, *Chiyoda* was assigned, together with *Chitose* and *Zuiho*, to the 3rd Aircraft Carrier Division of the Mobile Fleet. On 1 March, she departed Yokosuka for Guam, Saipan, Palau, Balikapan and Davao to provide support, together with *Ryuho*, to the Japanese troops stationed in the Mariana Islands, returning to Kure on 10 April. On 11 May, *Chiyoda* departed with Air Group 653 for Tawi-Tawi, where the Mobile Force was deploying for the defence of the Mariana Islands. From 18–21 June she took part in the Battle of the Philippine Sea, and on 20 June was slightly damaged by a bomb which killed twenty crewmen.

She departed for repairs at Kure on 22 June, remaining there until the end of July. On 20 October, *Chiyoda*, together with *Zuikaku*, *Chitose* and *Zuiho* of the 3rd Carrier Division, departed Oita in Japan as part of Admiral Jisaburo Ozawa's Decoy Force intended to lure American aircraft carriers away from the landing beaches in Leyte Gulf. At 1000hrs on 25 October, *Chiyoda* was attacked off Cape Engaño by thirty-six aircraft from the aircraft carriers *Lexington*, *Franklin* and *Langley*. She suffered four bomb hits or near misses that left her dead in the water due to flooding in the starboard engine room.

Attempts by the battleship *Hyuga* to take her in tow, as well as that by the cruiser *Isuzu* to bring her crew to safety, were frustrated by further air attacks. *Chiyoda* was finished off by gunfire from the American cruisers *Wichita*, *New Orleans*, *Santa Fe* and *Mobile*. No survivors were rescued as she went down at 1655hrs with the entire crew of 1,470 officers and men.

Chitose

After her conversion was completed on 1 February 1944, *Chitose* was assigned, together with *Chiyoda* and *Zuiho*, to the 3rd Aircraft Carrier Division of the Mobile Fleet. With the exception of a few journeys to Singapore and Saipan, she remained in the Inland Sea of Japan until April 1944. In early May she embarked the aircraft of Air Group 653, then on 11 May departed for Tawi-Tawi in the southern Philippines, where the Mobile Force tasked to defend the Mariana Islands was concentrating. On 22 May, while conducting air training, *Chitose* was attacked by the American submarine *Puffer*, which fired a spread of torpedoes which missed, exploding in her wake.

On 13 June, she departed Tawi-Tawi for the Marianas with the Mobile Fleet. She took part in the Battle of the Philippine Sea from 18–21 June, emerging unscathed. After the Japanese defeat, *Chitose* withdrew to Okinawa and then to Kure, where she arrived on 1 July. She became part of the 3rd Aircraft Carrier Division, joining *Zuikaku*, *Chiyoda* and *Zuiho*. When American forces landed in Leyte, *Chitose* was attached to Admiral Jisaburo Ozawa's Decoy Force, tasked to lure the US Task Force 38 aircraft carriers away from Leyte so as to allow the Japanese battleships, cruisers and destroyers to attack the American landing force.

During the resulting Battle of Leyte Gulf, at around 0835hrs on 25 October, *Chitose* was bombed off Cape Engaño by aircraft from the aircraft carriers *Essex* and *Lexington*. She was damaged by

The *Unryu*-class aircraft carrier *Kasagi* still incomplete at Sasebo on 27 September 1945. She was scrapped there between 1946 and 1947. (NHHC)

three near misses and a torpedo hit on port side forward of the bow aircraft elevator; this caused a 25° list, which was able to be reduced to 15°. At 0855hrs, the forward starboard engine room flooded, reducing her speed to 14 knots.

At 0925hrs, *Chitose* went dead in the water, with a list of 30°. She capsized at 0937hrs and sank bow-first, taking with her 903 crewmen. The cruiser *Isuzu* and destroyer *Shimotsuki* rescued, respectively, 480 and 121 survivors.

Taiho

After commissioning, *Taiho* was assigned to the 3rd Fleet and attached, together with the *Shokaku*s, to the 1st Aircraft Carrier Division of the 1st Mobile Fleet (*Dai ichi Kido Kantai*). On 20 March 1944, after two weeks of training in home waters, *Taiho*, escorted by the destroyers *Hatsuzuki* and *Wakatsuki*, set sail for Linga (Singapore), where the rest of the Mobile Fleet was concentrated. On 15 April, Vice Admiral Jisaburo Ozawa, commander of the 3rd Fleet, transferred his flag from *Shokaku* to *Taiho* to take advantage of the improved command facilities of the new carrier. On 12 May, the Mobile Force left Linga and arrived two days later at Tawi-Tawi (Philippines), in order to bring the Japanese fleet as close as possible to the oil fields where the ships could refuel.

On 13 June, after a series of air drills hindered by the presence of American submarines, *Taiho* left Tawi-Tawi for Guimaras in the Philippines. The move was intended to place the 1st Mobile Fleet in an advantageous position in the event of an American attack on the Marianas (Operation Forager). After the beginning of the American attacks against Saipan, the commander of the Combined Fleet, Admiral Soemu Toyoda, ordered the 1st Mobile Fleet to start Operation A-Go. The Japanese force crossed the San Bernardino Strait and reached the waters of the Marianas on 19 June, thus starting the clash known as the Battle of the Philippine Sea, involving nine Japanese aircraft carriers. At 0810hrs on the same day, after launching forty-two aircraft as her contribution to Ozawa's attack waves, *Taiho* was attacked by the American submarine *Albacore*, which fired six torpedoes, scoring one hit on the starboard side, just forward of the island.

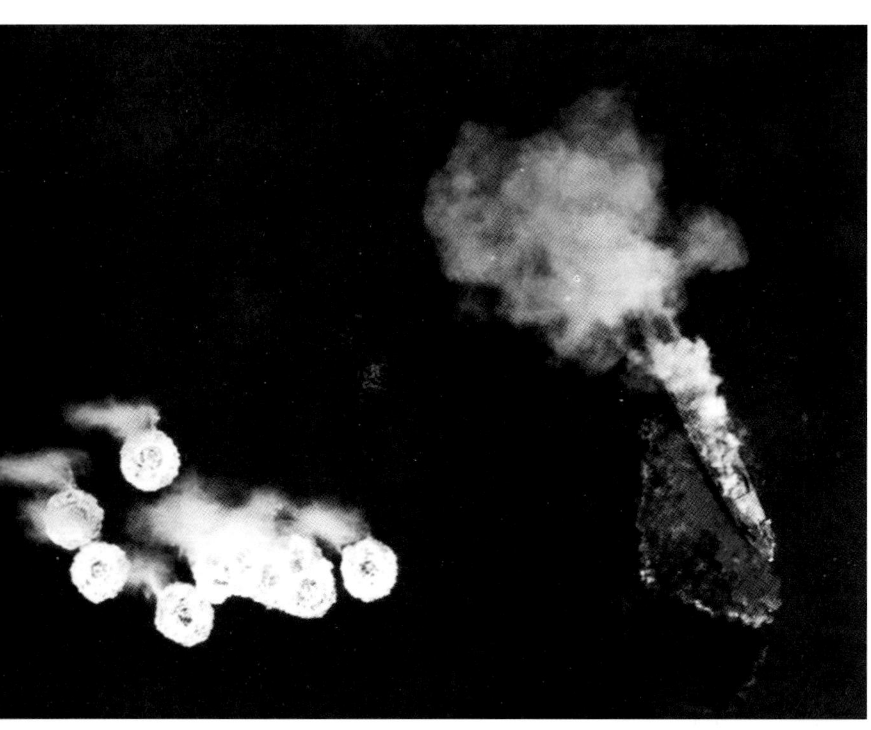

The carrier *Ikoma* (right) under attack by US Navy aircraft in Kobe on 19 March 1945. Her construction had been suspended on 9 November 1944 when 60 per cent complete. *Ikoma* was finally scrapped between July 1946 and March 1947. (NHHC)

Initially, the damage did not seem serious enough to compromise *Taiho*'s efficiency, so air operations continued. However, the impact jammed the forward elevator and damaged the petrol tanks. As a consequence, the hangar was soon filled with petrol fumes, while the forward elevator pit was filled by a mixture of seawater, oil and petrol. In spite of the efforts of the damage-control teams, the upper and lower hangar decks were soon permeated by vaporising petrol and fumes.

With *Taiho*'s hangars completely enclosed, mechanical ventilation was the only means of exhausting fouled air. The chief damage-control officer eventually ordered the general ventilation system switched to full capacity and all doors, portholes and hatches opened to try to get rid of the fumes. However, as a result of this, the areas previously unexposed were also filled by petrol vapours, increasing the chances of accidental ignition.

At 1428hrs, about six-and-a-half hours after she was hit, the carrier was jolted by a huge explosion, causing the destruction of the flight deck (where thirteen planes were still ready for launch) and the collapse of the ship's sides. Completely engulfed by fire, which had also reached the magazines, *Taiho* sank stern-first at 1628hrs. Admiral Ozawa wanted to go down with the ship, but his staff convinced him to escape and transfer his flag to the cruiser *Haguro*. The destroyers *Wakatsuki*, *Isokaze* and *Hatsuzuki* managed to rescue about 500 men, but losses numbered some 660 officers and sailors.

Ryuho

On 18 April 1942, four months after the works to transform the former submarine tender *Taigei* into an aircraft carrier were started, *Ryuho* was damaged by a 500lb bomb from B-25 aircraft that, led by Colonel James H. Doolittle, had taken off from the aircraft carrier USS *Hornet*. Her first war mission was transporting thirty aircraft, including twenty light bombers, and their crews to Truk. The carrier left Yokosuka on 11 December 1942, escorted by the destroyer *Tokitsukaze*. The following day, she was hit by a single torpedo from the submarine *Drum* (SS-228). The damage was not serious, but it still forced *Ryuho* to return to Yokosuka for emergency repairs.

Once the repairs were completed, she resumed ferry missions to occupied islands in the South Pacific. In June 1943, she embarked the air group of *Hiyo*, which had been torpedoed by an American submarine.

Some details of the incomplete carrier *Ibuki* at Sasebo in October 1945, where she was seized by the American occupation force. The picture on the right shows three small *Ha-101*-class submarines – *Ha-109, Ha-105* and *Ha-106* – moored alongside the carrier. (NHHC)

In July, *Ryuho* became part, together with the carriers *Hiyo* and *Junyo*, of the 2nd Aircraft Carrier Division of the 3rd Fleet, carrying out training activities mainly in home waters, with the exception of two overseas missions, the first to Singapore and the second to Truk (October/December 1943), before returning to Kure on 2 January 1944. In May 1944, as Operation A-Go approached, *Ryuho* was sent to Tawi-Tawi to join the Combined Fleet. She participated in the Battle of the Philippine Sea, where she was slightly damaged on 19 June by near misses by Avenger torpedo bombers from the carrier USS *Enterprise*.

The following month, as part of the reorganisation of the Japanese carrier force, *Ryuho* was transferred to the 1st Carrier Division and then to the 4th Division of the 3rd Fleet. On 21 October, she sailed from Kure together with the escort carrier *Kaiyo* and the escort destroyers *Momi*, *Ume* and *Momo* on a ferry mission to Keelung, Formosa, where she unloaded aircraft and other equipment. In November, following the dissolution of the Mobile Fleet, the carrier was transferred to the 1st Division of the Combined Fleet. On 31 December, *Ryuho* sailed for Formosa as part of a convoy of nine oil tankers and five destroyers, with a load of fifty Ohka rocket-powered kamikaze aircraft. *Ryuho* then departed for Japan on 2 January 1945, arriving at Kure on 18 January. On 19 March, she was attacked by aircraft from Task Force 58, suffering three 500lb bomb strikes and two rocket hits, which caused serious damage and killed twenty crew members. Considered a total loss, *Ryuho* was moored as an abandoned wreck off Etajima (Kure) until the Japan surrender, and was scrapped in 1946.

Shinano

At 1800hrs on 28 November 1944, just nine days after being handed over to the Imperial Japanese Navy, *Shinano* left Yokosuka for Kure, escorted by the destroyers *Hamakaze*, *Isokaze* and *Yukikaze.* Captain Toshio Abe, the commanding officer, had asked for a delay, as fitting out was not yet completed. Most of the watertight doors had still to be installed, many holes in the compartment bulkheads for electrical cables, ventilation ducts and pipes had not been sealed and essential systems such as fire-fighting were still inoperable.

Four of her twelve boilers had not yet been installed, limiting the top speed to 25 knots. Furthermore, most of the crew lacked experience, and there were also some 300 shipyard workers still aboard. At 2048hrs, while *Shinano* was sailing at 18 knots, she was sighted by the American submarine *Archerfish* (SS-311), which began to pursue the carrier on the surface on a parallel course. At 0304hrs on 29 November, *Archerfish* submerged in preparation to attack. She launched six torpedoes at the carrier at 0315hrs, scoring four hits on the starboard side and causing extensive flooding and a consequent 10° list. With a trained crew, the damage could still have been managed, but a series of events and wrong decisions prevented the carrier from being saved.

Damage to the hull near the forward compressor room, forward boiler and engine rooms and stern spaces were the main cause of the ship's loss. Damage control teams were forced to split up, without the necessary coordination and underestimating the danger of their situation, while Captain Abe, overconfident in the ship's structural strength, ordered the carrier to maintain its maximum speed of 20 knots. His decision only accelerated flooding and delayed the counterbalancing efforts that, as a commission of inquiry later established, could probably have saved the ship. Consequently, a few hours after being hit, *Shinano* was unable to halt the flooding and her list increased. Eventually, at 1057hrs, she sank stern-first about 160 miles south-east of Cape Muroto in approximately 13,000ft of water, taking 1,435 officers, men and civilians with her. There were just 1,080 survivors. A report by the US Navy

Technical Commission stated: 'The shock that struck the Japanese Navy Ministry is easier to imagine than to describe.'

Unryu

Once completed, *Unryu* was assigned to the 1st Carrier Division of the 3rd Fleet. Due to the lack of aircraft and trained pilots, she remained in home waters for training and tests until December 1944. In November, after the Mobile Fleet was disbanded, she was transferred to the 1st Carrier Division and tasked to carry out support missions in the Philippines. On 17 December, two days after the American landings on Mindoro, *Unryu* departed Kure for Manila, escorted by a fleet destroyer (*Shigure*) and two escort destroyers (*Momi* and *Hinoki*). The carrier was tasked with transporting a mixed cargo, including thirty Ohka rocket-propelled kamikaze aircraft, Daihatsu landing barges, towed howitzers and civilian and military personnel, to reinforce the Japanese garrison on Luzon island. On the afternoon of 19 December, while sailing about 200 miles south-east of Shanghai in the South China Sea, *Unryu* was sunk by the American submarine *Redfish*, which fired four torpedoes. Two hits were scored on the starboard side, the first near the island and the second abreast the forward elevator. The carrier, torn apart by the explosion of petrol fumes and ammunition, sank between 1657 and 1701hrs with heavy human losses (1,172 crewmen). Only 145 men, some of them seriously wounded, were rescued by *Shigure*. *Unryu* was the last Japanese aircraft carrier to be sunk on the open seas.

Amagi

Once completed in August 1944, *Amagi* was assigned to the 1st Aircraft Carrier Division. Due to a shortage of aircraft and trained pilots, she remained in the Inland Sea and was assigned to training duties. On 19 March 1945, while stationed in Kure, *Amagi* was attacked by aircraft from Task Force 58, and was hit by small-calibre bombs on the starboard side of the flight deck. The carrier was only slightly damaged, but one bomb, penetrating the hangar, led to the jamming of the aft elevator, which was never repaired. In April, *Amagi* was classified, like her sister ship *Katsuragi*, as a '4th rank reserve ship' and extensively camouflaged. On 24 July, she was attacked by aircraft from Task Force 38, which inflicted serious damage. A 2,000lb bomb penetrated the flight deck and detonated in the upper hangar. The flight deck between the elevators buckled for a length of about 60m, the upper hangar walls were perforated and a 50m-long section was blown overboard.

Fragments from further near misses perforated the hull near the boiler rooms, with consequent flooding and progressive loss of stability. Four days later, another attack carried out by Task Force 38 aircraft and B-24 bombers caused additional damage, with the ship listing further to port, until at 1000hrs on 29 July *Amagi* capsized, part of her flight deck falling overboard. The wreck remained in Kure until the end of the war, with the bow submerged and the starboard propellers protruding from the sea. Salvage work began in December 1945, the carrier being refloated in July 1946 and scrapped in Kure by December 1947.

Katsuragi

After completion, *Katsuragi* was assigned to the 1st Carrier Division. Subsequently, due to a lack of pilots and aircraft, she mainly remained stationed in the Inland Sea. On 19 March 1945, a raid by aircraft from Task Force 58 caused slight damage. A month later, she was classified as a '4th rank reserve ship', like her sister-ship *Amagi*, and was moored at Mitsuokojima (Kure) and camouflaged. On 28 July, an air attack from Task Force 38 damaged her again. A 2,000lb bomb hit the flight deck and detonated in the upper hangar, blowing out a large section of the port wall and part of the flight deck, but the hull and engine rooms remained unharmed.

At the end of the war, *Katsuragi* was designated a Special Transfer Ship and used for the repatriation of Japanese soldiers and civilians. On 15 November 1946, she was stricken from the Japanese Navy List and five days later was placed under the jurisdiction of the Ministry of the Interior for disposal. Scrapping began at Osaka in December 1946 and was completed in November 1947.

Kasagi

After launch, she was towed to Sasebo for further fitting out. Work was suspended on 1 April 1945 when 84 per cent complete. The hull was broken up in 1947.

Aso

Work on *Aso* was suspended on 9 November 1944 when 60 per cent complete. On 24 July 1945, an attack by aircraft from Task Force 38 damaged her hull. Thereafter she was used as a target ship for kamikaze suicide weapons. She was scrapped at Kure in 1947.

Ikoma

Work was suspended on 9 November 1944 when *Ikoma* was 60 per cent complete. On 24 July 1945, aircraft from Task Force 38 caused severe damage. *Ikoma* was broken up at Tamano in 1947.

Ibuki

Construction was stopped in March 1945, when *Ibuki* was 80 per cent complete. *Ibuki* was scrapped at Sasebo between November 1946 and August 1948.

The hull of the aircraft carrier *Aso* was scrapped at Tainouchi, Kure, in 1946. (USN)

APPENDIX 1 – SHIPS' NAMES

Akagi	named after Mount Akagi, a dormant volcano in the Kanto region
Amagi	named after Mount Amagi, a range of volcanic mountains in the Izu peninsula
Aso	named after Mount Aso, the largest active volcano in Japan (on Kyushu Island)
Chitose	meaning 'Thousand years'
Chiyoda	named after a special ward in central Tokyo, where the Imperial Palace is located; literally meaning 'Field of a thousand generations'
Chuyo	meaning 'Hawk which soars'
Hiryu	meaning 'Flying dragon'
Hiyo	meaning 'Dragon which flies far away'
Hosho	meaning 'Flying Phoenix'
Ibuki	named after Mount Ibuki, a mountain on the border between Shiga and Gifu Prefectures
Ikoma	named after Mount Ikoma, a mountain on the border between Nara and Osaka Prefectures
Junyo	meaning 'Peregrine Falcon'
Kaga	named after the ancient Kaga Province (literally meaning 'Supreme cheerfulness')
Kaiyo	meaning 'Sea hawk'
Kasagi	named after Mount Kasagi, a mountain located in Kyoto Prefecture
Katsuragi	named after Mount Katsuragi, a mountain located on the border between Osaka and Gose Prefectures
Ryuho	meaning 'Dragon Phoenix'
Ryujo	meaning 'Prancing dragon'
Shinano	named after the ancient Shinano Province
Shinyo	meaning 'Divine hawk'
Shoho	meaning 'Auspicious Phoenix'
Shokaku	meaning 'Soaring crane'
Soryu	meaning 'Blue-grey dragon'
Taiho	meaning 'Great Phoenix'
Taiyo	meaning 'Big hawk'
Unryu	meaning 'Cloud dragon'
Unyo	meaning 'Cloud hawk'
Zuiho	meaning 'Auspicious Phoenix'
Zuikaku	meaning 'Auspicious crane'

Hosho ('Flying Phoenix'), the first Japanese aircraft carrier, during sea trials in December 1922. (Kure Naval Museum, digitally coloured image, courtesy J Irotoko)

Amagi (named after a volcano on the Izu peninsula) in the Bay of Kure in December 1944. (Kure Naval Museum, digitally coloured image, courtesy J Irotoko)

APPENDIX 2 – NAVAL GUNS

Calibre (mm)	200/50
Model	Type 3
In-service date	1924
Weapon weight (breechblock included)	17.90t
Projectile weight	110kg
Muzzle speed	870m/s
Horizontal range (at 45°)	28,000m
Max depression	-5°
Rate of fire	5rpm
Used on	*Akagi*, *Kaga*

Calibre (mm)	140/50
Model	Type 3
In-service date	1914
Weapon weight (breechblock included)	5.60t
Projectile weight	38kg
Muzzle speed	850m/s
Horizontal range (at 20°)	15,800m
Max depression	-5°
Rate of fire	6–10rpm
Used on	*Hosho*

Calibre (mm)	127/40
Model	Type 89
In-service date	1932
Weapon weight (breechblock included)	3.06t
Ammunition weight (full round)	34.32kg
Muzzle speed	720m/s
Horizontal range	13,200m
Vertical range (theoretical, at 90°)	8,100m
Vertical range (actual, at 90°)	7,400m
Max depression	-8°
Rate of fire (theoretical)	14rpm
Rate of fire (actual)	11–12rpm
Used on	almost all aircraft carriers taking part in Second World War

Calibre (mm)	120/45
Model	Type 10
In-service date	1926
Weapon weight (breechblock included)	2.98t
Ammunition weight (full round)	32.50kg
Muzzle speed	825m/s
Horizontal range	15,600m
Vertical range (theoretical, at 75°)	10,065m
Vertical range (actual, at 75°)	8,450m
Max depression	-10°
Rate of fire (theoretical)	10–11rpm
Rate of fire (actual)	6–8rpm
Used on	*Akagi*, *Kaga*, *Taiyo*

Calibre (mm)	100/65
Model	Type 98
In-service date	1940
Weapon weight (breechblock included)	3.05t
Projectile weight	13kg
Horizontal range (theoretical)	19,500m
Horizontal range (actual)	14,000m
Vertical range (theoretical, at 90°)	14,700m
Vertical range (actual, at 90°)	11,000m
Max depression	-10°
Rate of fire (theoretical)	19rpm
Rate of fire (actual)	15rpm
Used on	*Taiho*, modified *Taiho*

Calibre (mm)	76.2/60
Model	Type 98
In-service date	1940
Weapon weight (breechblock included)	1.31t
Projectile weight	5.99kg
Muzzle speed	900m/s
Horizontal range	13,600m
Vertical range (at 90°)	9,100m
Max depression	-10°
Rate of fire	25rpm
Used on	*Ibuki*

Calibre (mm)	76.2/40
Model	Type 3
In-service date	1916
Weapon weight (breechblock included)	0.6t
Projectile weight	5.99kg
Muzzle speed	670m/s
Vertical range (theoretical, at 75°)	6,800m
Vertical range (actual, at 75°)	5,300m
Max depression	-5°
Rate of fire	13rpm
Used on	*Ibuki*

Calibre (mm)	25/60
Model	Type 96
In-service date	1936
Weapon weight	0.115t
Projectile weight	0.243–0.262kg
Muzzle speed	900m/s

Horizontal range (at 50°)	7,500m
Max vertical range (at 80°)	5,250m
Actual anti-air range	1,500m
Rate of fire (theoretical)	220–240rpm
Rate of fire (actual)	110–120rpm
Max depression	-10°
Used on	all aircraft carriers taking part in Second World War

Calibre (mm)	**13.2/76**
Model	Type 93
In-service date	1935
Weapon weight	0.042t
Projectile weight	0.44–0.51kg
Muzzle speed	800m/s
Horizontal range (at 50°)	6,400m
	4,500m
Actual anti-air range	1,000m
Rate of fire (theoretical)	450rpm
Rate of fire (actual)	250rpm
Max depression	-10°
Used on	some aircraft carriers

The carrier *Akagi* in 1926, shortly after commissioning. Two twin 200/50 turrets, part of the main armament, were fitted on the sides of the intermediate flight deck.

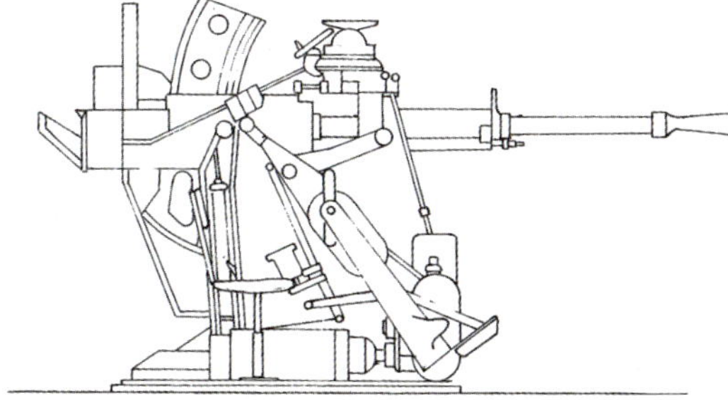

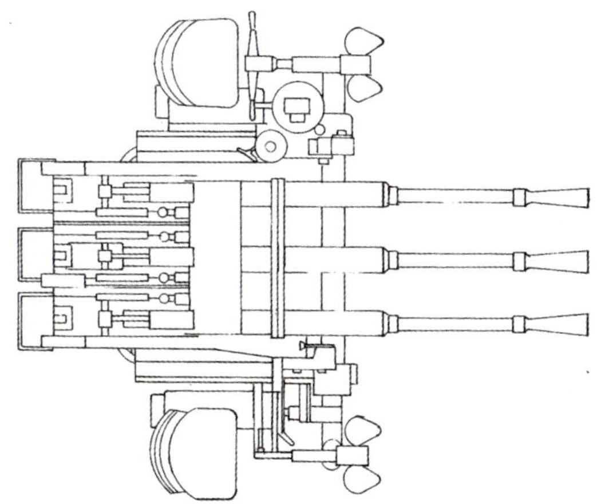

Side and top views of the 25/60 Type 96 triple mount, present on almost all Japanese warships of the Second World War. The Japanese Navy was lacking an intermediate-calibre anti-aircraft weapon between the 25/60 and the 127/40, similar to the 40/56 Bofors used by the US Navy and Royal Navy. (Drawing by J Lambert, from J Campbell, *Naval Weapons of World War Two*)

A 127/40 anti-aircraft twin mount on the starboard side of the carrier *Soryu* in a picture taken in November 1937. (Kure Naval Museum – digitally coloured image, courtesy J Irotoko)

APPENDIX 3 – NAVAL RADARS

Only after the war began was the Imperial Japanese Navy able to employ radars, although their performance was not up to the standard of the equivalent US Navy systems. The first Japanese naval radar to enter service was the Type 21 in August 1943, followed shortly thereafter by Type 22. Type 13, considered by the operators as the most reliable equipment, became available only in early 1944.

In parallel with the development of radar, much effort was directed towards the best arrangement of the ships' spaces intended for such use, and to ensure the best performance when the ships operated in tropical waters.

At the same time, experiments were carried out to develop radar-based fire control systems. The light cruiser *Kiso* was intended as a test platform for this purpose, but after the Battle of the Marianas (June 1944), time and resources to follow on this path were no longer available.

Type 21 (No 2 Type 1)	
Purpose	Air search
In-service date	August 1943
Weight	840kg
Wavelength	1.5m
Frequency	200MHz
Peak power	5kW
Max range	150km
Actual range	70–100km
Minimum range	5km
Precision	1–2km
Resolution	2km
Operators	2

Type 22 (No 2 Type 2)	
Purpose	Surface search
In-service date	December 1943
Weight	1,320kg
Wavelength	0.01m
Frequency	3,000MHz
Peak power	2kW
Max range	60km
Actual range	17–35km
Minimum range	1.5km
Precision	250–500m
Resolution	1.5km
Operators	3

Type 13	
Purpose	Air search
In-service date	February 1944
Weight	110kg
Wavelength	2m
Frequency	150MHz
Peak power	10kW
Max range	150km
Actual range	150–100km
Minimum range	2–3km
Resolution	3km
Operators	2

APPENDIX 4 – PAINTING SCHEMES by Maurizio Brescia (*)

Unlike the other major belligerent naval forces, the Imperial Japanese Navy did not make extensive use of camouflage for its ships during the Second World War. Only schemes designed for specific types of ships were widely used, along with camouflage methods used mainly for stationary or not fully operational vessels. Starting from the end of the First World War, the painting of Japanese warships was based on a uniform grey, substantially similar to the dark ash grey adopted by the Royal Italian Navy during the Second World War. The colour was applied to all vertical and horizontal surfaces, with the exception of upper decks and forecastles, which were mostly covered with rectangular sheets of brown-ochre linoleum measuring 2 x 4m. Brass strips were applied to the joints between the sheets in order to give greater solidity to the entire covering and probably to improve the aesthetic appearance.

Most of the ships of the Imperial Japanese Navy operated with this colour scheme throughout the Second World War. During the conflict, as part of periodic refitting cycles, the painting scheme of numerous ships – while maintaining the general standards described above – was completed with a lighter shade of grey.

In the pre-war period and up until 1942, aircraft carriers of the Imperial Japanese Navy were painted with the classic dark grey colour scheme described above. The flight decks were covered with unpainted wooden planks: there was usually a continuous white line along the centreline, flanked on both sides by dotted white lines. The aft end of the deck was painted with stripes of contrasting colours that could be arranged either longitudinally or transversely. At least in a couple of cases, these stripes were white and red.

Along with the continuous white line there were often two or three groups of white lines arranged in a 'fan' shape, at the top of which was a hole to release steam, allowing the pilots, during landing, to identify the direction of the wind across the flight deck. It is very likely that on some Japanese aircraft carriers that took part in the Battle of Midway (such as *Hiryu* and *Soryu*), a large red circle with a white border – the classic '*Hinomaru*' – was painted on the forward part of the flight deck. This seems to be confirmed both by the testimony of numerous American airmen and by some photographs – unfortunately not clear enough to be indisputable proof – taken from a great height by US Navy reconnaissance aircraft in the run-up to the battle. Finally, on the aft part of the flight deck, the first syllable of the ship's name was painted in white *katakana*† characters.

Between March and July 1944, a committee of twenty technical officers began to address the problem of aircraft carrier camouflage at the Yokosuka Navigation School. The members of the committee initially worked on aircraft carrier models about 1 metre long, whose flight decks were painted in various colours. These models, floated in the vicinity of the old battleship *Fuji* – used at the time as a training ship – were then observed through binoculars used in reverse mode (ie using the lens as an eyepiece), in order to simulate observation from a great distance.

This experimental phase resulted in a colour scheme probably based on two tones of grey, which was then applied to the flight deck of the aircraft carrier *Unyo*. The scheme was intended to mislead an observer as to the true nature of the target, roughly simulating the view from above of a merchant ship. At the direction of the committee, additional aircraft carriers (*Taiyo*, *Chitose*, *Unryu* and, later, *Unyo*) had their decks painted with similar, though more complex, schemes (See page 2). Various shades of green (as well as black) were used, and an effective similarity with the plan view of a merchant vessel was sought by graphically reproducing the holds, central superstructure, rounded bow and stern and, in some cases, even the derricks.

In the following months, the flight decks of other aircraft carriers were painted with similar schemes, and in some cases (for example, *Zuiho* at the time of the Battle of Leyte Gulf), the detail of the camouflage is supported by photographic evidence attributable to American sources. These pictures had been taken either by US Navy reconnaissance aircraft or by attacking American fighter-bombers.

At the same time, the hull sides of the aircraft carriers were painted with a colour scheme derived from the one that had been applied to Japanese merchant ships and auxiliary vessels since the summer of 1943. The 'no 1' and 'no 2' tones of green were used to create, on a light green background ('no 1'), the stylised silhouette of a merchant ship with a central superstructure by using the darker 'no 2' green tone (See page 2, *Amagi* after the war).

From the second half of 1944 until the end of the conflict, these schemes were applied to the flight decks and hull sides of practically all operational Japanese aircraft carriers. The few newly built aircraft carriers commissioned in the last year of the war also received similar colour schemes. An exception was *Shinano*, which at the time of her sinking (29 November 1944) was apparently painted with 'no 2' green.

In the final phase of the conflict, several large ships were still under repair or being fitted out in ports and the main Japanese naval bases. Lack of fuel prevented their transfer to secondary or more protected anchorages, with these ships forced to rely on shore installations for the supply of power, steam, water and so on.

The aircraft carrier *Junyo* was immobilised at Sasebo, while *Ryuho* (formerly the submarine support ship *Taigei*), *Kaiyo* (formerly the merchant ship *Argentina Maru*), *Amagi* and *Katsuragi* were at the

(*) From M Brescia, *Mimetiche navali giapponesi* (*Japanese naval camouflage* – see Bibliography).

(†) *Katakana* is one of the two Japanese syllabic alphabets (the second is *Hiragana*). Both consist of forty-seven symbols.

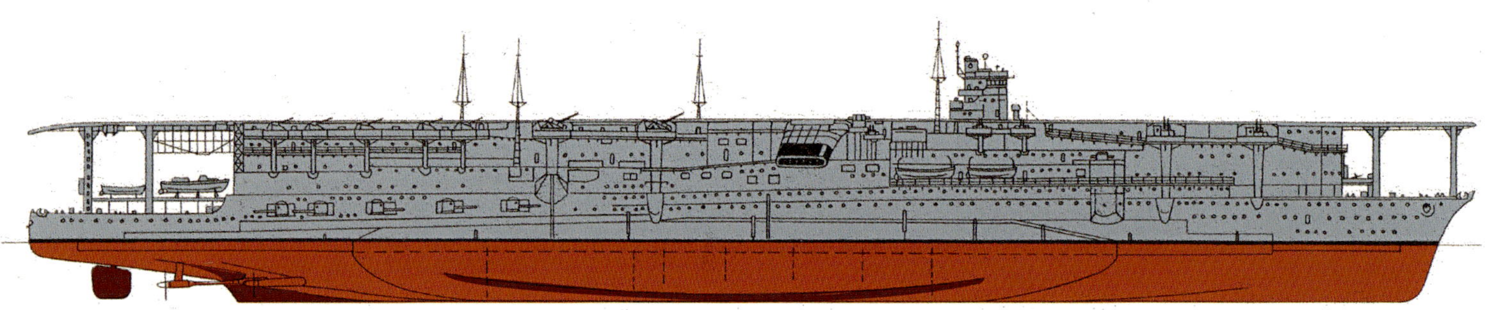

The aircraft carrier *Kaga* in its final configuration in spring 1942, with the typical colour scheme of all Japanese warships during the early Second World War. Note the different position of the *Hinomaru* and the white and red stripes at the aft end of the flight deck, compared to the same details of *Akagi*. (Drawings by A Nani, digitally coloured by M Brescia)

0 20 40 60 m

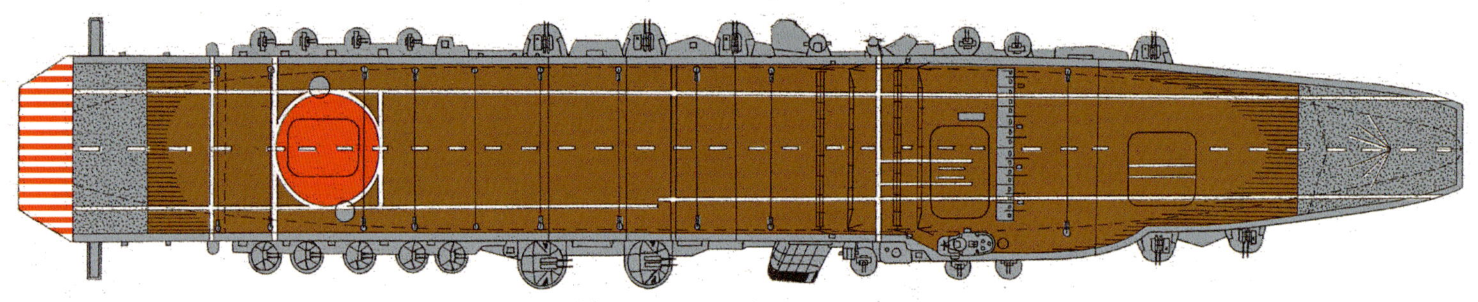

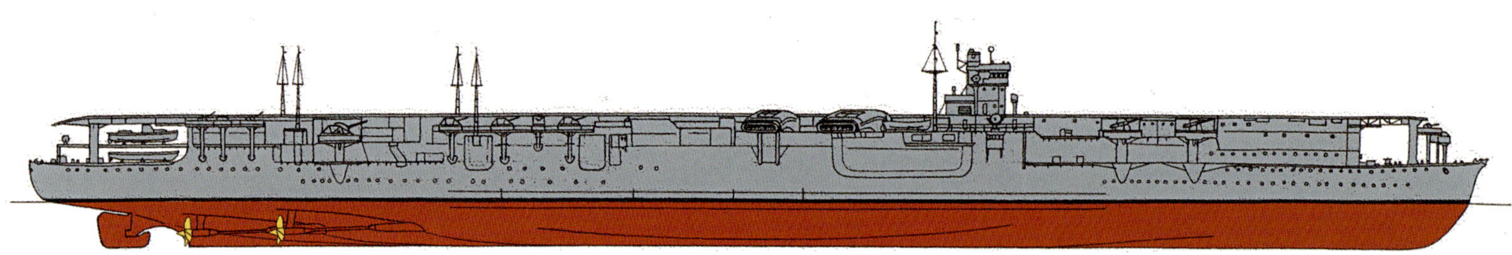

Starboard side and top views of *Soryu* in spring 1942. (Drawings by A Nani, digitally coloured by M Brescia)

0 20 40 60 m

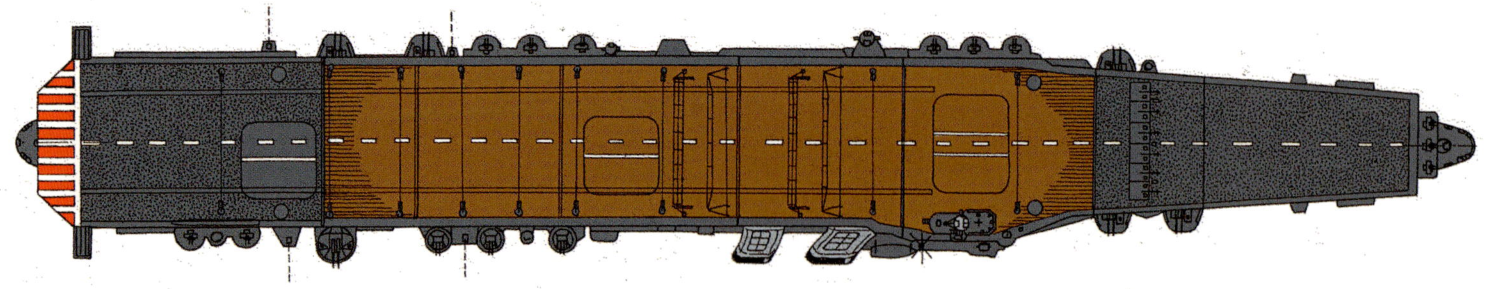

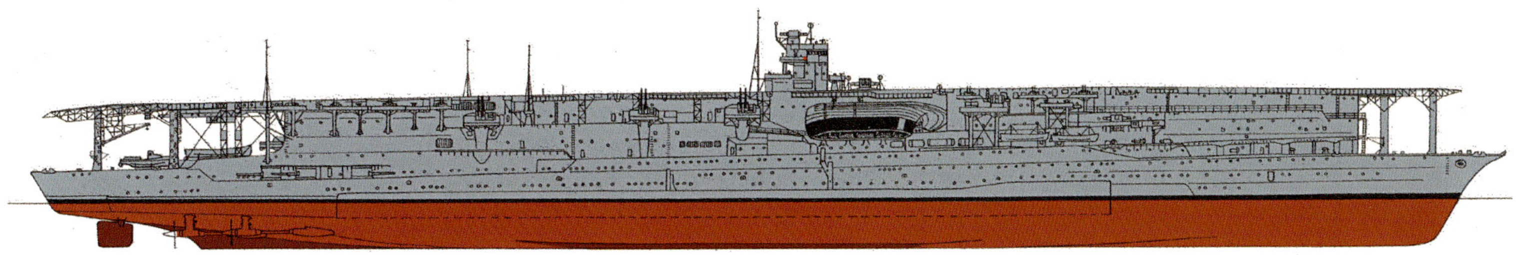

The aircraft carrier *Akagi* in her final configuration, before she was sunk at the Battle of Midway. Note the *Hinomaru* (a red disk bordered in white) on the forward flight deck. (Drawing by A Nani, digitally coloured by M Brescia)

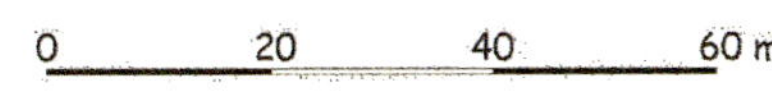

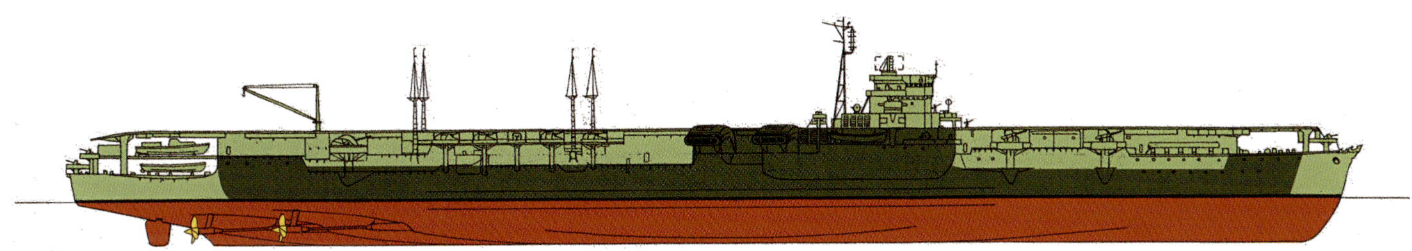

The camouflage scheme of *Zuikaku* (the same on both sides), as reconstructed from original photos, around mid-1944. The simplified silhouette of a merchant vessel (painted in order to mislead an observer about the real type of the ship) is in dark blue, rather than in dark green as was common practice at the time on Japanese warships. (M Brescia)

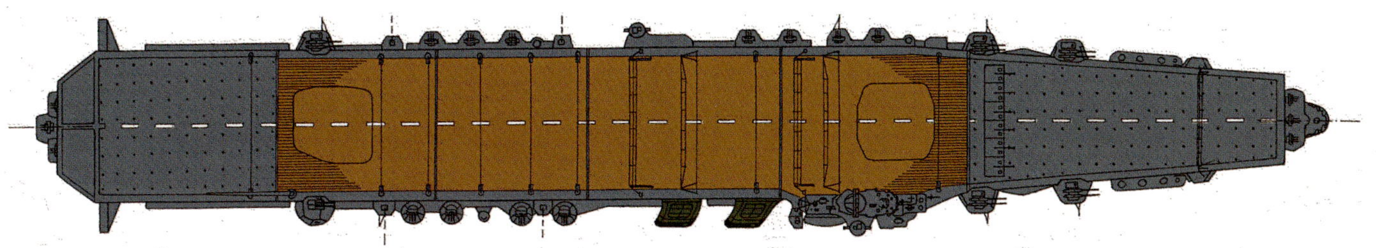

The carrier *Unryu* in the first half of 1944. A merchant ship's silhouette, painted in dark green no 2, is superimposed on both sides of a light green no 1 applied to the rest of the hull and the island. (Drawings by A Nani, digitally coloured by M Brescia)

A well-known image of *Zuiho,* taken from a US aircraft shortly before the carrier was sunk at the Battle of Cape Engaño on 25 October 1944. (US Navy)

Kure Arsenal between January and March 1945. On the instructions of the Commander in Chief of the Combined Fleet, the crews of all these carriers undertook an extensive camouflage operation which, in the case of *Katsuragi*, was particularly complex and elaborate. After reaching Kure in mid-February, *Katsuragi* was slightly damaged by American air attacks, which continued until August. It was then extensively examined, first by means of photographs taken by US air reconnaissance aircraft (*) and then, after the end of hostilities, directly by members of the US Naval Technical Mission to Japan (†).

Katsuragi had been moored with her bow facing north about 50 metres from the north-eastern side of the island of Mitsuko Jima, where the water depth was 15 metres, so as to facilitate recovery in the event of sinking. The aircraft carrier *Amagi*, moored close to the southern coast of the same island, was secured in a similar way. The outer (starboard) side, bow and stern of *Katsuragi* was covered by a curtain of bamboo supported by steel cables stretched along the edge of the flight deck. Branches and foliage were applied to the bamboo curtain in order to increase the camouflage's effectiveness. Nets, supported by steel cable, were stretched between the port side of *Katsuragi* and the coastline, and covered with additional branches, reeds and brushwood. Two motor torpedo boats were moored a short distance off the starboard side of *Katsuragi* and additional camouflage nets were stretched between their decks and the carrier's hull side, to simulate two small docks connected to the mainland. This was to make *Katsuragi* appear to be part of the island. To this end, structures resembling houses and warehouses were built from wood and sandbags on the flight deck. The ingenuity of the Japanese did not stop there: fake sand 'roads' were laid across the flight deck, along with additional foliage and several large trees that were placed in an upright position. The island of *Katsuragi* was covered with camouflage nets, while some anti-aircraft machine guns – originally

(*) See report for the reconnaissance of 24–28 July 1945 (*Photographic Interpretation Report 816 {Interpron Two}, Shipping Report of Kure for 24–28 July 1945*).

(†) See *US Naval Technical Mission to Japan, Miscellaneous Targets – Camouflage of Japanese Ships and Naval Installations*, edited by Lt (jg) W E Champion, W M Kluss and R B Palmer, USNR, San Francisco, December 1945.

The carrier *Katsuragi* underwent a complex camouflage operation in early 1945 to make her appear to be part of the coast of the island of Mitsuko Jima, in the hope of thus preventing air attacks. In this graphic reconstruction, based on photographs taken by US air reconnaissance, trees, small houses and other structures are visible on *Katsuragi*'s flight deck. (From M Brescia, *La mimetizzazione delle navi italiane 1940–1945*, Parma, Albertelli, 2006)

installed on the edges of the flight deck – were removed and placed near the 'roads', similar to what was done for land emplacements. The camouflage underwent various changes over time: in its latest version, it included additional 'houses' made with tents in the central area on the flight deck and, scattered everywhere, piles of scrap metal (also present on the island in the vicinity of the aircraft carrier).

During the bombing of Kure on 24 and 28 July 1945, the flight deck of *Katsuragi* was hit by bombs and damaged, but within a few days the hole caused by the explosion was covered with tarpaulin, on which fake structures were restored. In September 1945, when the naval base of Kure was occupied by American forces, *Katsuragi* was still in the same condition. In addition to *Amagi*, similar camouflage had been applied in the first half of 1945 to the battleship *Hyuga*, the light cruisers *Kuma* and *Natori*, and other minor vessels present in the arsenal and the Bay of Kure.

An unusual starboard bow view of the aircraft carrier *Ryujo* in September 1934. She is painted in the dark grey that was used at the time, and until late in the Second World War, on all units of the Imperial Japanese Navy. (Kure Naval Museum)

APPENDIX 5 – NAVAL AIRCRAFT TECHNICAL DATA

Like the US Navy and Royal Navy, the Imperial Japanese Navy also had in service different types of aircraft, built by the main domestic aeronautical industries, for use on its aircraft carriers. Due to the space limitations of this publication, only a concise data sheet accompanied by a photograph is provided for each aircraft in service between 1920 and the end of the Second World War.

MITSUBISHI IMF3 TYPE 10

Type	Fighter
Commissioning	1923
Empty weight	940kg
Take-off weight	1,280kg
Wing span	8.50m
Length	6.90m
Height	3.10m
Wing area	n/a
Engine	Mitsubishi Type Hi, 8-cylinder V, 300hp
Maximum speed	213km/h
Ceiling	7,000m
Climb rate	10 minutes to 3,000m
Endurance	2 hours 30 minutes
Armament	2 x 7.7mm machine guns
Crew	1

NAKAJIMA A1N2 TYPE 3

Type	Fighter
Commissioning	1930
Empty weight	882kg
Take-off weight	1,375kg
Wing span	9.70m
Length	6.50m
Height	3.30m
Wing area	26.35m^2
Engine	Mitsubishi Type Jupiter, 9-cylinder star, 450hp
Maximum speed	241km/h
Ceiling	7,000m
Climb rate	6 minutes and 10 seconds to 3,000m
Range	846km
Armament	2 x 7.7mm machine guns, 2 x 60kg bombs
Crew	1

NAKAJIMA A2N1-3 TYPE 90

Type	Fighter
Commissioning	1934
Empty weight	1,045kg
Take-off weight	1,709kg
Wing span	9.37m
Length	6.18m
Height	3.03m
Wing area	19.74m^2
Engine	Nakajima Type Kotobuki 2, 9-cylinder star, 460hp
Maximum speed	293km/h
Ceiling	9,000m
Climb rate	5 minutes and 45 seconds to 3,000m
Range	500km
Armament	2 x 7.7mm machine guns, 2 x 30kg bombs
Crew	1

NAKAJIMA A4N1 TYPE 95

Type	Fighter
Commissioning	1936
Empty weight	1,307kg
Take-off weight	1,760kg
Wing span	10.00m
Length	6.66m
Height	2.98m
Wing area	22.89m^2
Engine	Nakajima Type Hikari 1, 9-cylinder star, 670hp
Maximum speed	352km/h
Landing speed	111km/h
Ceiling	7,700m
Climb rate	3 minutes and 30 seconds to 3,000m
Range	846km
Armament	2 x 7.7mm machine guns, 2 x 30kg or 60kg bombs
Crew	1

MITSUBISHI A5M4 TYPE 96 MOD 4 (Allied codename CLAUDE)

Type	Fighter
Commissioning	1938
Empty weight	1,216kg
Take-off weight	1,671kg
Wing span	11.00m
Length	7.56m
Height	3.23m
Wing area	17.80m^2
Engine	Nakajima Type Kotobuki 41, 9-cylinder star, 710hp
Maximum speed	435km/h
Ceiling	9,800m
Climb rate	3 minutes and 35 seconds to 3,000m

Range	1,200km
Armament	2 x 7.7mm machine guns, 2 x 30kg bombs
Crew	1

MITSUBISHI A6M2 TYPE 0 MOD 21 (ZEKE)

Type	Fighter
Commissioning	1940
Empty weight	1,754kg
Take-off weight	2,421kg
Wing span	12.00m
Length	9.06m
Height	3.05m
Wing area	22.44m^2
Engine	Nakajima Type NK1C Sakae 12, 14-cylinder, 950hp
Maximum speed	534km/h
Ceiling	10,000m
Climb rate	7 minutes and 27 seconds to 6,000m
Range	3,100km
Armament	2 x 20mm and 2 x 7.7mm machine guns, 2 x 60kg bombs
Crew	1

MITSUBISHI A6M3 TYPE 0 MOD 32 (HAMP)

Type	Fighter
Commissioning	1941
Empty weight	1,807kg
Take-off weight	2,535kg
Wing span	11.00m
Length	9.06m
Height	3.51m
Wing area	21.53m^2
Engine	Nakajima Type NK1F Sakae 21, 14-cylinder, 1,100hp
Maximum speed	544km/h
Ceiling	11,000m
Climb rate	7 minutes and 5 seconds to 6,000m
Range	2,380km
Armament	2 x 20mm and 2 x 7.7mm machine guns, 2 x 60kg bombs
Crew	1

MITSUBISHI A6M5 TYPE 0 MOD 52 (ZEKE)

Type	Fighter
Commissioning	1943
Empty weight	1,8764kg
Take-off weight	2,733kg
Wing span	11.00m
Length	9.05m
Height	3.50m
Wing area	21.33m^2

Engine	Nakajima Type NK1F Sakae 21, 14-cylinder, 1,100hp
Maximum speed	565km/h
Ceiling	7 minutes and 1 second to 6,000m
Range	1,920km
Armament	2 x 20mm and 2 x 7.7mm machine guns, 2 x 60kg bombs
Crew	1

MITSUBISHI A7M2 MOD 22 REPPU (SAM)

Type	Fighter
Commissioning	not achieved
Empty weight	3,265kg
Take-off weight	5,920kg
Wing span	14.00m
Length	10.98m
Height	4.23m
Wing area	30.86m^2
Engine	Mitsubishi Type Ha-43 Mk9A, 12-cylinder double star, 2,2000hp
Maximum speed	627km/h
Ceiling	5 minutes and 57 seconds to 6,000m
Endurance	3 hours 30 minutes
Armament	either 2 x 20mm and 2 x 12.3mm machine guns and 2 x 60kg bombs, or 4 x 20mm machine guns and 2 x 60kg bombs
Crew	1

AICHI D1A1 TYPE 94

Type	Dive bomber
Commissioning	1934
Empty weight	1,400kg
Take-off weight	2,400kg
Wing span	11.37m
Length	9.40m
Height	3.45m
Wing area	34.05m^2
Engine	Nakajima Type Kotobuki 2 Kai-1, 9-cylinder star, 580hp, or Nakajima Type Kotobuki 3 Kai-1, 640hp
Maximum speed	281km/h
Ceiling	7,000m
Climb rate	9 minutes and 30 seconds to 3,000m
Range	1,055km
Armament	3 x 7.7mm machine guns, 1 x 250kg and 2 x 30kg bombs
Crew	2

AICHI D1A2 TYPE 96

Type	Dive bomber
Commissioning	1937
Empty weight	1,516kg
Take-off weight	2,500kg
Wing span	11.40m
Length	9.30m
Height	3.41m
Wing area	34.70m^2
Engine	Nakajima Type Hikari, 9-cylinder star, 730hp
Maximum speed	306km/h
Ceiling	8 minutes to 3,000m
Range	926km
Armament	3 x 7.7mm machine guns, 1 x 250kg and 2 x 30kg bombs
Crew	2

AICHI D3A1 TYPE 99 MOD 11 (VAL)

Type	Dive bomber
Commissioning	1939
Empty weight	2,410kg
Take-off weight	3,650kg
Wing span	13.40m
Length	10.20m
Height	3.85m
Wing area	34.90m^2
Engine	Mistubishi Type Kansei 44, 14-cylinder double star, 1,070hp
Maximum speed	390km/h
Ceiling	9,300m
Climb rate	6 minutes and 27 seconds to 3,000m
Range	1,472km
Armament	3 x 7.7mm machine guns, 1 x 250kg and 2 x 60kg bombs
Crew	2

AICHI D3A2 TYPE 99 MOD 22 (VAL)

Type	Dive bomber
Commissioning	1942
Empty weight	2,570kg
Take-off weight	3,800kg
Wing span	14.40m
Length	10.20m
Height	3.90m
Wing area	34.90m^2
Engine	Mistubishi Type Kansei 54, 14-cylinder double star, 1,300hp
Maximum speed	429km/h
Landing speed	122km/h
Ceiling	10,500m
Climb rate	5 minutes and 48 seconds to 3,000m
Range	1,352km
Armament	3 x 7.7mm machine guns, 1 x 250kg and 2 x 60kg bombs
Crew	2

YOKOSUKA D4Y1 MOD 11 SUISEI (JUDY)

Type	Dive bomber
Commissioning	1943
Empty weight	2,440kg
Take-off weight	3,650kg
Wing span	11.50m
Length	10.24m
Height	3.63m
Wing area	23.60sqm
Engine	Aichi Type AE1A Atsuta 21, 12-cylinder V, 1,200hp
Maximum speed	552km/h
Landing speed	140km/h
Ceiling	11,000m
Climb rate	8 minutes and 57 seconds to 5,000m
Range	1,574km
Armament	3 x 7.7mm machine guns, 1 x 500kg or 2 x 250kg bombs
Crew	2

YOKOSUKA D4Y2 MOD 12 SUISEI (JUDY)

Type	Dive bomber
Commissioning	1944
Empty weight	2,635kg
Take-off weight	3,835kg
Wing span	11.50m
Length	10.22m
Height	3.67m
Wing area	23,60m^2
Engine	Aichi Type AE1P Atsuta 32, 12-cylinder V, 1,400hp
Maximum speed	580km/h
Landing speed	144km/h
Ceiling	10,720m
Climb rate	7 minutes and 40 seconds to 5,000m
Range	1,520km
Armament	3 x 7.7mm machine guns,1 x 500kg or 2 x 250kg bombs
Crew	2

MITSUBISHI 1MT1N TYPE 10

Type	Torpedo bomber
Commissioning	1922
Empty weight	1,370kg
Take-off weight	2,500kg
Wing span	13.26m
Length	9.78m
Height	4.43m
Wing area	43.00m^2
Engine	Napier-Lyon, 12-cylinder double V, 430hp
Maximum speed	209km/h
Ceiling	6,000m
Climb rate	13 minutes and 30 seconds to 3,050m
Endurance	2 hours 30 minutes
Armament	1 x 445mm torpedo
Crew	1

MITSUBISHI B1M1 TYPE 13-1

Type	Torpedo bomber/bomber
Commissioning	1924
Empty weight	1,442kg
Take-off weight	2,697kg
Wing span	14.76m
Length	9.77m
Height	3.50m
Wing area	59.00m^2
Engine	Napier-Lyon, 12-cylinder double V, 450hp
Maximum speed	209km/h
Ceiling	n/a
Climb rate	n/a
Endurance	2 hours 36 minutes
Armament	2 x 7.7mm machine guns, 1 x 450mm torpedo or 2 x 240kg bombs
Crew	2

MITSUBISHI A1M3 TYPE 13-3

Type	Torpedo bomber/bomber
Commissioning	1931
Empty weight	1,750kg
Take-off weight	2,900kg
Wing span	14.78m
Length	10.12m
Height	3.52m
Wing area	57.00m^2
Engine	Mitsubishi Type Hi, 12-cylinder V, 450hp
Maximum speed	198km/h
Ceiling	n/a
Climb rate	n/a
Endurance	n/a
Armament	4 x 7.7mm machine guns, 1 x 450mm torpedo or 2 x 240kg bombs
Crew	2

MITSUBISHI B2M2 TYPE 89

Type	Torpedo bomber/bomber
Commissioning	1932
Empty weight	2,180kg
Take-off weight	3,600kg
Wing span	14.98m
Length	10.18m
Height	3.50m
Wing area	49.00m^2
Engine	Mitsubishi Type Hi, 12-cylinder V, 650hp
Maximum speed	228km/h
Ceiling	n/a
Climb rate	12 minutes to 3,000m
Range	1,759km
Armament	2 x 7.7mm machine guns, 1 x torpedo or 800kg of bombs
Crew	2

YOKOSUKA B3Y1 TYPE 92

Type	Torpedo bomber/bomber
Commissioning	1933
Empty weight	1,850kg
Take-off weight	3,200kg
Wing span	13.50m
Length	9.50m
Height	3.73m
Wing area	50.00m^2
Engine	Hiro Type 91, 12-cylinder double vee, 600hp
Maximum speed	218km/h
Ceiling	n/a
Climb rate	n/a
Endurance	4 hours 30 minutes
Armament	2 x 7.7mm machine guns, either 1 x torpedo or 1 x 500kg bomb or 2 x 250kg bombs or 6 x 30kg bombs
Crew	2

YOKOSUKA B4Y1 TYPE 96 (JEAN)

Type	Torpedo bomber/bomber
Commissioning	1935
Empty weight	2,000kg
Take-off weight	3,600kg
Wing span	15.00m
Length	10.15m
Height	4.38m
Wing area	50.00m^2
Engine	Nakajima Type Hikari 2, 9-cylinder star, 700hp
Maximum speed	278km/h
Ceiling	6,000m
Climb rate	14 minutes to 3,000m
Range	1,574km
Armament	1 x 7.7mm machine gun, either 1 x torpedo or 1 x 500kg bomb or 500kg of smaller bombs
Crew	2

NAKAJIMA B5N1 TYPE 97 MOD 11 (KATE)

Type	Torpedo bomber/bomber
Commissioning	1937
Empty weight	2,106kg
Take-off weight	3,700kg
Wing span	15.52m
Length	10.30m
Height	3.70m
Wing area	37.70m^2
Engine	Nakajima Type 3, 9-cylinder star, 770hp
Maximum speed	369km/h
Landing speed	115km/h
Ceiling	7,400m
Climb rate	7 minutes and 55 seconds to 3,000m

Range	1,093–2,259km (depending on type of mission)
Armament	1 x 7.7mm machine gun, either 1 x 800kg torpedo or 800kg of bombs
Crew	3

NAKAJIMA B5N2 TYPE 97 MOD 12 (KATE)

Type	Torpedo bomber/bomber
Commissioning	1939
Empty weight	2,279kg
Take-off weight	3,800kg
Wing span	15.52m
Length	10.30m
Height	3.70m
Wing area	37.70sqm
Engine	Nakajima Type Sakae, 14-cylinder double star, 1,000hp
Maximum speed	378km/h
Landing speed	113km/h
Ceiling	8,260m
Climb rate	7 minutes to 3,000m
Range	1,020–1,993km (depending on type of mission)
Armament	1 x 7.7mm machine gun, either 1 x 800kg torpedo or 800kg of bombs
Crew	3

NAKAJIMA B6N2 MOD 12 TENZAN (JILL)

Type	Torpedo bomber/bomber
Commissioning	1943
Empty weight	3,010kg
Take-off weight	5,650kg
Wing span	14.9m
Length	10.86m
Height	3.80m
Wing area	37.20m^2
Engine	Mitsubishi Type MK4T Kaisei 25, 14-cylinder double star, 1,850hp
Maximum speed	481km/h
Landing speed	133km/h
Ceiling	9,040m
Climb rate	10 minutes and 24 seconds to 5,000m
Range	1,746km
Armament	1 x 13mm and 1 x 7.7mm machine guns, either 1 x 800kg torpedo or 800kg of bombs
Crew	3

AICHI B7A1 RYUSEI (GRACE)

Type	Torpedo bomber/dive bomber
Commissioning	not achieved
Empty weight	3,150kg
Take-off weight	4,942kg
Wing span	14.40m
Length	11.47m
Height	3.97m
Wing area	35.50m^2

Engine	Nakajima Type NK9B Homare 11, 18-cylinder double star, 1,800hp
Maximum speed	563km/h
Ceiling	n/a
Climb rate	7 minutes and 30 seconds to 4,000m
Range	1,852km
Armament	1 x 20mm and 1 x 7.92mm machine guns, either 1 x 800kg torpedo or 500kg of bombs
Crew	2

AICHI B7A2 RYUSEI (GRACE)

Type	Torpedo bomber/dive bomber
Commissioning	not achieved
Empty weight	3,614kg
Take-off weight	5,625kg
Wing span	14.40m
Length	11.50m
Height	4.07m
Wing area	35.40m^2
Engine	Nakajima Type NK9C Homare 12, 18-cylinder double star, 1,825hp
Maximum speed	567km/h
Landing speed	130km/h
Ceiling	11,250m
Climb rate	6 minutes and 55 seconds to 4,000m
Range	1,852km
Armament	1 x 20mm and 1 x 13mm machine guns, either 1 x 800kg torpedo or 500kg of bombs
Crew	2

MITSUBISHI 2MR1 TYPE 10

Type	Spotter
Commissioning	1923
Empty weight	980kg
Take-off weight	1,320kg
Wing span	12.03m
Length	7.92m
Height	2.90m
Wing area	37.70m^2
Engine	Mitsubishi Type Hi, 8-cylinder V, 300hp
Maximum speed	203km/h
Ceiling	6,000m
Climb rate	17 minutes to 3,000m
Endurance	3 hours 30 minutes
Armament	4 x 7.7mm machine guns, 3 x 30kg bombs
Crew	2

NAKAJIMA C3N1(S) TYPE 97

Type	Spotter
Commissioning	1937
Empty weight	1,805kg
Take-off weight	3,000kg
Wing span	13.95m
Length	10.00m
Height	n/a
Wing area	30.00m^2
Engine	Nakajima Type Hikari 2, 9-cylinder star, 750hp
Maximum speed	387km/h
Ceiling	6,670m
Climb rate	n/a
Range	2,278km
Armament	1 x 7.7mm machine gun
Crew	3

YOKOSUKA D4YC1-C TYPE 2 MOD 11 SUISEI (JUDY)

Type	Spotter
Commissioning	1942
Empty weight	n/a
Take-off weight	n/a
Wing span	11.50m
Length	10.20m
Height	3.67m.
Wing area	23.60m^2
Engine	Aichi Type AETA Atsuta 21, 12-cylinder V, 1,200hp
Maximum speed	546km/h
Ceiling	9,860m
Climb rate	9 minutes 28 seconds to 5,000m
Range	1,783km
Armament	3 x 7.7mm machine guns
Crew	2

NAKAJIMA C6N1 MOD 11 SAIUN (MYRT)

Type	Spotter
Commissioning	1942
Empty weight	2,875kg
Take-off weight	4,500kg
Wing span	12.50m
Length	11.00m
Height	3.96m
Wing area	25.50m^2
Engine	Nakajima Type NK9H Homare 21, 18-cylinder double star, 1,990hp
Maximum speed	609km/h
Landing speed	139km/h
Ceiling	10,470m
Climb rate	8 minutes to 6,000m
Range	3,080–5,308km
Armament	1 x 7.92mm machine gun
Crew	3

BIBLIOGRAPHY

Annuals

All the World's Fighting Ships 1906–1921 (London, Conway Maritime Press, 1986)

All the World's Fighting Ships 1922–1946 (London, Conway Maritime Press, 1987)

Books and Periodicals

Baker III, A D, 'Japanese naval construction', in *Warship International*, n 1 (1987)

Boyd, A, *The Royal Navy in Eastern Waters* (Barnsley, Seaforth, 2017)

Brescia, M, 'Mimetiche navali giapponesi', in *Storia Militare Dossier*, n 36 (September 1996)

———, 'Radar navali 1939–1945', in *Storia Militare*, n 139 (April 2005)

Brescia, M & Galbiati, F, 'La battaglia delle Midway', in *Storia Militare Briefing*, n 21 (June 2020)

Breyer, S, *Schlachtschiffe und Schlachtkreuzer 1905–1970* (Munich, Lehmanns Verlag, 1970)

Brown, D, *Aircraft Carriers* (London, MacDonald & Jane's, 1977)

———, *Warship Losses of World War Two* (London, Arms and Armour Press, 1990)

———, *Carrier Operations in World War II* (Barnsley, Seaforth, 2005)

Dickson, W D, 'Fighting flat-tops, the Shokaku', in *Warship International*, n 1 (1977)

Draminski, S, *The Japanese Aircraft Carrier Akagi* (Lublin, Kagero, 2015)

Evans, D C & Peattie, M R, *Kaigun* (Annapolis, US Naval Institute Press, 1997)

Francillon, R J, *Japanese Carrier Air Groups 1941–45* (London, Osprey Publishing, 1970)

Friedman, N, *Naval Radar* (Annapolis, US Naval Institute, 1981)

Fukui, S *et al*, *Naval Vessels 1887–1945 Mitsubishi Zosen Built* (Tokyo, Nippon Kobo Co, 1956)

———, *Nihon no Gunkan* (Tokyo, Shuppan Kyodo, 1957)

———, *Japanese Naval Vessels at the End of World War II* (London, Greenhill Books, 1992)

Giorgerini, G *et al*, *Storia della Marina* (Milan, Fabbri Editori, 1978)

Gòralski, W, *The Japanese Aircraft Carrier Shinano* (Lublin, Kagero, 2016)

Jentschura, H et al, *Die Japanischen Kriesschiffe 1869–1945* (Munich, Lehmanns Verlag, 1970)

Jordan, J, *Warships after Washington* (Barnsley, Seaforth, 2015)

Lacroix, E, 'The development of the Imperial Japanese Navy', in *The Belgian Shiplover* (1968–75)

Ledet, M, *Samourai sur porte-avions* (Outreau, Lela Press, 2006)

Lengerer, H, 'Akagi & Kaga', in *Warship*, n 22–23–24

———, *BB Kongo class & CV Unryu class* (Katowice, Model Hobby, 2010)

———, 'Katsuragi and the failure of mass production of medium-sized aircraft carriers', in *Warship* (2010)

———, 'The IJN Ryujo', in *Warship* (2014)

———, 'The light carrier Ibuki', in *Warship* (2017)

———, *The Aircraft Carriers of the Imperial Japanese Navy and Army* (vol 1) (Katowice, Model Hobby, 2019)

Lengerer, H & Takahara, T R, 'The Japanese aircraft carriers Junyo and Hiyo', in *Warship*, n 33–34–35

Martino, E, 'Le portaerei di squadra giapponesi', in *Storia Militare*, n 282–283 (March/April 2017)

———, 'Le navi da battaglia giapponesi (1909–1945)', in *Storia Militare Dossier*, n 43 (May 2019)

Martino, E & Nani, A, 'L'evoluzione della portaerei di squadra nella seconda guerra mondiale', in *RID Rivista Italiana Difesa* (November 1997)

———, 'Le navi che non combatterono (1939–1945)', Supplement to *Rivista Marittima* (March 2001)

Matsumoto, K, *Design and Construction of the Battleships Yamato and Musashi* (Tokyo, Haga Publishing, 1961)

Milanovich, K, 'Hosho, the first aircraft carrier of the Imperial Japanese Navy', in *Warship* (2008)

Millot, B, *La guerra del Pacifico* (Milan, Mondadori, 1972)

Nani, A, *Navi portaerei 1930–1970* (unpublished notes)

O'Hara, V P *et al*, *On Contested Seas: The Seven Great Navies of the Second World War* (Annapolis, US Naval Institute Press, 2010)

Okumiya, M, Horikoshi, J & Caidin, M, *Les ailes japonaises en guerre 1941–1945* (Paris, Presses Pocket, 1965)

Overy, R, *La strada della Vittoria* (Bologna, il Mulino, 2002)

Santoni, A, 'Nascita e tramonto del navalismo e dell'imperialismo giapponese', in *Rivista Italiana Difesa* (February 1987)

Skwiot, M, *The Japanese Aircraft Carriers Soryu and Hiryu* (Lublin, Kagero, 2015)

Skwiot, M & Jarski, A, *Akagi* (Gdansk, A-J Press, 1994), *Kaga 1920–1942* (Lublin, Kagero, 2014)

Toland, J, *L'eclisse del Sol Levante* (Milan, Mondadori, 1971)

Watts, A J & Gordon, B G, *The Imperial Japanese Navy* (London, MacDonald, 1971)

TEXT NOTES

1. See M Brescia, '*USS Lexington and USS Saratoga*', in *Storia Militare* No 311 (August 2019).
2. Thus Great Britain would have the battlecruisers *Courageous* and *Glorious* available for conversion into aircraft carriers, which was in fact carried out. France, in turn, converted *Béarn*, the last of the five *Normandie*-class super-dreadnoughts, whose construction was interrupted at the outbreak of the First World War.
3. The US Navy had six *Lexington*-class battlecruisers being built or planned, and the Japanese Navy had the four 41,200-ton *Amagi*s.
4. The British collier *Lethington*, captured by the Japanese during the war against Russia, was renamed *Wakamiya* and employed until 1914 as a transport ship, and later operated as a seaplane support ship. Classified as an aircraft carrier in April 1920, she had the following characteristics: standard displacement, 7,470 tons; dimensions, 111.30 x 14.70 x 5.80m; propulsion power, 1,590hp; speed, 10.5 knots; armament, 2 x 76mm/40, 2 x 47mm, 4 seaplanes (2 in reserve). She was decommissioned on 1 April 1931.
5. This plan, which remained a paper project for both industrial and financial reasons, foresaw the building of as many as 282 units, including 9 battleships, 3 aircraft carriers, 40 cruisers, 16 flotilla leaders, 144 destroyers and 70 submarines.
6. Following this concept, from 1931–4, the US Navy built the *Ranger* (CV-4), with a full load displacement of 17,500 tons and capable of carrying around sixty aircraft. As a fleet carrier, however, she was lacking other essential characteristics such as armament, protection (including underwater) and endurance. *Ranger* was slow and not very stable, and therefore she was not considered suitable for operating in the Pacific. During the Second World War, she carried out limited operations in the Atlantic, then moved to training and air transport duties.
7. Article 9 of the Treaty of London read as follows: 'The replacement rules contained in Annex I of this Part II are applicable to warships whose displacement does not exceed 10,000 standard tons, with the exception of aircraft carriers whose replacement is governed by the provisions of the Washington Treaty.'
8. Article 23 of the Washington Treaty established its validity until 31 December 1936, unless one of the signatory parties expressed the intention to withdraw before 31 December 1934.
9. This article stated that: 'The Treaty shall remain in force until 31 December 1936, but the provisions relating to aircraft carriers shall remain in force until the expiration of the Washington Treaty (31 December 1936). Unless the contracting parties decide otherwise, following a more general agreement regarding naval armaments, they will meet during 1935 for the purpose of concluding a new Treaty which would replace the present one and serve the same purposes.'
10. After the failed putsch of February 1934, the cabinet chaired by Keisuke Okada had been replaced by a new government led by the former Foreign Minister, Koki Hirota, who had appointed Admiral Osami Nagano as Minister of the Navy.
11. Together with the new construction, the following measures were also approved: the refurbishment of the demilitarised battleship *Hiei*, in accordance with works which had already been carried out in the sister ships, *Kongo*, *Haruna* and *Kirishima*; the modification of the main armament in the four *Mogami*-class light cruisers, replacing their five 155mm triple turrets with the same number of 203mm twin turrets; the modernisation of the *Furutaka*-, *Aoba*- and *Takao*-class heavy cruisers; and the construction of a new type of experimental submarine capable of reaching an underwater speed of 25 knots. Known by the designation No 71, the latter was short-lived, but served as the basis for future fast submarines such as *I-201* and *Ha-201*.
12. After the construction of the lead ship had already been approved, with the Law of 14 June 1940 and the 'Two Ocean Navy Act' of 19 July 1940, ten additional *Essex*-class aircraft carriers were ordered, namely: *Bonhomme Richard*, later the second *Yorktown* (CV-10); *Intrepid* (CV-11); *Hornet* (CV-12); *Franklin* (CV-13); *Ticonderoga* (CV-14); *Randolph* (CV-15); *Cabot*, later the second *Lexington* (CV-16); *Bunker Hill* (CV-17); *Oriskany*, later the second *Wasp* (CV-18); and *Hancock* (CV-19).
13. The following warships were authorised: 2 battleships (the 3rd and 4th of the *Yamato* class); an aircraft carrier (*Taiho*); 6 cruisers (4 of the *Agano* and two of the *Oyodo* class); 22 destroyers (3 *Kagero*s, 12 *Yugumo*s, 6 *Akitsuki*s and the *Shimakaze*); and 2 submarines.
14. On 26 July 1939, the US government had rescinded the 1911 Japanese–American trade treaty, which would have expired on 26 January 1940.
15. The Fifth and Sixth Programmes envisaged the following capital ships: a fifth *Yamato*-class battleship (No 797), six 'super-*Yamato*' battleships (Project A-150) and six battlecruisers (Project B-65).
16. The *Kai-Maru-Go* Plan envisaged the following construction (figures in brackets indicate those completed before the end of the war): eighteen (two) aircraft carriers; two (nil) cruisers; thirty-one (nil) destroyers; 139 (four) submarines; three (nil) seaplane support ships; three (nil) submarine support ships; thirty (three) submarine chasers; fifteen (nil) tankers; ten (nil) supply ships; one (nil) cable vessel; five (one) target ships; two (nil) factory ships; one (nil) hydrographic vessel; one (nil) icebreaker; twelve (nil) minelayers; eighteen (nil) motor torpedo boats, thirty-six (nil) minesweepers; thirty-four (twelve) escort ships.
17. The passenger ship *Brazil Maru*, sister ship of *Argentina Maru*, was never converted as she was sunk on 5 August 1942 while still operating as a transport.
18. The *Shirekoto* class comprised seven vessels, built from 1920–23

and named *Shirekoto*, *Notoro*, *Erimo*, *Sata*, *Shiriya*, *Tsurumi* and *Iro*. Their normal displacement was 15,450 tons and their speed was 12 knots. They were able to carry 8,000 tons of crude oil.

19. Although the British aircraft carrier *Hermes* had been laid down on 15 January 1918, two years earlier than *Hosho*, she was not completed until February 1924.
20. HMS *Eagle* was the former Chilean battleship *Almirante Cochrane*, ordered from the Armstrong-Whitworth yard on the Tyne. At the outbreak of the First World War, her construction was halted. At the end of 1917, she was redesigned as an aircraft carrier for the Royal Navy and purchased by Britain on 28 February 1918. She was launched on 8 June 1918, but her completion was delayed by labour troubles and the possibility that she might be repurchased by Chile. She was eventually completed in April 1920.
21. Despite the positive remarks from aircrews, the production of Mitsubishi Type 10 torpedo bombers, entirely made of wood and intended to be used from shore-based airfields, was ended after the construction of about thirty aircraft.
22. In May/June 1942, *Hosho* operated six Type 96 torpedo bombers for anti-submarine duties.
23. The enlargement of the flight deck, which protruded 6m forward and aft, led to dangerous stability issues. Therefore, to avoid capsizing in bad weather, *Hosho*'s operations were limited to the Inland Sea (located between the islands of Honshu, Shikoku and Kyushu), and then only in favourable circumstances.
24. *Furious* was a battlecruiser which epitomised former First Sea Lord Admiral Fisher's theories for this kind of warship. With a full load displacement exceeding 22.890t, she was armed with two 457/40 single mounts, achieved 32 knots and featured a light protection. Shortly before her commissioning, she was converted to a 'semi-carrier', with a forward take-off platform replacing the forward 457/40 mount. A further conversion was approved in 1921 and completed in 1925 at the Devonport Dockyard. As a result, *Furious* was fitted with an upper continuous flight deck, a slightly inclined lower flight deck, two hangars with as many elevators, ten 140mm guns and six 102mm guns. Horizontal smoke ducts exhausted in the stern areas. Telescopic devices were available for signalling, communication and observation. Command and control equipment was placed below the upper flight deck.
25. Thickness of the VC steel armour belt originally planned for the *Kaga*s and the *Amagi*s was 280mm and 254mm, respectively.
26. The embarked air wing usually did not exceed eighty aircraft. At Midway, for example, this number was reduced to sixty to facilitate air operations.
27. This experiment was probably short-lived. The Japanese, whose planes stood out for their low weight and low wing loading, considered catapults superfluous for the take-off of many aircraft in a short time span.
28. The commissioning of new torpedo bombers presented serious problems linked to their significant weight increase. A B6N2 Jill was more than one-third heavier than a B5N2 Kate (5,650kg against 3,800kg). Conversely, only minor differences affected the dive bombers: the weight of the D4Y2 Judy was almost equal to that of the D3A2 Val (3,835kg against 3,800kg).
29. At the time, the workforce of the Sasebo Arsenal was focused on the second modernisation of the battleship *Kirishima*, as well as the construction of destroyers and submarines.
30. At the time, the Yokosuka Arsenal was carrying out the modernisation of the battlecruiser *Kongo* and the construction of the heavy cruiser *Takao*, the latter to be delivered on 31 May 1932.
31. When completed, and due to pressure from the Department of Naval Aviation, *Ryujo* was equipped with large windbreaks on both sides of the flight deck, in order to compensate for its reduced length. Later, this solution proved ineffective, so during *Ryujo*'s first modernisation it was eliminated and no longer proposed for any other aircraft carrier.
32 On 12 March 1934, the torpedo boat *Tomozuru*, delivered just seventeen days earlier, ran into a violent typhoon during an exercise in the area east of Nagasaki and capsized. In this state, she was skilfully towed by the cruiser *Tatsuta*, which also managed to save three shipwrecked survivors. Back in Sasebo, *Tomozuru* was docked and floated, and ten other crew members were miraculously found alive inside.
33. On 26 September 1935, during an exercise 250 nm east of Miyako, the 4th Fleet was hit by a violent typhoon. Many warships were damaged, including two aircraft carriers and several cruisers and destroyers.
34. Pitch: the repeated oscillation of a vessel around its horizontal axis, due to the combination of the waves' motion and that of the vessel itself. Shear: longitudinal deflection of the hull when it receives a strong upward thrust at its fore and aft sections, not compensated at the central section.
35. In addition to the aircraft carriers *Soryu* and *Hiryu*, the construction of the following warships was planned: the heavy cruisers *Tone* and *Chikuma*, fourteen destroyers (four *Shiratsuyu* and ten *Asashio* class) and four submarines.
36. *Chitose* and *Chiyoda* were later converted to aircraft carriers. *Mizuho* retained her original role and was sunk on 2 May 1942 by the American submarine *Drum* (SS-228) off Cape Omaisaki (Honshu Island).
37. The first auxiliary ship to be converted into an aircraft carrier was the fast oiler *Takasaki*, requisitioned while still on the slipway and completed in December 1940 as *Zuiho*.
38. A total of 890 passengers in the liners were split as follows: 220 in 1st class, 120 in 2nd class and 550 in 3rd class.
39. The official order, including the government decision to proceed with the purchase of the two ships, was issued on 10 February 1941.
40. These carriers are known as the *Hiyo* class because of their launch dates.
41. After the Battle of the Philippine Sea (June 1944), *Junyo*'s petrol tanks were shielded with concrete. The use of concrete for hull protection was not new. At the beginning of the twentieth century, it had been envisaged to fit the hull of the never-completed Italian *Caracciolo*-class super-dreadnoughts with a layer of concrete in a watertight void.
42. Refuelling stations in the hangar and on the flight deck provided two types of aviation fuel: Type A high octane, for

take-off operations and top speed; and Type B low octane, for cruising speed.

43. Due to its size, this type of island was adopted only on the large carriers *Taiho* and *Shinano*. On the *Unryu*s, the Japanese Navy adopted the traditional solution (funnels, at the level of the flight deck, inclined outwards and oriented downwards), probably to avoid stability problems arising from a large island and consequent heavy top weight.
44. 2nd Division (*Junyo*, *Hiyo*, *Ryuho*); 3rd Division (*Chitose*, *Chiyoda*, *Zuiho*).
45. Okumiya, Horikoshi and Caidin, Les ailes japonaises en guerre 1941–45, pp 243–4.
46 At the time, this shipyard was carrying out the construction of two *Unryu*-class aircraft carriers, three *Akitsuki*-class fleet destroyers, six Type D corvettes and several War Emergency-type 10,000t oilers.
47. The 1934 Programme also included a third seaplane carrier, *Mizuho*, with characteristics similar to the *Chiyoda*s, the only difference being its machinery. The *Chiyoda*s had a combination of steam turbines and diesel engines, while *Mizuho* had only diesel engines. A fourth unit of the type, *Nisshin*, planned in the '1937 Third Replacement Construction Programme' (*Maru-San*) and with features similar to her predecessors, was built between 1938 and 1942, but was sunk on 22 July 1943 (17 miles west of Cape Alexander) by American aircraft.
48. The Japanese, in a bid to reduce the anticipated American quantitative superiority, had elaborated an operational theory focused on simultaneous operation of all four seaplane carriers. Each of them would carry twelve midget submarines so as to form, by launching each at intervals of 1,000m, a 48km-wide barrier. Ninety-six 17.9in torpedoes (two per submarine), employed in conjunction with the larger-calibre guns of battleships and heavy cruisers, would thus be available to intercept and destroy the enemy battleships.
49. In addition to improving stability, these bulges were supposed to increase underwater protection. Some sources report that the *Chiyoda*s' petrol tanks also had light armour.
50. It is very likely, although there is no certain evidence, that, after having completed the *Taiho*'s preliminary design, the Japanese were satisfied when they learned of the exceptional resistance demonstrated by HMS *Illustrious* on 10 January 1941 in the Mediterranean, when she was attacked by German Stukas. In this regard, it is worth underlining that the American technicians of the Norfolk Arsenal were amazed by the extent of the damage *Illustrious* had resisted, so much so that it cannot be excluded that this contributed to the decision to build the *Midway*s, the first large American aircraft carriers fitted with an armoured flight deck.
51. While the British carrier designers enclosed the flight deck and hangar (including its sides and ends) in an armoured citadel, the Japanese limited the flight deck armour to the area between the two elevators.
52. Starting from the second half of 1943, due to the shortage of suitable wood and to speed up fitting out, the flight decks of Japanese aircraft carriers were covered with a latex-based rubbery compound.
53. The decision to give up the middle elevator was motivated by the desire not to interrupt the structural continuity of the flight deck with another opening.
54. This protection scheme for steering gear spaces was also adopted on the *Agano*-class light cruisers.
55. Due to the extreme danger they posed, petrol tanks were also shielded by 1m-wide oil tanks, separated from them by an empty space.
56. Due to the poor performance of the Type 13 Mod 10 diesel engines, the Japanese were forced to give up equipping the *Yamato*s with a combined power plant (steam turbines and diesel engines).
57. *Taigei*'s original diesel engines developed 14,000shp for a maximum speed of 20 knots.
58. As a floating base, *Shinano* was to be equipped with 120 bombs of 500–800kg, 240 bombs of 250kg, 458 bombs of 60kg, 144 bombs of 30kg and eighty torpedoes.
59. The table on page 290 of Matsumoto's book, *Design and Construction of the Battleships Yamato and Musashi*, contains a printing error so far uncritically accepted by all authors. In fact, the hull weight was not 33,346t but 23,346t, resulting from the summary of weights shown above. This demonstrates that even when referring to a primary source – the author was part of K Fukuda's team that designed the *Yamato*s – errors are always possible.
60. The construction plans included the following frontline warships (units completed in brackets): one modified-*Hiryu* fleet aircraft carrier (one); two *Suzuya*-class heavy cruisers (nil); sixteen *Yugumo*-class destroyers (eight); ten *Akitsuki*-class anti-aircraft destroyers (six); six I-15-class submarines (six); six I-16-class submarines (three); twelve RO-35-class submarines (eight); and nine RO-100-class submarines (nine).
61. Provisions initially included seventy-two 800kg bombs, 240 250kg bombs, 360 60kg bombs, 144 30kg bombs and thirty-six Type 91 Mod 6 torpedoes. Later, the following changes were made: forty-eight 800kg bombs, forty-eight 500kg bombs, ninety-six 250kg bombs, 144 60kg bombs, and thirty-six Type 91 Mod 3 and/or Type 91 Mod 6 torpedoes.
62. Some sources report machinery identical to that of *Kagero*-class destroyers, others to that of *Akitsuki*-class anti-aircraft destroyers.
63. Placement of air intakes on the opposite side to the funnels had proved to be a serious mistake. At Midway, hot air and fire was sucked into these spaces, suffocating most of the engineering personnel, for whom there were no emergency exits.
64. The second unit of the type, provisionally named *No 301*, was laid down on 1 June 1942, just three days before Midway, at the Mitsubishi shipyards in Nagasaki. Some sources attribute to her the name *Ikomache*, but this was never officially done.
65. Although the *Tone*s could be considered the most successful of the Japanese heavy cruisers in terms of effectiveness and habitability, it was nevertheless decided to repeat the *Suzuya*s, which had shown structural and stability problems, in order not to give up two 7.9in guns. See Martino, *Gli incrociatori leggeri giapponesi*, *Storia Militare*, pp 269–70.
66. See M. Brescia, 'Le portaerei leggere classe "Independence"', *Storia Militare* n. 318–19.